BRUTALITY ON TRIAL

NEW PERSPECTIVES ON MARITIME HISTORY AND NAUTICAL ARCHAEOLOGY

UNIVERSITY PRESS OF FLORIDA

Florida A&M University, Tallahassee
Florida Atlantic University, Boca Raton
Florida Gulf Coast University, Ft. Myers
Florida International University, Miami
Florida State University, Tallahassee
University of Central Florida, Orlando
University of Florida, Gainesville
University of North Florida, Jacksonville
University of South Florida, Tampa
University of West Florida, Pensacola

NEW PERSPECTIVES ON MARITIME HISTORY AND NAUTICAL ARCHAEOLOGY

James C. Bradford and Gene A. Smith, Series Editors

The Maritime Heritage of the Cayman Islands, by Roger C. Smith
(1999; first paperback edition, 2000)

The Three German Navies: Dissolution, Transition, and New Beginnings, 1945–1960,
by Douglas C. Peifer (2002)

The Rescue of the Gale Runner: *Death, Heroism, and the U.S. Coast Guard*,
by Dennis L. Noble (2002)

*Brown Water Warfare: The U.S. Navy in Riverine Warfare and the Emergence
of a Tactical Doctrine, 1775–1970*, by R. Blake Dunnavent (2003)

*Sea Power in the Medieval Mediterranean: The Catalan-Aragonese Fleet in
the War of the Sicilian Vespers* by Lawrence V. Mott (2003)

An Admiral for America: Sir Peter Warren, Vice-Admiral of the Red, 1703–1752,
by Julian Gwyn (2004)

Maritime History as World History, edited by Daniel Finamore (2004)

Counterpoint to Trafalgar: The Anglo-Russian Invasion of Naples, 1805–1806,
by William Henry Flayhart III (first paperback edition, 2004)

Life and Death on the Greenland Patrol, 1942, by Thaddeus D. Novak,
edited by P. J. Capelotti (2005)

X Marks the Spot: The Archaeology of Piracy, edited by Russell K. Skowronek
and Charles R. Ewen (2006)

*Industrializing American Shipbuilding: The Transformation of Ship Design
and Construction, 1820–1920*, by William H. Thiesen (2006)

Admiral Lord Keith and the Naval War against Napoleon,
by Kevin D. McCranie (2006)

Commodore John Rodgers: Paragon of the Early American Navy,
by John H. Schroeder (2006)

*Borderland Smuggling: Patriots, Loyalists, and Illicit Trade in the Northeast,
1783–1820*, by Joshua M. Smith (2006)

*Brutality on Trial: "Hellfire" Pedersen, "Fighting" Hansen, and
the Seamen's Act of 1915*, by E. Kay Gibson (2006)

E. KAY GIBSON

Foreword by James C. Bradford and Gene A. Smith, Series Editors

UNIVERSITY PRESS OF FLORIDA
Gainesville · Tallahassee · Tampa · Boca Raton · Pensacola · Orlando · Miami · Jacksonville · Ft. Myers

BRUTALITY ON TRIAL

"HELLFIRE" PEDERSEN,

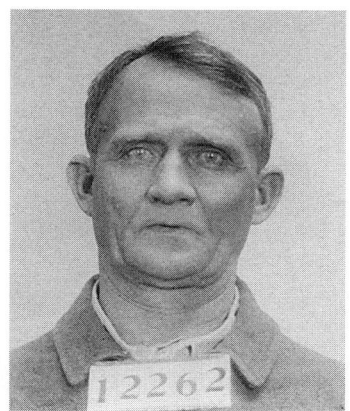

"FIGHTING" HANSEN,

AND THE SEAMEN'S ACT OF 1915

Copyright 2006 by E. Kay Gibson
Printed in the United States of America on acid-free paper
All rights reserved

11 10 09 08 07 06   6 5 4 3 2 1

A record of cataloging-in-publication data is available
from the Library of Congress.
ISBN 0-8130-2991-0

The University Press of Florida is the scholarly publishing agency
for the State University System of Florida, comprising Florida A&M
University, Florida Atlantic University, Florida Gulf Coast University,
Florida International University, Florida State University, University
of Central Florida, University of Florida, University of North Florida,
University of South Florida, and University of West Florida.

University Press of Florida
15 Northwest 15th Street
Gainesville, FL 32611-2079
http://www.upf.com

CONTENTS

List of Plates   ix
Foreword   xi
Preface and Acknowledgments   xv
Introduction   1
1. Cape Town, 1917   4
2. Vancouver-Victoria, B.C., April 1918   14
3. Off Cape Town, August 27, 1918   22
4. Digesting the Official Logbook   39
5. The "Plot" Enlarges   49
6. The Search for the Truth   56
7. Transportation Secured   65
8. Captain and Son Indicted for Murder   89
9. The Government's Second Round   94
10. The Defense   108
11. Summations   119
12. Judge Jack's Charge of the Court   127
13. Appeal Denied   130
14. "Fighting" Hansen   142
15. Four Davids Take On Goliath   150
Epilogue   159
Author's Reflections   165

APPENDIX 1. The Evolution of Maritime Laws
Affecting Seamen, 1790–1915   167

APPENDIX 2. The Seaman's Diet   181

APPENDIX 3. An Attempt to Weaken the Seamen's Act of 1915   182

APPENDIX 4. Lyrics from *Songs of the Workers:
To Fan the Flames of Discontent*   185

Glossary of Technical and/or Obscure Terms   189

Notes   193

Bibliography   209

Index   215

PLATES

Plates follow page 71.

1. Hind, Rolph & Co. advertisement, 1903
2. Captain Adolph Cornelius Pedersen and wife
3. Barkentine *Puako*, loaded dockside
4. Barkentine *Puako* setting her sails
5. Chart showing six known positions for *Puako*
6. Cape Town docks and Table Bay anchorage, circa 1920
7. Consular form no. 192 reporting death of Stewart
8. Death notice of Bjarne Olsen in Cape Town
9. Consul general's certificate of discharge of seaman
10. Roeland Street Gaol, Cape Town
11. Consul General George H. Murphy
12. Bilge pump of *Puako*'s sister ship
13. Mug shot of Pedersen, April 1921
14. Pedersen's prison processing paperwork
15. Mug shot of Frederick "Fighting" Hansen
16. Leonard Roy Pedersen (1889–1992)
17. Adolph Eric Pedersen (1900–1991)
18. Banner of "The Red Record"
19. Andrew Furuseth

FOREWORD

Water is unquestionably the most important natural feature on earth. By volume, the world's oceans compose 99 percent of the planet's living space; in fact, the surface of the Pacific Ocean alone is larger than that of the total surface of all land bodies. Water is as vital to life as air. Indeed, to test whether other planets or the moon can sustain life, NASA looks for signs of water. The story of human development is inextricably linked to the oceans, lakes, and rivers that dominate the earth's surface. The University Press of Florida's series New Perspectives on Maritime History and Nautical Archaeology is devoted to exploring the significance of the earth's water while providing lively and important books that cover the spectrum of maritime history and nautical archaeology broadly defined. The series includes works that focus on the role of canals, rivers, lakes, seas, and oceans in history; on the economic, military, and political use of those waters; and on the people, communities, and industries that support maritime endeavors. Limited by neither geography nor time, volumes in the series contribute to the overall understanding of maritime history and can be read with profit by both general readers and specialists.

E. Kay Gibson's study reveals the true nature of the violence and brutality that took place aboard the barkentines *Puako* and *Rolph*, both owned by Hind, Rolph & Co. of San Francisco—one of the few companies that had supported the Seamen's Act that Woodrow Wilson signed into law in March 1915 with the intention of protecting seamen against abusive officers.

Gibson's study examines the social and legal circumstances of seamen during the waning days of the era of sail. During the summer of 1917 the *Puako*, under the command of Captain Adolph Cornelius "Hellfire" Pedersen, carried two mates and twelve crewmen—three Americans, six Chileans, a Finn, and two Chinese. When the ship arrived in Cape Town that June, the two Chinese requested a discharge, prompting the U.S. consul general to investigate conditions on board the ship. Apparently, during the voyage Captain Pedersen had violently assaulted both Chinese, hitting, kicking, and choking them. Although Pedersen denied the charge, a diary kept by one of the Chinese seamen basically substantiated the harsh penalties meted out by Pedersen for relatively minor infractions of ship rules and regulations. Soon afterward, the Chilean and American seamen added their own complaints of violence to those of their Chinese shipmates and reported being underfed during the voyage. Consular officials secured transfers for the Chinese and helped address the other complaints. On July 27, after recruiting a replacement for a cook who had swum ashore, the *Puako* departed Cape Town. After the ship's departure, the consul general drafted a lengthy report to Secretary of State Robert Lansing, insisting that Pedersen should not be commanding an American vessel in foreign trade. A U.S. government committee conducted a brief hearing before concluding that Captain Pedersen should not be charged with mistreatment of his subordinates.

In April 1918 the *Puako* made a return voyage to Cape Town, this time with tragic results. Captain Pedersen, considered an extremely hard-driving officer, was still in command of the vessel, which by anyone's standards was this time inadequately manned. U.S. entry into World War I the year before had created an extremely tight labor market for crews of sailing ships, including masters, mates, and seamen. The *Puako* did not escape the effects of this shortage, and although the ship was nominally up to strength, it was the lack of skilled manpower that set the tone for a voyage that ultimately changed the fortunes of Hind, Rolph & Co.

By the time a British transport ship intercepted the *Puako* off Cape Town, two seamen had died and most of the remaining crewmen were in irons facing charges of mutiny. Pedersen claimed that he and his mates—his two teenaged sons—had foiled a mutiny incited by German spies among the seamen who planned to seize the ship and blow it up. The men in chains denied the charges and countered by accusing the drunkard Pedersen of subjecting them to unwarranted violence. Gibson's account explains how the crew of the *Puako*, with the assistance of the U.S. consulate and British officials in Cape Town, were able to successfully press their accusations against Captain Pedersen and his two sons, who were eventually prosecuted for illegal exercise of corporal punishment. A year later, four seamen of another Hind, Rolph barkentine, the *Rolph*, who had been viciously and repeatedly assaulted by the vessel's mate, Frederick Hansen, were equally successful in the courtroom.

While the literature of American maritime history contains many accounts of unpunished abuse of crews of both naval and commercial vessels, only in the rarest of instances did merchant seamen secure justice for the pain and suffering that they experienced. Gibson's account is significant because it analyzes two of the few cases in which seamen succeeded in obtaining redress for abuse suffered at the hands of ships' officers.

At the heart of this book is Gibson's riveting account of good versus evil—basically good seamen confronting mean and vindictive masters and mates. By documenting how the officers mistreated the seamen and the difficulties experienced by those victims in seeking justice, Gibson wins sympathy for Jack Tar's last sons. The vindication won in the courtroom by those brutalized seamen resulted from a combination of factors—recent passage of the federal law designed to protect seamen from abuse; the diligence of the U.S. consuls at Cape Town and at Antofagasta, Chile; assistance rendered by government officials; the skill of the prosecuting attorneys; the fairness of federal judges in New York, San Francisco, and Seattle. Gibson provides an absorbing legal perspective on the arguments and evidence presented by the attorneys hired by labor unions and by the shipowner—and, in the process, offers a broad insight into social conditions during the waning days of the Age of Sail.

James C. Bradford, Texas A&M University
Gene A. Smith, Texas Christian University
Series Editors

PREFACE AND ACKNOWLEDGMENTS

Thirty-some years ago, I first heard mention of Captain Adolph Cornelius Pedersen and a ship called *Puako* while my husband, Charles Dana Gibson, and I were visiting with Dana's father, Langhorne Gibson Sr. At that time my father-in-law passed along several yellowed *New York Times* clippings from 1919 which announced that Captain Pedersen and his two young sons, Leonard and Adolph Eric Pedersen, were being held in jail in New York for crimes they had committed while serving respectively as master and mates on a four-month voyage of the *Puako*. The crimes of which the Pedersens were accused ranged from illegal exercise of corporal punishment to murder. My husband, a master mariner, had just written his first book; the story of the Pedersens seemed opportune for a second writing project. From the Department of State he obtained a wealth of files, and work began on the assembly of trial records. However, before Dana could launch into writing the story of the Pedersens and the *Puako*, other endeavors intervened.

A few years later we had a chance meeting with Harold Huycke, a maritime historian and retired master mariner from the West Coast, who had once met the younger of the Pedersen boys and who knew something of the *Puako* affair. When my husband told him what files he had gathered to date, Harold became enthusiastic about writing the story, which at that juncture had its main focus on *Puako*. We shipped the records off to him. Before proceeding with the project, Harold made an attempt to develop further background. In that process, he located and separately interviewed both of the Pedersen boys, who were by then shriveled old men well into their eighties (see plates 16 and 17). Harold was joined in the interview process by the late Karl Kortum, director of the National Maritime Museum (now the San Francisco Maritime National Historical Park). The Pedersen boys talked freely of their father and the old days right up until the interviewers posed a question concerning the *Puako*. Each of the brothers had seemingly developed a selective amnesia that enabled him to talk around the *Puako* but never address directly the ship or the events on board her between April and August of 1918. Despite his inability to get any firsthand connection to the *Puako*, Harold continued his interest in the project, but he never found the time to start the process of writing. After visiting with Harold again in 2002, and realizing how committed he had become to other research projects, I impulsively blurted out to my husband that I would like to give it a try, never dreaming the directions or the depths to which the endeavor would take me. And so in due course Harold shipped the records back to us.

My initial focus was on the 1918 *Puako* voyage which had proved fatal for two of the crewmembers and traumatic for most of the rest. As a result of the deaths and injuries caused by the brutality of the ship's officers, the Pedersens were brought to New York, indicted, and then tried in separate proceedings in federal court. As my research progressed, other legal actions involving the *Puako*'s seamen came to light. These were initiated on behalf of the seamen for damages suffered to their persons. Under admiralty law, actions for damages are known as libels. These libels pitted the *Puako* seamen libellants against the ship's owner, a company headed by James Rolph Jr. At the time, Rolph was mayor of San Francisco and a powerful political figure in California who would go on to serve as governor. During the course of researching the *Puako* libels, it came to my attention that seamen from another Rolph-owned vessel, the *Rolph*, had also gone to federal court seeking damages for the brutal beatings they had endured from a drunken first mate, Frederick Hansen.

At this point, I began to realize that the actions against the Rolph enterprises had significance that reached beyond the brutality of ships' officers and libels against owners. The libels appear to have been the first tests of what was until then a little known provision of the Seamen's Act of 1915. That provision allowed seamen employed upon U.S.-flag vessels to seek fiscal redress for injury or death brought on by the illegal action of a ship's officer. The successful judgments in favor of the injured seamen from the *Puako* and the *Rolph* against such a visible party as James Rolph Jr. sent a loud and clear message throughout the shipping industry that owners could be and would be held responsible for the actions of their ships' officers, and that henceforth greater diligence should be taken in the hiring of masters and mates. The result was an occupational protection not heretofore enjoyed by American merchant seamen.

To fully appreciate the legal circumstances and remedies that existed for merchant seamen sailing aboard American-flag vessels in the early years of the twentieth century as against those of an earlier time, I found it helpful to examine the evolution of United States maritime law. The gist of that research forms my appendix 1, which documents the relationship that had historically existed between seamen and the ships' officers under whom they served. Some writers have equated this relationship with that of master and slave, a description not far off the mark. For some masters and mates who had been sailing since the late 1800s and who had grown used to the way of the iron fist, the greatest challenge to that relationship was passage of the Seamen's Act in 1915.

In the 1970s when my husband initiated his research of the *Puako*-Pedersen matter, he was assisted by Roger Sandack, then an associate with the New York law firm Cadwalader, Wickersham, and Taft, which has an admiralty division. With the aid of archivist Dr. Milton O. Gustafson of the National Archives and Records Administration (NARA), hundreds of pages of a Department of State case file were also located. These included copies of Office of Naval Intelligence reports that, up to the time of Dana's request, had not been declassified, which indicated they had not been previously accessed. The then (1970s) warden at the federal penitentiary in Atlanta, J. D. Henderson, forwarded most of the information that the prison archive had on Inmate 12262-131, a/k/a Pedersen, Adolph C.

Since taking over the project in 2002, I discovered that outside of the few clippings passed down by my late father-in-law, there no longer exists any public record of the most sensational *Puako*-related trial in New York, which involved a charge of murder: *United States vs A. C. Pedersen and A. E. Pedersen*. The Department of State files, which contain voluminous interrogation statements taken by police and consular officials in Cape Town, enabled me to piece together the circumstances that had brought about the murder charges of which the two Pedersens were acquitted. The trial record Roger Sandack had located in the 1970s covered a separate trial, which involved charges against all three of the Pedersens for the illegal exercise of corporal punishment and which ended with verdicts of guilty. Those verdicts were appealed. It was from the printed appeal transcript that I worked, as the original record of that trial also could not be located. As I began to write, I discovered that Mr. Sandack had located only the first half of the corporal punishment trial transcript. Sarah Mitchell, librarian with Cadwalader, Wickersham, and Taft, located the rest of it for me at NARA, New York City. Other trial transcripts I studied came from repositories in San Bruno, California, and Seattle, Washington.

I wish to thank four experts in the fields of maritime history and maritime law who took time from their busy schedules to read and critique my manuscript: Rear Admiral Thomas A. King, USMS, Retired, former superintendent of the United States Merchant Marine Academy; Dr. Charles Schultz, archivist at Texas A&M University; Dr. William Still, professor emeritus, East Carolina University; and William H. Welte, Esq., proctor in admiralty.

I am especially grateful to my husband and to Harold Huycke, who have both continued their interest in my research and writing. Dana, author of eight published histories, whom I consider my sternest critic, has been particularly helpful in keeping me focused.

NARA archivists who have helped me locate critical documents include Dr. Milton O. Gustafson, Dr. Michael Hussey, and John K. Vandereedt, Civilian Records, Suitland, Maryland; Kim Y. McKeithan, Old Military and Civil Records, Textual Archives Services Division, Suitland; Arlene Royer, East Point, Georgia; Joseph Sanchez and Peggy Tran-Le, Pacific Region, San Bruno; John Fitzgerald, Pacific-Alaska (Seattle) Region. I also received assistance from Anne Diestel, U.S. Department of Justice, Federal Bureau of Prisons, and from Marise Bronkhorst at the National Archives of South Africa, Cape Town Archives Repository. To my surprise, I was told by those archivists who helped root out the pertinent Department of State and federal trial transcripts that those files had never been previously accessed.

Museums, libraries, and librarians that offered expertise and assistance include Camden Public Library, Camden, Maine (Dottie Morales); Department of State Library, Reference (Michele Powell); E. P. Foster Library, Ventura, California; Humboldt County Library, Eureka, California; Maine Maritime Museum, Bath (Nathan Lipfert); Maritime Museum of Victoria, British Columbia (Richard MacKenzie); Maritime Museum, Vancouver, British Columbia (Susan Buss); Pleasant Hill Library, Contra Costa County, California (Ellen Jones and Carmen Meneses); San Francisco Maritime National Historical Park Library (Bill Kooiman); State of Maine Law and Legislative Reference Library, Augusta (Lynn Randall); U.S. Merchant Marine Academy Library, Kings Point, New York (George Billy).

Others who have assisted include, but are not limited to, Sheila Dodge; Ken Gross; Rick James; Stephanie Leclerc; Pat Maloney, Board of Pilot Commissioners, San Francisco; Jay H. McDowell, former partner at Cadwalader, Wickersham, and Taft; Stephen J. Nolan, American consul general, Cape Town; Kelly G. Shannon, Department of State; Graydon S. Staring, Esq., of counsel to Nixon Peabody, LLP, San Francisco; Captains John Winterling and Bob Porteous, retired San Francisco bar pilots, who both worked with Adolph Eric Pedersen and shared their memories of him; Walter Bulski, grandson of Captain Helms; and Jack Pearson and Dick Stafford, grandsons of Captain Pearson, who also shared memories.

I have reserved for last a special thank-you to Meredith Morris-Babb, director of the University Press of Florida, who in the beginning had more faith in me than I had in myself and offered me the opportunity to submit my work for UPF review. No one could have guided me with more skill and professionalism than Meredith and her staff, which included Gillian Hillis and Michele Fiyak-Burkley, who always cheerfully made themselves available to me throughout the publication process. Finally, I thank Ann Marlowe whose eyes found many things that needed extra attention. Together this was a wonderful team to work with.

To each and all, and to others unnamed who in a variety of ways have assisted me in my work, I extend a large thank-you. I could not have succeeded without your help.

INTRODUCTION

During the nineteenth century, the United States Congress passed numerous laws intended to protect America's seamen from the abuse and misuse of corporal punishment by ships' officers. But even into the first decades of the 1900s, the legislation had only limited effect in reining in that small segment of masters and mates—men referred to as buckos—who, once at sea, were determined to keep the upper hand over seamen even if it meant using such devices as knuckle dusters, belaying pins, clubs, marline spikes, rope ends, even boots—in short, anything at hand that could be turned into a weapon or a "training tool." In theory, all that was to change when on March 4, 1915, President Woodrow Wilson signed into law legislation commonly known as the Seamen's Act.

The full title of the Seamen's Act of 1915 was "An Act to promote the welfare of American seamen in the merchant marine of the United States; to abolish arrest and imprisonment as a penalty for desertion; and to secure the abrogation of treaty provisions in relation thereto; and to promote safety at sea." Certain of those sections are particularly relevant:

Section 2 set the standards for watches, both at sea and in safe harbor. When masters failed to comply, seamen were entitled to wages earned and to discharge from such vessel.

Section 4 allowed a seaman to receive on demand up to one-half of his wages due at each port where the vessel stopped during the course of the voyage. Failure of the master to comply with a seaman's request released the man from his contract and entitled him to full payment of wages earned.

Section 7, paragraphs 4, 5, and 6, addressed criminal penalties for willful disobedience, including striking an officer. Among the penalties were forfeiture of wages and placement in irons. The minimum rations mandated in *Section 10* (see appendix 2) could be reduced to bread and water, with regular rations to be given every fifth day during the voyage. Upon subsequent conviction by a civil court, terms of imprisonment could range from one month to two years, depending on the severity of the disobedience.

Section 8 gave authority to U.S. Department of State consular officers in foreign ports to intervene in cases of insubordination by seamen and, when appropriate, to request the assistance of local authorities including police. This section also gave consular officers the authority to discharge seamen and officers, including masters.

Section 9 restated the prohibition of flogging on vessels of commerce, which was initially abolished by Section 1 of the Act of September 28, 1850. That provision was recodified into Section 22 of the Act of December 21, 1898, the White Act, and later into Section 9 of the Act of March 4, 1915, the Seamen's Act. These latter two acts prohibited not only flogging but "all other forms of corporal punishment" as well. It was the duty of masters to surrender any violating officer to proper authorities as soon as practicable. The penalty for violation of Section 9 was a term of imprisonment not to exceed two years for each violation. Failure of the master to use due diligence could render "the master, or the vessel, or the owner of the vessel" liable for damages. This provision, in the last sentence of Section 9, was intended to force shipowners to be more responsible in their hiring practices. For the story unfolding here, that last sentence of Section 9 is of paramount importance.

There was considevvrable opposition among shipowners, who strongly lobbied against passage of the 1915 act. One of the few who stood out as a supporter was San Francisco's mayor, James Rolph Jr., president of the shipping firm Hind, Rolph & Co. It is unclear from documents I have studied whether Rolph, when he backed the bill, was cognizant that the last provision of Section 9 could make shipowners fiscally liable for the illegal actions of their officers.

If Captain Adolph Cornelius "Hellfire" Pedersen of the barkentine *Puako* was an example of the type of officer employed by Hind, Rolph & Co. prior to passage of the act, then at that juncture the company probably felt it had nothing in particular to worry about. If it did have any concerns about Pedersen, who was considered in the industry to be a "hard driver," the company chose to overlook them. This may have been for practical reasons. By 1917 the steamship was well on its way toward replacing the outmoded sailing vessel, and young men with the desire to follow a seagoing career were looking unfavorably on the arduous life under sail. In fact, licensed chief mates of sail vessels over 700 gross tons had become so scarce that a decade earlier, on January 25, 1907, Congress had rescinded the part of the Act of

December 21, 1898, that required chief mates of sail vessels to be licensed. By 1915 when the Seamen's Act was passed, without an underlying cadre of certifiably qualified mates to replace aging sail masters, shipping companies were being forced to keep on masters who for one reason or another should have been let go or retired.

The shortage of masters and mates in sail was compounded following 1917 by the entry of the United States into the First World War, as vast numbers of trained seamen, including officers, found it more attractive to serve on steamships with their higher pay and improved living standards. Additionally, by April 1918 military conscription had taken its toll of both officers and fo'c'sle hands, leaving a dwindling labor pool of seamen from which to draw.

It was in this atmosphere of strengthened legislative regulations, a tight labor market, and a declining demand for sailing ships that in early 1918 the Hind, Rolph barkentine *Puako* under the command of Captain Adolph Cornelius Pedersen began loading lumber at Vancouver, British Columbia. The upcoming voyage was one that company president James Rolph Jr. could not have envisioned when he had stood practically alone among shipowners and openly supported passage of the Seamen's Act. In a matter of months, provisions of that act would be harshly invoked against Rolph's shipping enterprises. In a few short years—in large part because of the penalties stipulated by Section 9—Hind, Rolph & Co. would be but a memory.

Brutality on Trial is more than a tale of the sea. It is an affirmation that individuals with an admirable goal can make a great positive difference in the lives of their fellow men. To maritime labor lobbyist Andrew Furuseth, a strong proponent of the Seamen's Act of 1915, and others who had similar aspirations to make the sea a safer place, this book is dedicated.

CHAPTER 1

CAPE TOWN, 1917

After suffering for days under the wrath of Captain Adolph Cornelius Pedersen, John Henry Stewart could take no more. Stewart, the ship's cook, walked out of the galley, jumped over the side, and, without attempting to grab the log line, disappeared under the surface of the sea. Suicide had been his only recourse. Weeks later, with Second Mate Adolph Eric Pedersen in hot pursuit, it was Axel Hansen's turn. Once in the water, Hansen changed his mind, grabbed the log line, and called for help. The order went out for the *Puako* to maintain her course. Soon from the stern of the ship the only sound was the rush of water creating the ship's wake.

Adolph Cornelius Pedersen, master of the barkentine *Puako* when these events transpired, was born March 9, 1865, in Norway. In 1893 he became a naturalized American citizen. Seven years later Pedersen, a short, chunky man standing about 5'6" and weighing around 160 pounds, landed a position as mate on a vessel owned by Hind, Rolph & Co., a shipping firm formed in January 1898 by George U. Hind and James Rolph Jr. The firm's advertisements (for example, plate 1) described the company as shipping and commission merchants with offices at 302 California Street, San Francisco, and 212 Merchant Street, Honolulu.

By the time the thirty-six-year-old Pedersen obtained his first master's license in 1902, the company's partners, Rolph and Hind, considered him a loyal and trusted employee. Consequently, when the ailing Captain William Fownes was forced to retire from the company's barkentine *Challenger*, A. C. Pedersen was selected to take over that command.

On October 26, 1905, the *Challenger* sailed for Osaka, Japan, from Killisnoo Bay, Alaska, carrying a cargo of fish fertilizer. Aboard, in company to Captain Pedersen, were his three young sons and his attractive wife, Gertrude Thornlun Pedersen (see plate 2), who was pregnant at the time with their fourth child. About four weeks out and halfway to Japan, the fertilizer began smoldering, the result of spontaneous combustion. Pedersen ordered that the hatches be battened down in an attempt to smother the fire by keeping air from entering the cargo spaces. Despite those efforts, for nearly a month the fire burned, fanned by "furious weather." Upon sighting land, Pedersen headed toward the beach, where he hoped he could extinguish the fire and thus save the ship. A gale blew the *Challenger* ashore, where she broke into pieces. Although he had lost the ship, Pedersen did manage to save his family and all hands.[1]

In its column "Sea Breezes," a weekly feature for sailing ship lovers, the *Portland (Oregon) Shipping Telegraph* of Saturday, October 28, 1944, carried details of the *Challenger* incident. The author, John G. Rowe, quoted from an undated *Tacoma Sunday Ledger* story written by a reporter who claimed to have received the facts of that voyage firsthand from Pedersen:

> When the fire and storm were at their worst, the watch below refused to a man to come on deck when it was called. . . . Pedersen slipped a revolver into his pocket and went down into the forecastle. It was much like venturing into a cage of wild animals, for a crew that has mutinied is neither gentle nor reasoning, and the crew now acted as sulky lions do when their trainer cracks his whip. "On deck with you! Every one of you on deck!" Not a man stirred. Instead the entire watch crouched in a corner, one or two growling that they were dead beat and had had enough of it.

According to Rowe's story, Pedersen ordered them all to be put in irons (handcuffs) and locked inside the forecastle. The other watch would now do double duty through the night. Near dawn, shouts came from the forecastle. The fire had spread to the forehold, and smoke was entering the forecastle, choking the shackled crew. Only when they promised to work and obey orders did Pedersen allow their release. Thereafter, Pedersen was known along the waterfront as "Hellfire." Long after his passing, many would remember him by that name, although the sobriquet would more often be associated with his later shipboard demeanor. Most never knew it stemmed from his no-holds-barred attempt in 1905 to save his burning ship.

Within the corporate headquarters of Hind, Rolph & Co., Pedersen was no doubt considered a hero and a valuable master in view of the extraordinary measures he had undertaken to save the *Challenger*. On or about September 17, 1907, he was rewarded, not surprisingly, with a new assignment

Cape Town, 1917

as master of the skysail barkentine *Puako*, taking over that command from George Seeley.[2]

The *Puako*, of 1,011 net tons, was built in 1902 for Hind, Rolph by W. A. Boole and Son of Oakland. She was constructed of oak and Oregon pine with galvanized fastenings and is described as having a billet-head and an elliptical stern (see plates 3 and 4). Her dimensions were: length overall 240', length between perpendiculars 221', breadth 42', depth 17'.[3] The *Puako*'s first Certificate of Registry was issued at the Port of San Francisco on December 5, 1902.[4]

Following the loss of the *Challenger*, Pedersen seems to have kept out of the public eye for several years until a paragraph appeared in the *Coast Seamen's Journal* on February 3, 1915, a month before passage of the legislation that has commonly become known simply as the Seamen's Act:

"Captain A. C. Pedersen must answer charges filed against him at [Port Townsend], Washington, with the United States Commissioner of Navigation by German members of the crew of the American barkentine *Puako* who were paid off January 9 at Winslow, following the vessel's arrival from the Hawaiian Islands. The Germans accuse Captain Pedersen of ill-treatment, abuse, and violence."

The charges, which had been mailed to Washington while the barkentine was discharging coal at Mahu-Kona, Hawaii, were probably dropped, as Pedersen's license file contains no mention of any action against him or his license. Two years would pass before Pedersen's activities again attracted notice.

In June of 1917 the *Puako* arrived at Cape Town from Victoria, British Columbia, with a full load of lumber. Besides Pedersen, her officer complement consisted of Fred Wann, first mate, and J. Bulman, second mate. Making up the rest of the crew were three Americans, six Chileans, a Finn, and two Chinese. One of the Americans, ordinary seaman Adolph Eric Pedersen, then a boy of sixteen, was the master's second son.

Soon after the ship arrived, the *Puako*'s two Chinese crew members, Wai Lee (also known as Waly Lee) and Cheng Kee, requested that they be discharged. The United States consul general at Cape Town, George H. Murphy (see plate 11), was first made aware of their situation by a local Chinese merchant, Sam Lee, who was accompanied to Murphy's office by his attorney, J. B. Shacknovis. Sam Lee and Shacknovis gave Murphy a statement dated June 27, 1917, signed by Sam Lee, in which he paraphrased what he knew of the shipboard situation of the two men.

> During the voyage, the captain struck Waly Lee with his fists, kicked him with his booted foot on the head and threatened to throw him overboard. A number of assaults were committed by the captain on the said Waly Lee during the voyage. The said Waly Lee has marks on his head and body which show that he was violently assaulted by the said Captain Pedersen. During the voyage the said captain tried to choke the said Cheng Kee by pushing a pillow into his mouth and struck him with his clenched fists and kicked him with his booted foot on his body causing very severe injuries. The captain also threatened to throw him overboard.[5]

Sam Lee went on to say that the two men feared for their lives and requested the protection of the United States Consular Service.

Under South African immigration law, discharging a seaman, especially an Oriental, in a South African jurisdiction was a costly affair for a vessel's owner. Because of that policy, Consul General Murphy usually made every attempt to keep crewmen from leaving their ships. But Murphy took seriously the accusations contained in Sam Lee's statement, and after consulting with South African Immigration authorities, he informed Pedersen in writing that he would visit the vessel the following day in order to personally speak with the Chinese seamen.

Before Murphy left for the *Puako*, Pedersen arrived at the consulate general "in an enraged, entirely unreasonable, and very offensive condition." Murphy was aghast at Pedersen's performance and in his departmental memorandum stated, "In my whole Consular experience of over thirty years, I have not met as badly behaved, unreasonable, and violent a master of an American vessel as Captain Pedersen. . . . His attitude and language . . . became so insulting that I was compelled to ask him either to alter his tone or leave the office." Before finally leaving, Pedersen said that upon his complaint, the two Chinese had been arrested and were being held at the Roeland Street Gaol. The complaint, according to Pedersen, was that Wai Lee had gone ashore at night without consent and in violation of local immigration regulations. Since that complaint seemingly involved only Wai Lee, it is unclear why both of the Chinese ended up in the Roeland Street Gaol.

On June 29 George Murphy, accompanied by Vice-Consul Charles H. Heisler and by merchant Sam Lee, who acted as interpreter, visited the two jailed Chinese crewmen. In his statement Wai Lee claimed that he and

Cheng Kee had been treated well at the start of the voyage but that since the beginning of April things had gone downhill. He claimed that at 4:30 on the morning of April 4, Pedersen knocked him down, causing blood to come from his ear, spotting his jersey, which he was still wearing and which he identified to Murphy. The master had said Wai Lee was no good as a cook, and on April 6 he threatened to kill both of the men. To the Chinese, Pedersen had claimed to be "king of the ship" with authority to do whatever he pleased. Because of the ill-treatment, once the *Puako* reached Cape Town, Wai Lee repeatedly requested permission to see the American consul general. Pedersen denied all the requests. On the night of the twenty-seventh, Pedersen had chained Wai Lee's hands behind him for a period of time. After that incident, a fearful Wai Lee left the ship and solicited the aid of local merchant Sam Lee. Wai Lee said he "would be in terror" of his life if he were returned to the ship, and he asked to be discharged.

Cheng Kee, the Chinese cabin boy, made similar accusations, claiming Pedersen had struck him and kicked him down a ladder during an encounter in mid-April. "I offered coffee to Pedersen. He asked if the coffee was good, and I replied, 'Yes.' Before he even tasted the coffee, he told me to come in and stand nearer him. He then struck me with his fist on the chest and called me by a vile name. He called his son Adolph Eric and closed the door. He knocked me down on the floor, and I fainted. Afterward my breast was very sore. Eric then pressed a pillow over my mouth, and the captain whipped me with a whip. He made me go down on my knees before him, and he did not stop [whipping me] until I held up my hands to him, palm to palm."

Cheng Kee said he also would be afraid of his life if forced to return to the ship, and he too requested to be discharged. To augment statements by the two men, Wai Lee produced a diary containing entries made in Chinese characters. These entries were purported to contain dates and details of numerous other violent assaults made against the two men. Most of the assaults had occurred in the master's cabin without eyewitnesses.

Pedersen denied to Murphy that he had used violence against anyone during the voyage, but according to a consular memorandum, Pedersen's own logbook entry refuted that. The entry stated that the Chinese had been seen "pouring dirty dishwater into the master's coffee." This act allegedly had been reported to Pedersen by one of the Chileans. Based on that report, Pedersen had justifiably "disciplined" the men, although Murphy did not relay specific details of the discipline meted out by Pedersen.

Murphy was in a quandary. If he could prove that the rights of the Chinese had been violated, he could grant the men discharges from the ship. In such a case, the vessel and her owners would be responsible for the high fees that would be due to the South African Immigration authorities. Murphy scheduled a hearing for July 2, but in the hope he would not unnecessarily delay the *Puako*, he attempted to arrange a settlement before the hearing commenced. Pedersen obviously did not want the Chinese on board, as he considered them unsatisfactory, and the Chinese wished to be discharged. Wai Lee even threatened suicide if he were forced to resail with Pedersen. Murphy and Vice-Consul Heisler discussed the situation with Pedersen and his attorney, a Mr. Low, pointing out that if Pedersen were found guilty at the hearing, he would lose the respect of the remainder of his crew and could find it difficult to locate replacements. Further, the ship would be required to make costly deposits for the deportation of the Chinese. Pedersen then agreed to release the two men if they would drop all charges.

There was, however, another problem. President Woodrow Wilson's signing of a declaration of war with Germany on April 6, 1917, had immediately resulted in an increased demand on shipping for war-related needs. This demand was concentrated on runs between the United States and Europe and siphoned off ships from such out-of-the-way places as Cape Town. This made it virtually impossible for Murphy to find transportation directly to the United States or Canada for the Chinese crewmen. The most Murphy could hope for was shipment to perhaps an Asian port from where the Chinese could transship to their home destinations in British Columbia. Despite repeated attempts, it was not until July 11 that Vice-Consul Heisler was able to locate transportation for the two men to Japan, from where they could more easily get passage to the United States or Canada. Since there were no open crew slots, the Chinese used their wages to purchase their passage.[6] Space was so scarce that the men were forced to travel to Japan on separate vessels—Wai Lee on the *Iyo Maru* and Cheng Kee on the *Tacoma Maru*.

Before they departed Cape Town, a Mr. O'Hare, their official escort provided by South African Immigration, accompanied Wai Lee and Cheng Kee to the *Puako* to get their belongings. O'Hare later related to Heisler that Pedersen and all others on board were drunk and disorderly. Wai Lee was struck by one of them. Fearing further problems, O'Hare announced that if either of his charges was struck again, everyone on board, including Captain Pedersen, would be arrested and jailed.

The Chinese were not the only *Puako* problem. When the Chilean and American crewmen had presented themselves at the United States Consulate General on July 2 as potential witnesses in the matter of the two Chinese, they lodged their own complaints and asked to be discharged:

"We, the undersigned, members of the crew of the American sailing ship *Puako*, wish to complain to the American Consul General at Cape Town regarding the amount of food issued to us while at sea, the allowance being far below the amount prescribed by law. Moreover, the supply of food has not only been entirely insufficient but has been exceedingly poor in quality."

Pedersen countered this most recent charge by claiming the provisions had been plentiful and that what he supplied daily to the cook was in excess of the minimal provisions mandated (see appendix 2). He said the problem was Wai Lee's bad cooking, and that after fresh supplies were exhausted, the men went hungry because they had thrown their food overboard. When the complainants were told by Murphy that the matter would have to be investigated by no less than three inspectors and that the crewmen themselves would have to bear the cost of the investigation if the complaint proved unfounded, the men backed down. As a group, the six Chileans agreed to stay on board and return to the United States with Pedersen, editing their initial complaint by saying that things had in fact improved since the ship arrived in Cape Town and that even prior to their arrival there had been no problem with the food so long as the ingredients had been provided to the Chinese cook by Bulman, the second mate. It was when Captain Pedersen began supplying the materials to the cook that "there was at once a great and improper falling off in the quantity of their food which resulted in their often being hungry."

Although the Chileans were no longer of concern to Murphy, the American crewmen V. G. Chambers and George Corron continued to press for discharges. Chambers stated that Pedersen had a reputation as "the most brutal master on the Pacific Coast of America where he is commonly called Hellfire." Chambers's remark seems to indicate that by 1917, Pedersen's sobriquet had more to do with his personality on board the *Puako* than with the difficult fire that had occurred aboard the *Challenger* in 1905. Although Murphy found an opening for one of the men on the American schooner *Sophie Christenson*, Pedersen refused to release either man, claiming he needed their service for the return trip.[7]

At some point following July 2, Pedersen filed charges against three of the Chileans, Rivera, Gusman, and Salina, claiming they had attempted to destroy the *Puako* by lighting matches in the vicinity of the vessel's petroleum supply. Although the *Puako* was sail propelled, she had aboard a gasoline engine that powered the ship's main bilge pump.[8] When Vice-Consul Heisler visited the three in jail, they again asked to be discharged. Two of them stated that Pedersen had struck them. Like the incidents with the Chinese, these alleged assaults had occurred in the master's cabin without witnesses and would therefore be hard to prove. Heisler knew Pedersen would not grant discharges to the three Chileans. He made every attempt to placate them and finally persuaded them to return to the ship.

On July 7 the first mate, Fred Wann, was discharged by mutual consent and replaced by Victor J. Van Trojen. In his official report Murphy spoke highly of Wann, describing him as a "sober, reliable man." Prior to leaving Cape Town as a passenger on the Swedish steamer *Siljan*, bound for New Orleans, Wann told Murphy "he could not be satisfied to remain on that ship with a violent and immoral man like Captain Pedersen whom he described as a disgrace to the American merchant marine."

A week or so later Pedersen and his new mate, Van Trojen, showed up at the consulate general, "both very much under the influence of liquor." Pedersen "swore so loudly that his words, 'God damn your soul' were clearly heard by Murphy and Vice Consul John W. Dye," who was in Murphy's office some distance from the public reception area. Heisler met with Pedersen and promised to go to the ship that afternoon to settle the *Puako*'s new difficulties, which seemed in part to have resulted from yet more accusations against the master by the Americans George Corron and V. G. Chambers, who feared that they would be treated violently during the pending voyage to San Francisco via Manila. When Heisler reached the ship, Van Trojen assured him as well as Corron and Chambers that so long as the men attended to their duties, they had nothing to fear. Based on this understanding, Heisler had no grounds on which to authorize the discharge of either man. As Heisler was preparing to leave the ship's cabin where he had met with the mate, Pedersen came on board, so drunk "it was almost impossible for him to stand alone." Pedersen ordered Van Trojen out of the cabin and began ranting to Heisler, but in his drunken state, coherent discussion proved impossible. Pedersen became very abusive and charged that the consular staff at Cape Town was unjustifiably interfering with him. He would run his ship to suit himself. When Heisler made no comment to Pedersen's tirade, the master angrily shouted to the vice-consul that "all at this office could go to Hell." As Heisler was leaving the ship, Pedersen appeared on deck and "with expressions of indifference as to whatever might happen to the ship, stated he was going back up town. An automobile was, as usual, waiting for the master, and Mr. Heisler saw him drive away in it with two women while the master's minor son [Adolph Eric Pedersen] sat crying on the deck."

On the same day, Ernest Allen Bruce made a statement regarding Pedersen to Vice-Consul Dye at the Consulate General. Bruce, a resident of Scotland, had been employed temporarily on July 14 as cook and steward on the *Puako*, with plans to remain permanently as soon as arrangements could be made with South African Immigration. According to Bruce, Pedersen directed: "You run the God damn ship as cheap as you can, and I will see you all right." Bruce stated that there had been no bread and that the amount of food was insufficient at Sunday's noon dinner. Sunday's supper consisted of about "two spoons full of hash for each man, and one-quarter loaf of bread for six men, and tea with no milk." That same Sunday the fifteenth, Pedersen told Bruce that it was "the God damn Americans who are making all the trouble aboard about the food; I will fix their hash when we get outside." Bruce told Dye that as he had not yet signed articles, and as he had not been able to get enough to eat, he had left the vessel about 8:30 Sunday night.

On the evening of the twentieth, Captain Pedersen was ashore when he received a note from Van Trojen informing him that at 5 a.m. the newly shipped Negro cook had jumped overboard "and had swum ashore, wearing a life belt and carrying a valise containing his clothing." At this point the *Puako* was at Cape Town's anchorage area known as Table Bay (see plate 6), preparing for departure. Pedersen arranged for yet another cook, who apparently stayed on board, as on July 27, 1917, to the great relief of George Murphy, Pedersen secured clearance papers from Vice-Consul Heisler. In parting, the master stated to Heisler that he expected to return to Cape Town in nine months. Had George Murphy known what the next six years would bring, he might have viewed those words more as a threat than a promise and considered asking for a transfer.

Although Captain Pedersen was out of sight once the *Puako* left Cape Town, he was not out of the minds of George Murphy and others in Cape Town with whom he had had dealings. The staff at the United States Consulate General was of the opinion that Pedersen was hated by the crew and that those who had remained on board had decided not to make formal charges against him fearing "unpleasant results" if the charges and evidence were not sufficient for the accusers to be discharged from the ship by the American consul general.

While memories were fresh, Murphy submitted a lengthy dispatch dated July 30, 1917, to Secretary of State Robert Lansing in which he discussed for the record the recent visit of the *Puako* and all the problems that he and his staff had just experienced with her master. In an almost regretful tone, he said he believed that the Chinese seamen had probably been repeatedly and brutally assaulted by Pedersen; however, there had been no eyewitness to present direct evidence, "although some of the seamen said that they had heard screams proceeding from that room." Even though Murphy did not have enough evidence with which to charge Pedersen and remove him from the *Puako*, he and his vice-consuls all shared the opinion, based on Pedersen's general behavior, that he "is not a man who is fit to creditably command an American vessel in foreign trade."[9]

A later dispatch dated December 14 from Murphy to Secretary Lansing was probably the result of a visit Heisler had from a Mr. Osborn, the manager of Lemm's Outfitting Store. Osborn brought up the subject of the Chinese seamen. To the vice-consul's surprise, Osborn claimed to have witnessed an assault by Pedersen against one of the Chinese while the *Puako* was unloading at Cape Town. Osborn said the assault had taken place in the master's cabin. In this memo Murphy stated, "I am satisfied that at the time of his visit to this port, Mr. Pedersen's naturalization had not sufficiently affected his attitude to fit him for the command of an American vessel or to induce him to respect the provision of American law."

Pedersen returned to the United States with the *Puako* in January 1918. At the instigation of the Department of State, an in-house governmental hearing was held in Washington—probably by the Bureau of Navigation's Steamboat Inspection Service—to review the information contained in Murphy's consular dispatches of July 30 and December 14, 1917.[10] Without available witnesses, it was felt that charges could not be brought against Pedersen and that, at least for now, he would remain in charge of the *Puako*.

CHAPTER 2

VANCOUVER-VICTORIA, B.C., APRIL 1918

At the same time that maritime labor leader Andrew Furuseth was organizing seamen and pushing for legislative remedies to make life aboard American vessels less abusive and more humane and thus more attractive to a higher grade of sailor, William D. Haywood was crusading for the general working class following his formation of the union known as the Industrial Workers of the World (IWW). Unlike Furuseth, who brought together the workers of one particular industry, the IWW had a broader approach aimed at mobilizing the working classes of many industries, including the maritime industry, under the banner "One Big Union." The IWW's members—known as Wobblies—were particularly active in the western states, where their message was disseminated by soapbox orators and singers whose defiant ballads were contained in the IWW songbook titled *Songs of the Workers: To Fan the Flames of Discontent*. (For a sampling of those songs, see appendix 4.) The message of the IWW also appeared in their publications *Industrial Worker* and *Solidarity* as well as in Jack London's *The Iron Heel*, Edward Bellamy's *Looking Backward*, and Laurence Gronlund's *Cooperative Commonwealth*. In November 1909 the revolutionary character of the Wobblies brought the movement into national focus when hundreds of its members swarmed into Spokane, Washington, to protest the practices of employment agents and lumber camp managers who, they claimed, were swindling workers in the timber industry. Within a week's time, the Spokane jail and a school overflowed with IWW prisoners. "They came into court bloody from beatings; they were put to hard labor on bread and water, jammed into cells like sardines, and in the name of sanitation hosed with ice water and returned to unheated confinement."[1] Like locusts, more and more Wobblies continued to pour into Spokane while those in jail sang their ballads through the nights, staged hunger and work strikes, and defied their captors. By March 1910 the taxpayers of Spokane had had enough. They rebelled against the cost of confining the Wobblies in jail, and the prisoners were all set free.

The IWW was especially attractive to those who could fit under the umbrella of "migrant"—men who moved from job to job and place to place, following the harvests, construction cycles, timbering, mining, and even "a spell of sea life in the forecastle of a merchant ship." Wherever they went, they sang their songs, dispersed their literature, and plastered millions of stickers on everything from pickaxes to boxcars. One of those stickers appearing between 1915 and 1917 displayed the union's symbol of industrial sabotage, the wooden shoe, and the message "Slow Down. The hours are long, the pay is small, so take your time and buck 'em all." In return for their growing radicalism, the Wobblies continued to receive rough treatment, one western sheriff bragging, "Just knock him over the head with a night stick and throw him in the river. When he comes up, he beats it out of town." For several years following 1914, Wobblies were regularly jailed, beaten, shot, and tortured, especially in communities along the Pacific coast of the United States. In the midst of this, on April 6, 1917, the United States declared war on Germany. Following this declaration, new IWW stickers exhorting "Don't be a soldier; be a man" made this movement even more feared and despised by the United States government as well as by upper- and middle-class America.

Even though deep-sea masters—especially those sailing from West Coast ports—were out of touch a good deal, employers would have stayed abreast of this dangerous radical labor movement and in turn would have kept their masters informed via cabled messages to shipping agents located worldwide.[2] With the world at war and the Industrial Workers of the World infiltrating the maritime industry, this was a period during which a ship's master had a great deal to be concerned about.

On July 28, 1917, the *Puako* cleared Cape Town. After making stops in Australia and the Philippines, she returned to San Francisco in early January of 1918. Following the settling of the ship's account with Hind, Rolph & Co., Pedersen spent three weeks at home with his wife, Gertrude, and their family. On February 10 the *Puako* was towed to Vancouver, where she was hauled, cleaned, and painted prior to loading lumber for her next trip.

The *Puako* had a carrying capacity of 1.4 million board feet of lumber, some of which was carried as deck load (see plate 3).[3] With the weight of lumber changing seasonally because of its fluctuating water content, the actual number of board feet carried could vary. Since the *Puako* took on her cargo in Canada and was to discharge it in South Africa—both included in the British Commonwealth—she may have come under the 1870s British loading guidelines. Had she loaded in a United States port, the amount she carried would have been at Pedersen's discretion, since the United States Congress had been slow to establish freeboard restrictions. In fact, it was not until March 2, 1929, that Congress passed the Load Line Act which established loading guidelines for U.S.-flag seagoing vessels over 150 gross tons.

The first crew members Captain Pedersen signed were two of his sons, Leonard Roy, age eighteen, and Adolph Eric, age seventeen. Both boys were the same height as their father, 5'6". William Mattson, age sixty-five and 5'9", was also on board. Mattson, a native of Finland, had sailed with Pedersen for the past seven years as the ship's carpenter, and he considered the master a friend.

As loading commenced, Captain Pedersen began trying to fill the remaining crew slots. Experienced seamen who knew Pedersen's reputation as a hard driver and a brute were reluctant to sign on with him at any time, but especially in 1918 when jobs were plentiful. One reason for the tight labor market was that military conscription in the United States and in Canada had taken thousands of young men who otherwise might have sought employment at sea. Within weeks after the United States passed the Selective Service Act of May 18, 1917, nearly 10 million males between the ages of twenty-one and thirty-one had been enrolled. By the time the armistice was signed on November 11, 1918, nearly 3 million men had been mobilized. A substantial number of them were drafted shortly after passage of the Selective Service Act. Conscription had cut an even deeper swath through the male population of the British Empire, where males between eighteen and forty were subject to be drafted. The manpower drain was made worse by the competing and predominant steamship segment of the merchant marine, which was paying higher wages than the $60 a month Pedersen was offering an able-bodied seaman.[4]

Once the *Puako* was loaded, she was towed across the Strait of Georgia from Vancouver to Victoria. From there the voyage commenced following the formality of signing on the crew that Pedersen finally managed to cobble together.

> I, R. M. Newcomb, Vice Consul of the United States of America at Victoria, British Columbia, Canada, do hereby certify that on this 24th day of April A.D. 1918

L. R. Pedersen
A. E. Pedersen
William Mattson
L. A. Smithson
William Jones
John Walter Campbell
James Campbell
John Henry Stewart
Peter Jorgensen
Lester A. Jensen
Axel H. B. Hansen
Jack Joe
Bjarne Olsen
Frank Grielen

all personally known to me, appeared before me, and in my presence signed the within agreement [ship's articles] with my sanction and in all respects complied with the requirements of law, each for himself acknowledging that he had read or had heard read the said agreement and understood the same, and that while sober and not in a state of intoxication he signed it freely and voluntarily for the uses and purposes therein mentioned.

Given under my hand and seal of office the day and year first above written.

[signed] R. Newcomb, Vice Consul
United States of America

Accompanying Newcomb's certification was U.S. consular form no. 79, "Roll or List of the Crew of the Barkentine *Puako* of San Francisco, Cal., whereof A. C. Pedersen is Master, Bound to South Africa...."[5] Included with form 79 was consular form 82, Certificate of Shipment of Seamen to be Attached to Crew List and Shipping Articles. The following was compiled from both of those forms, which were signed by Newcomb on April 24, 1918.

Name of Seaman	Station	Monthly Wage
L. R. Pedersen	First Mate	$110
A. E. Pedersen	Second Mate	$100
William Mattson	Carpenter	$90
John Henry Stewart	Cook	$100
L. A. Smithson	Cabin Boy	$40
William Jones	A.B.	$60
John Walter Campbell	O.S.	$40
James Campbell	A.B.	$60
Peter Jorgensen	A.B.	$60
Lester A. Jensen	O.S.	$40
A. H. B. Hansen	A.B.	$75
Jack Joe	A.B.	$60

Vancouver-Victoria, B.C., April 1918

| Bjarne Olsen | Boatswain | $80 |
| F. Grielen | A.B. | $60 |

According to a cable dated September 24, 1918, from Hind, Rolph & Co. to Secretary of State Robert Lansing, Captain Pedersen was paid $150 a month plus unspecified bonuses.[6]

Absent from both crew lists prepared by Newcomb was one Edward Reilly, who was irregularly shipped by Pedersen and later added to the ship's articles once the *Puako* reached international waters.

On April 25, 1918, the *Victoria Daily Times* reported: "After an unusually long period of detention in port by reason of the great scarcity of seamen, the American 4-masted barkentine *Puako*, is expected to get away today on her voyage to Cape Town. A full crew has finally been signed, and Captain A. C. Pedersen is congratulating himself that his troubles are over for the present."

The news item went on to discuss the acute manpower shortage within the maritime industry, stating that if not obviated, vessels loaded in North America with cargo destined for Britain and her allies would stagnate in port. One realizes from that report that the *Puako* was lucky. She was loaded, crewed, and ready to sail. She had on board a full load of lumber—Oregon pine that Hind, Rolph & Co. had purchased in British Columbia for $30,000. Added charges, including stevedore services and transportation of the cargo to South Africa, brought the lumber's total delivered value to $156,000 on arrival at Cape Town.

After receiving his clearance from Newcomb, Pedersen went before the collector of customs where he was cautioned—at least according to a later statement he made—that "German [surface] raiders might be operating off the west coast of Mexico and in the South Pacific Ocean and that floating mines had been reported along the South African coast."[7]

The *Puako* was towed to Cape Flattery by the Canadian tug *Clayburn* on April 27. Once the barkentine dropped the hawser around seven o'clock that evening, the *Puako* and the fifteen souls aboard were on their own.[8]

By the time the *Puako* reached Cape Town, her first port of call, two of the crew were dead and most of the rest were in irons facing serious charges made by the master. The following information about the seamen was obtained from the shipping articles and Department of State files:

L. A. Smithson, 5'7", was a nineteen-year-old United States citizen born in Cleveland, Ohio.

Peter Jorgensen, 5'7", age thirty, was a Danish citizen and allegedly a deserter from the Canadian navy.

John Henry Stewart, 5'6", age forty-one, was a United States citizen born in San Francisco, California.

Axel H. B. Hansen, 5'4", age twenty-eight, was a Danish subject. The higher monthly wage Hansen was paid as an able-bodied seaman suggests that he had previous seagoing experience.

Forty-seven-year-old William Jones, 5'10½", had perhaps the most varied background. He was a native of South Wales who had spent most of his life as a miner, although in 1902 he had made a trip as a crewman on the four-masted British bark *Puritan*, traveling for 154 days from Tacoma, Washington, to Dunkirk, France, via Cape Horn. He first left South Wales in 1889 and settled in Luzern County, Pennsylvania, where he worked at the Bordantown Colliery as a coal miner. About a year later he was in Colorado, working various coal mines before moving on to the state of Washington, where he stayed about three years. Thereafter he worked in mines in California, Utah, Arizona, and New Mexico before returning to South Wales in 1902. He remained in South Wales until 1906, after which he had spent most of his time in Canada working in various types of mines, although in 1914 and 1915 he temporarily left the mines to work in Canada's vast wheat fields. Jones, who could never stay in one place very long, had developed a desire to travel to and work in the mines of South Africa. He thought he had found his opportunity when he read a newspaper ad placed by Jack Clear, a shipping agent in Victoria used by Captain Pedersen. At the time, Jones was suffering from miner's consumption, today known as black lung, and he thought a long sea voyage would be a great health benefit. Although Jones signed on for the complete voyage, he later claimed that he had a verbal understanding with Captain Pedersen that he would leave the ship in Cape Town.

John Walter Campbell, age twenty-one, 5'8½", was a country boy born in Maquoketa, Iowa, where his father was a member of the Jackson County Board of Supervisors. He joined the *Puako* on March 1 when she was loading lumber in Vancouver and prepared to embark on his first sea voyage. Although he was signed on as an ordinary seaman, Campbell did not share the forecastle with the rest of the crew. He lived aft with the ship's officers, the carpenter, and the cabin boy, L. A. Smithson.

James Campbell, age twenty-eight, 5'9", a British subject born in Kingston, Ontario, was in 1918 a legal resident of Calgary, Alberta, where he shared a home with his widowed mother. Prior to joining the *Puako* he had been working on the Canadian west coast as a seaman on a small steamboat. The Canadian draft had designated James Campbell as Class A but had deferred him because he was his mother's sole source of support. Even with that deferment, he had to obtain permission from the British military to sign on board the *Puako* for what would be his first deep-sea voyage under sail.

Lester Jensen, a 5'6" United States citizen, was twenty years of age when he signed on board. Jensen was born in Utah, where his widowed father still lived. In April 1918 he was working near Seattle as a waiter in a logging camp but was looking for a change. When he registered with the U.S. Employment Bureau in Seattle, he saw a notice that sailors were wanted for a trip to Manila. The sign directed him to the office of shipping agent Maxwell Levy, where he was waylaid by Pedersen. That night after obtaining seaman's papers, Jensen accompanied Pedersen to Victoria aboard the ferry *Sol Duc*.[9]

At 5'0", forty-three-year-old Jack Joe was the smallest and least educated man on board. Jack Joe's stated age of thirty-four on the shipping papers seems to have been the result of a typographical error reversing the numbers. Pedersen was at a hotel in Victoria asking around for seamen when Jack Joe approached him and said he would like to make the trip as quartermaster, claiming he was good at the wheel. Jack Joe was able to make only his mark rather than a signature. He knew very little about his origins. His aunt had told him his mother was from Honolulu and that his father was Chilean. His seaman's pass identified him as Hawaiian. Jack Joe's hands were crippled by rheumatism, a condition that Pedersen must have known would limit his ability to help others on watch in pulling lines and tending sails. That the master hired a man with Jack Joe's physical disability is an indication of how desperate he was to have bodies with which to fill the crew roster.

Bjarne Olsen, called Barney by his shipmates, was a 6'0", 190-pound, twenty-seven-year-old Norwegian. Some documents incorrectly listed him as Swedish. Barney, an experienced seaman, was signed on as boatswain at a wage of $80 but was shortly afterward reduced by Pedersen to able-bodied seaman.

Twenty-eight-year-old Frank Grielen, a native of Rotterdam, Holland, stood 5'4". He was the last man signed on the articles in Victoria before Vice-Consul Newcomb. Grielen, a stocky man at the start of the trip, had sailed transatlantic on passenger steamships where he had served both as a steward and as a printer. He also had worked on an ore boat operating in the Great Lakes. In 1913 Grielen began drifting around, working a few months as a hotel porter in New York, followed by some time in Michigan working for the Quincy Mining Company. By 1914 he was in Minnesota working seasonally at various timber camps and wheat fields. Altogether he had spent about five years working in the United States and Canada before deciding to ship on the *Puako*.

Edward Reilly, a twenty-five-year-old, six-foot Irishman, met Pedersen at Maxwell Levy's office in Seattle. He and Pedersen and Lester Jensen traveled on the ferry *Sol Duc* to Victoria. Reilly, a British subject with some seagoing experience, was exempted from military service because of a rupture and was thus free to sign on the *Puako*. Since he had no passport and there was no time to obtain other identification papers, Pedersen could not officially enter him on the shipping articles before leaving Victoria. Once the ship was in international waters, Reilly signed the articles. Pedersen told Reilly that he would claim him as a stowaway since the seaman had no papers. If Reilly confirmed the story, all would be well. At least, that is what Reilly was allegedly told by Pedersen, who "spoke to me like a father" in Victoria. The concocted story might have gone well for Pedersen in Cape Town, but without proper papers, Reilly undoubtedly would have quickly found a home in the local prison awaiting deportation.

CHAPTER 3

OFF CAPE TOWN, AUGUST 27, 1918

Four months after the *Puako*'s departure from Victoria, lookouts aboard the British troop transport SS *Magdalena* spotted a four-masted barkentine signaling Y-F: "want assistance; mutiny."[1] The barkentine's name board identified her as *Puako* out of San Francisco. A ship's boat from the *Magdalena* under the command of her second mate was lowered away and rowed over to investigate. Accompanying the boat crew was an armed ten-man boarding party. Adolph Cornelius Pedersen told the boarding officer that the crew had repeatedly attempted to kill him and his sons. According to an affidavit that boarding officer William George Martin gave before Commissioner of Oaths A. J. Larpent two months later on October 21, 1918, following his arrival in England, he looked around the *Puako* and observed eight men, later determined to have been Olsen, James Campbell, Jones, Grielen, Jensen, Jorgensen, Smithson, and Jack Joe. Four of those Martin remembered seeing were "battened down," or constrained, two of them in the after peak and two in the pump well; three others were on deck, and Jack Joe was at the wheel. Martin had either forgotten or did not see Mattson, John Walter Campbell, or Reilly. Reilly's deposition, taken within days of arrival of the *Puako* in Cape Town and reproduced later in this chapter, may be somewhat more accurate on this point than Martin's account. The two agree, though, that most of the men were covered in bruises. When Martin asked to see the face of the man at the wheel, Pedersen ordered his sons to "turn the bastard around and let the officer have a look at his face. One mate struck the man [Jack Joe] with his fist on one side of the jaw and the other mate struck the man with his fist on the other side of the jaw and turned him around.... After due observation," Martin reported, "I came to the conclusion that the master of the *Puako* was out of his mind."[2]

The January 12, 1919, London *Sunday Times* carried a lengthy, albeit embellished, story of the events. On March 3, 1919, the story was reproduced in the Cape Town *Cape Argus* under the sensational heading "War-time Episodes: Mutiny on the High Seas." The author, identified only as a subaltern, was probably a British Army officer who had been a passenger on the *Magdalena* when she intercepted the *Puako* near Cape Town. The author changed some of the details to make a good story even better.

Where the meeting of the smiling Indian and the turbulent Atlantic oceans cause a perpetual swell, the great liner [*Magdalena*] forges swiftly ahead. Her decks are crowded with as picturesque a throng as could be met within an Eastern bazaar. East and West are closely commingled. All have been through months of trying campaigning in East Africa. The black soldiers, with a goodly contingent of native carriers, are on their way to far-distant villages on the West Coast. The white officers and men are bound for Blighty [England]. All are on leave; some will return to Africa in due course; others will proceed to far-distant spheres of military operations.

For hours, not a ship has broken the monotony of the grey waste of waters. An occasional spouting whale, a huge albatross, or great flocks of migratory birds are the only signs of life. On board, the excitement of confusion and bustle incidental to our departure has subsided. In its place a reaction has set in, and the decks are strangely silent, except, perhaps, for an occasional groan from those who are paying involuntarily their tributes to Neptune's powers.

Presently, away half a mile on our port bow, a full-rigged sailing ship is seen wallowing in the swell. No clouds of snowy canvas make her a thing of beauty; a few sails here and there flap dejectedly in the smart breeze. Even to a landsman something is obviously wrong. Our glasses quickly tell us that she is not deserted. "Has she fever on board?" "Is she a decoy ship?" "What does the flag she is flying signify?" Quickly the answer is passed along—Mutiny! Are we living in the days of Clark Russell?[3] Mutiny on the High Seas!

The liner has come to a standstill. All is orderly bustle. An armed party of black soldiers is assembled; their eyes gleam and their faces glisten with sweat from sheer terror as soon as they realize they are to trust themselves in the small boat tossing alongside. Some of them pretend to be violently sick, but the ruse does not work. They tumble down a swaying rope ladder into the lifeboat as best they can. A more woebegone looking lot of warriors surely never was seen!

A couple of ship's officers clad in white, imperturbably sit in the stern seats. They alone seem unaffected by the excitement. The oars are manned by a white crew, the boat is cleared away. A thousand eyes eagerly watch her progress as she nears the apparently helpless vessel. She is alongside. A solitary figure leans over the bulwarks of the ship.

At the top of the gangway the officers in charge of the boat are met by a smiling, corpulent Yankee, who announces himself as the skipper. Sadly standing around are a few of the crew whose faces bear evidence of very great ill-usage. Explanations quickly follow: the ship is an American, 120 days out from _____ and bound for _____ [censored].

Very early in the voyage the suspicions of the captain had been aroused. There was nothing definite, but they were sufficient to put him on his guard. Finally an attempt by a large part of the crew to seize the ship was made. With the aid of a small loyal section, this was frustrated; the skipper does not say how, but one can imagine. Down below he had the mutineers in irons, and the worst of them were "up to their necks in bilge water at the bottom of the vessel." Investigation had shown that there were several German agents on board, plentifully supplied with money. This money they had lavishly distributed amongst the crew. Their intention was not only to seize the ship but to blow it up [along] with the officers and those of the men who had refused to join them. The skipper had not only secured the persons of the mutineers, but had made them disgorge their ill-gotten gains. With his greatly reduced crew it was impossible for him to work the ship, and hence his call for assistance.

Briefly told, with occasional adjectives, this was the story. But one wondered, as one looked at the smiling, cherubic face on the rotund captain, how much remained untold.

At Pedersen's request, the boarding officer signaled the *Magdalena* with semaphore flags asking the transport to send a wireless to Cape Town giving their position and requesting that a tug come out to assist the barkentine into port. The wireless was received in Cape Town by Captain Elliott Howe, who carried many titles including that of sub-inspector of the South African Police. Howe was also assistant provost marshal for the Cape Town

Docks Prohibited Area and a justice of the peace for the District of the Cape. American consul general George H. Murphy, having been notified by Howe, hired the tug *Ludwig Wiener* to take him and Captain Howe and an armed guard to the area designated by the *Magdalena*'s signal. The ship was not found—unsurprising, given the conditions of fog and heavy rain—and the tug returned to port. During the night the *Puako* made Cape Town on her own without escort, a violation of South Africa's wartime regulations. At six o'clock the next morning, as Murphy and his party were heading out by tug to renew the search, the *Puako* was spotted riding at anchor in Cape Town's Table Bay (see plate 6).

Howe, Murphy, a South African Customs officer, an official from South African Immigration, and fourteen or fifteen policemen armed with rifles immediately boarded the *Puako*. They were met by Pedersen, who delivered a sensational report of men jumping overboard and of others being German spies who had attempted to kill the ship's officers and destroy the vessel.

> I am the Master of the American Barkentine *Puako*. I left Victoria, B.C. on the 27th April 1918, bound for Cape Town with a cargo of timber. My crew consisted of 13 seamen, 2 mates who are my sons and myself. For the first few days the crew were seasick and after they got over this I found they were not seamen and instructed the mate to teach them their work.
>
> On the 21st May the Cook, John Henry Stewart came to my dining saloon at breakfast time, he walked through to the pantry. I heard him speak to the Cabin Boy, L. A. Smithson, and then he came out of the pantry holding a large carving knife in his right hand. He asked permission to speak to me and I said what do you want? He stammered for some time and did not ask me anything. He came closer to me all the time still holding the knife in his hand.
>
> I backed out of the Saloon into my cabin and closed the door and held the door slightly open and told him to get back to work. . . .
>
> On the 23rd May he came aft again on deck. I was on the poop deck and told him to go forward again. He was wearing a big coat. He turned around and went forward again.
>
> At 10 a.m. that morning I received a report from the second mate that this man had jumped overboard. I was in my cabin writing at the time. I went on deck and saw him in the water just level with the break of the Poop. He was under water and was sinking. The sea was calm and there was no wind and very little steering way.

Off Cape Town, August 27, 1918

From the 1st June 1918, I had occasion to find fault with the way in which the helmsmen were steering the ship when we were weathering the Society Islands which were on a lee shore and a danger to the ship. It appeared as though the intention was to put the ship ashore. All the crew took a turn at the wheel with the exception of Frank Grielen who could not take the wheel. The weather at this time was stormy with thunder and lightning and choppy seas.

The crew were on the point of mutiny and would not answer when told to get to work on a job and would not haul on the ropes.

On 10th June the second mate was spitting blood and complained of feeling bad. I gave him medicine. I examined the bread and found glass in it. I went to the store[room] and found that several lamp chimneys were missing.

From this date to the 22nd August I have had trouble with the crew and put eight of them in irons for disobedience of orders and behaving in a mutinous manner. I have taken statements from these men which they have signed and which have been witnessed and are now produced. My log-book contains entries of these matters.

On August 6th another seaman named Axel Hansen jumped overboard near Tristan da Cunha Islands.

[signed] A. C. Pedersen, Master[4]

The purported mutineers and spies—all in irons—were brought on deck after arrangements had been made between the consul general and the immigration officer to take them ashore for detention. Pedersen handed over to Elliott Howe the men's passports, the vessel's official logbook, and a sizable bundle of papers Pedersen identified as statements and confessions signed variously by the charged seamen.[5] Personal diaries that a few of the crew began writing at the beginning of the voyage had, their authors claimed, been confiscated by Pedersen. These either were taken ashore later and hidden by Pedersen or were destroyed by him even before the ship arrived in Cape Town.[6]

Captain Elliott Howe's report tersely sums up the physical condition of the crewmen: "In my seventeen years of experience as a police officer, I have never seen a body of men so badly knocked about."

Once they were ashore, Howe and Murphy arranged for a meal for the starving men at the Alfred Docks Police Station. After their hunger was satisfied, Howe explained to the men that since serious charges had been made against them by Captain Pedersen, they would have to be detained

Brutality on Trial

pending investigation. In company with two British naval officers, Howe took statements separately from Edward Reilly, "who told his story in an unconcerned manner"; William Jones, who "was practically in a state of physical collapse and was unable to finish"; and James Campbell, "who was in a highly nervous state and very emotional." Howe later also took a statement from Lester Jensen after the accused men were lodged in the Roeland Street Gaol (see plate 10).

Howe's authority to begin this investigation of foreign seamen removed at the request of the ship's master from a U.S.-flag vessel stemmed from the fact that these men, who Pedersen claimed were German spies, had come into territory controlled by the British military at a time when Britain and Germany were at war. As the investigation of events on the *Puako* widened, George Murphy continued to call on Howe for assistance under Section 8 of the Act of March 4, 1915, the Seamen's Act, which stated in part, "It shall be the duty of all consular officers to discountenance insubordination by every means in their power and, where the local authorities can be usefully employed for that purpose, to lend their aid and use their exertions to that end in the most effectual manner."

The most complete and depictive sworn statement gathered by Howe was made by Edward Reilly, an Irishman who had first come to the United States in November 1913.[7] The account from which the excerpts that follow are taken was transcribed by the Cape Town police stenographer. Reading them, one is amazed at how well-spoken Reilly was. At the beginning of his deposition, he explained that he had worked at a variety of jobs and had made two trips to Europe aboard the White Star liner *Adriatic* in 1915. On April 16 or 17, 1918, Reilly was in Seattle when he decided to go to sea again.

> The [U.S.] Government Employment Bureau . . . sent [me] down to Maxwell's Office on No. 1 Pier.[8] In Maxwell's office I met Captain Pedersen [who] asked if I wished to go to sea and . . . if I cared to make the trip to South Africa. . . . I said I had no experience of sailing vessels and he told me it would be all right. . . . He told me he was paying Ordinary Seamen $60.00 per month, and A.B.'s $95.00. He said "I will start you at $60.00 and when you get into the way of the ship I will give you more."
>
> On the night of the 18th April, Captain Pedersen, Lester A. Jensen, and I took a small coasting steamer [the ferry *Sol Duc*] from Seattle to Victoria B.C.

Off Cape Town, August 27, 1918

When immigration officials learned that Reilly was a British subject, he was examined to see if he qualified for military service. The doctors exempted him as he had a rupture.

> After the examination I again saw Captain Pedersen, and he told me to go aboard the sailing ship *Puako*. I went aboard at 2 p.m. on the 19th April 1918. I had no passport nor any papers from the American authorities; all I had was the captain's word that he would see me through all right.... I started work on board on the 20th April. Those on board ... were the first and second mates, the carpenter [Mattson] ..., William Jones, James Campbell, Peter Jorgensen, John Henry Stewart, Lester A. Jensen, and L. A. Smithson.

Two days after going aboard, and finding that things were not as he had anticipated, Reilly asked to be released. An angry Pedersen shouted, "You son-of-a-bitch, stay right where you are; I have paid your fare and am not going to let you go." When Reilly pointed out that he had not yet signed articles, Pedersen said he would take care of that once the ship was at sea. According to Reilly,

> On the evening of the 26th as the *Puako* lay in the [Esquimalt] Bay, a launch came out from shore with the captain and a military officer. The military officer remained in the launch. I saw him; he was too drunk to come aboard. The captain came aboard and we sailed on the morning of the 27th April from Victoria B.C....
>
> It was ... six days out at sea that I signed on. I was called aft to the cabin and asked "Well do you want to sign?" I said "Yes, I will sign from the day I came aboard, the 19th." He said, "No I cannot sign you on then, you are not a stowaway, but to clear myself with the authorities in South Africa I will sign you on as a stowaway as you have no passport".... The entry dated the 28th April to the effect that I came on deck at 10 a.m. as a stowaway and was then signed on is not correct. I never was a stowaway....
>
> The captain began abusing the crew ... as soon as the pilot left the ship. Then for a few days his behavior improved. After this he begun to daily abuse and assault John Henry Stewart, the cook. On occasions when I have been at the wheel, I have seen the captain kicking and smashing Stewart.... The cook often complained to me of his treatment and told me he ... would have to jump overboard.... The

captain told me that Stewart was trying to poison him.... From this time on he continually assaulted and abused Stewart till he jumped overboard.

I remember this day, I was at the wheel, it was calm, sails were set but not drawing. I did not see him jump over myself but heard the carpenter shout, "Cook gone overboard." The second mate ran aft and informed the captain. The second mate threw a line to Stewart, but I could not see if he caught hold.... No effort was made to launch a boat although the sea was dead calm....

I am not certain of the date Stewart jumped overboard. I had a pocket book with this and other dates in. This was taken from me by the captain the Sunday before we arrived at Cape Town....

A few days after Stewart's death the captain spoke to me.... "I went a bit too far with Stewart; but I will fix it up so that nobody will know what happened."

From other depositions, it is apparent that Reilly and the other seamen agreed that Stewart's death was the pivotal point when Pedersen began turning from master to monster. Reilly continued:

After Stewart's death the captain quieted down for about nine or ten days. Then he started abusing Lester A. Jensen who had been made cook in place of Stewart. I have seen on several occasions the captain and also the mates kick Jensen 'round the decks like a dog. ... The more [Jensen] complained the more thrashings he got.

As cook, Jensen satisfied us in the fo'c'sle better than Stewart, but nothing he did satisfied the officers. He was a well behaved quiet boy [who] used to cry when he was beaten. He was continually ill treated up to the time he was put in irons about a week before we landed at Cape Town....

I was ... left alone pretty well until about a week before we landed at Cape Town. I was on deck hauling sail when the first mate ... struck me on the back with an iron bar. The blow knocked me down, and then the second mate jumped on my stomach with both feet. ... They both kicked me as I was lying down [and] ... laughed [and] promised me a good beating coming.

Later that day, the mate told Reilly to report to the captain's cabin where the second mate was sitting at the table. The mate informed Reilly that he was "in for a beating."

Off Cape Town, August 27, 1918

> The captain then walked in and said, "Throw up your hands, you son-of-a-bitch." I threw my hands up, and he pointed the revolver straight in my face, the barrel touching my nose. He said, "I am going to shoot you tonight." He then handcuffed me behind the back. The second mate then got me by the collar of the coat and threw me into the hold. The hold is about 5 feet deep. I was knocked senseless and on coming to found myself still in the hold. This was on a Friday afternoon and I was kept there until Sunday morning without food or water.

Reilly was not alone in the hold. James Campbell had been there for a few days, and Frank Grielen had been there for nearly a month. The two men were shackled together with handcuffs. During the time Reilly was in the hold, none of them had anything to eat.

Between about the 11th and 22nd August, Grielen, Olsen, Jensen, Jack Joe, Jorgensen, James Campbell, and Smithson were all placed in irons. All but Grielen was taken out at various times and put to work and then put in irons again.

Within the certified copy of the logbook were confessions by Frank Grielen dated 24th and 25th July regarding a plot to destroy the vessel and murder the officers. Reilly witnessed these in the master's cabin and explained the circumstances.

> Grielen was forced to sign the confessions. He was weak from lack of food and had then been about ten days in irons. The captain also struck him on the head with a truncheon before he signed. The statement was read to me as I objected to sign as it was not true. The captain then winked at me to sign. Had I not done so I think I would also have been struck. I signed three times as witness to Grielen's signature. As far as I remember, an interval of several days happened between each occasion although in the logbook they appear together. Smithson also signed Grielen's confessions as a witness. It was hopeless to refuse to sign as a witness.
>
> I remember witnessing the statement appearing in the logbook August 11th regarding Olsen's implication in the plot. Grielen and Campbell also signed as witnesses. Grielen was in irons at the time and was brought from the hold to sign.
>
> Sometime after Stewart went overboard, the second mate sent Jack Joe up the rigging to help make up the main gaff topsail.... Joe did

his best but not quick enough for the mate who called him to the deck and started to kick and hit him. Joe complained he was crippled and doing his best, but he only got it worse. He said to the mate "I'll jump overboard." The mate said "Jump, you son-of-a-bitch." I was then standing about four yards away.... Joe made a run for the side; I jumped and got him by the back of the neck and prevented him going over; I ... told him we were all treated alike and he quieted down.

Whilst in irons the captain at the point of a revolver made the men in irons smash each other. I had to smash Jones and Jensen. John Campbell and the second mate also thrashed me.... John Campbell dragged me around the deck by my hair whilst the mate belabored me with a club.

The black eye which I still have was given me by the first mate the Monday before arriving at Cape Town; he did it with a sling shot.... The blow staggered me.... I was then sent to the wheel. As a result of the blow I bled a lot on to the deck, and for this the captain and both mates assaulted me. The captain used the tiller of the wheel and the mates had iron bars....

The statements signed by Grielen and Bjarne Olsen on the loose sheets [inserted into the logbook] ... which were witnessed by me were signed by these men under compulsion. Olsen had a gun pointed at his head by the captain. The statements were read over to us but were not written in my presence. As far as I can see the writing generally is that of the captain and two mates.

I am the only one of the nine under detention who has not been accused by the captain of plotting. After I had witnessed the statements the captain told me when we were alone that he would give me half the rewards for capturing German spies. To the best of my knowledge there is no truth in these statements I witnessed. My opinion is that the captain had mutiny and German spies on the brain and he intended claiming a reward for the capture of spies on his returning to America. I also think his offer to me of half the rewards was to keep me quiet as I knew too much about Hansen's death which occurred as follows:

Axel Hansen was sent by the second mate to set the royal yard on foremast. The second mate smashed and kicked him before he went up.... Hansen loosed the lee side of the sail and the second mate told him to hurry up. Hansen replied he was doing his best, and the second mate ordered him to come down. Hansen slid to the deck and the

Off Cape Town, August 27, 1918

second mate jumped on him at once and kicked him as he lay on the deck, and again ordered him aloft to finish the job. Hansen said, "All right, Sir, I'll finish it," and as he got up and was going up the mast the second mate again called him back and again kicked and struck him. Hansen said, "I can't stand this no longer, I will jump overboard." Hansen made a lurch to the side, and as he had his hand on the main rigging and making to jump, the second mate again kicked him and said "Go to it, you son-of-a-bitch," and Hansen then jumped.

As Hansen swam aft crying, "Save me; save me," the master was leaning over the rail shouting, "Drown, you son-of-a-bitch!" Reilly was at the mizzen rigging watching all of this happen. When Hansen grabbed hold of the log line, Reilly screamed,

> "Captain, he can be saved; all there is to do is to pull on the line." The captain replied, "Let the son-of-a-bitch drown." I replied, "I don't like to see a man drown when he can be saved," and I ran aft to grab the log line. He called me a son-of-a-bitch and ordered me forward to complete Hansen's work at the foremast.... Hansen was still hanging to the log line when I was in the foremast doing his work. Hansen was a good swimmer. At this time the breeze was freshening, the ship doing about 6 or 7 knots, there was a heavy sea running. I would not like to say it was possible to launch a boat, but I am sure he could have been saved with the log line with his knowledge of swimming to assist him....
>
> When I had finished Hansen's job at the foremast, the captain sent for me.... He was lying on his bed. The second mate was also there. The captain said "Well that sod is gone." I replied "He wouldn't have gone if you had let me save him, you heard him scream 'Save me!' and you made no attempt to do so." I was in an angry mood at the time and not afraid of the captain. The captain said I must make a statement as to what happened. [When] I told him what I had seen, he said, "That won't do, I'll get into trouble over that." He then told me to sit down.... The second mate got a pad and pencil. The captain then said, "This Hansen boy jumped over on account of being a bad character ashore; he knew we were coming near port and is afraid the authorities would lock him up."
>
> The second mate then wrote the statement produced ... which I ... objected to signing as the statement was not correct. The captain

said, "You sign it." I still refused. The captain said "You will get me into trouble." I replied, "I shall only perjure myself; get someone else to sign." He said "You'll have to sign it before you leave here. Sign and that will be all there is to it. If any questions are asked in South Africa, present this paper and that will be all."

When Reilly continued to refuse to sign the paper, Pedersen jumped off his bed, pulled out his revolver, and threatened to shoot the seaman.

> I was ... forced to sign to save my life. The statement is not correct and is an invention of the captain's except the description of the weather and the reference to my instructions to watch Hansen closely. These instructions were given me some days before [when] the captain had an idea that Hansen would start a mutiny. During these days Hansen never went anywhere without me, and he used to complain of his treatment and that he had been forced to sign statements. Hansen was a member of the Seamen's Union and the captain had no time for union men.[9] Hansen was well behaved and the best sailor in the fo'c'sle....
>
> The Monday before landing at Cape Town I was on deck with the carpenter. The captain called the carpenter aft, and I saw them talking for about half an hour with the mates and John Campbell. The captain then came up and told me to fix a watch tackle on the lee fore sheet. When hooking the tackle on the lower turn buckle and close to the water's edge the carpenter jumped right on my back and said, "You son-of-a-bitch; we'll get you." If I had not had one arm around the main rigging I am sure I would have gone overboard. I am sure this was a plot to get rid of me on account of my knowing about Hansen's death.

The next day, Pedersen signaled the SS *Magdalena*. Reilly related in his statement that when the ship's officer was coming on board, the mate told Reilly and Jones and Olsen to hide under an old sail and threatened to shoot them if they moved. By the time they were released, the steamer was out of sight and the seamen could see lights ashore. After the *Puako* anchored at Table Bay and the sails were lowered, Reilly and his shipmates were placed in irons and kept secured until the South African police came aboard and took them off the ship.

At the end of his statement, Reilly summarized for the police the overall behavior of Pedersen during the voyage, concluding with the remark

Off Cape Town, August 27, 1918

The captain was continually drinking throughout the voyage and his abuse of the crew became worse the more drink he had. My opinion is that he is mad, and his allegations about German spies and bribes to destroy the ship were inventions of his.

[signed] EDWARD REILLY

While the men were giving statements to police, Dr. Harold Augustus Engelbach, medical officer for the City of Cape Town, examined them and filed the following report.[10]

- L. A. Smithson: Contusions of scrotum, left thigh, left eye, and abrasion scalp.
- P. Jorgensen: Contusions, both eyes, abrasions face and nose, contusion both thighs and one lower right rib, contusion right arm.
- B. Olsen: Contusions both eyes, abrasion nose.
- W. Jones: Contusions left eye and nose, abrasions right cheek, nose, and left cheek. Very extensive bruises back. Abrasions both shins.
- L. A. Jensen: Contusions both eyes, both thighs.
- E. Reilly: Contusions both eyes.
- James Campbell: Left black eye, lacerated wound forehead, swelling lower left ribs.
- Jack Joe: Contusions both eyes, abrasions of face, extensive contusions of back, left arm, right arm, contusions of buttocks, abrasions scalp.
- F. Grielen: No marks.

Doctor Engelbach's report noted those wounds that were visible to the physician's eye but made no mention of internal injuries that might have been discovered by X-ray examination. He also made no mention of the emotional state of the men. Frank Grielen was in a particularly bad state following weeks of confinement, which had mostly been spent in the small boxlike storeroom. He paced nervously and seemed unable to assimilate back into the group of seamen.

In a lengthy memo sent August 31, Murphy discussed the physical condition of the men, especially Jones. "I saw his naked body. His whole back from shoulders to waist is blue with bruises. There are wounds on his face and head. There are others on his legs which he says were caused by kicks inflicted by the master and mates. There is not a single one of the men under arrest who is without visible signs of corporal punishment."[11]

Immediately on return to his office on the twenty-eighth, George Murphy had sent an urgent cable to Washington alerting the Department of State that the American barkentine *Puako* had arrived at Cape Town with a crew that was mutinous and that many of them were enemy agents. He reported in a second wire sent two days later:

> The authorities believe alleged enemy plots master's fabrication. Army captain taking testimony states conditions aboard apparently worse than any of Jack London's sea tales. In view of my fruitless reports of July 30 [and] December 14 last year upon this subject and desiring to obviate any doubt this master's brutal criminality, earnestly request special court of inquiry, impartial British naval officers and magistrate. I have seen seamen's bruised bodies, black eyes, the evidence [of] very cruel violence; also suspect murder. Mates are both master's minor sons.[12]

Following his meeting with Captain Howe on the twenty-ninth, Murphy sent to Washington details from Howe's report:

> (a) The men ate their meal ravenously, one of them eating fifteen rolls after the lunch was nominally completed;
>
> (b) He [Howe] was convinced by the testimony of the men that there was absolutely nothing in the master's charge that any of the men were enemy agents or had received payment to kill the master and his sons, or to sink the ship;
>
> (c) That the men, instead of being mutinous, were absolutely cowed, spiritless, and ready to do anything their tyrant ordered, even to the extent of signing documents incriminating themselves; and
>
> (d) That the master was practically guilty of murdering the two seamen who went overboard.[13]

On August 30, Murphy telegraphed Washington at the request of Captain Pedersen:

> Master *Puako* suggests inquiry as to whether seamen Bjarne Olsen and Frank Grielen each deposited thousand dollars last April Bank Montreal, Victoria. Olsen's deposit receipt valise Occidental Hotel, Victoria. Grielen's Johnson, Manager Northern Hotel, Victoria, and likewise Lester Jensen, Seattle State Bank, wife Blanche Jensen has the receipt, Seventh Avenue, South Great Falls, Montana, if it is true.

Payment money paid by alleged spy Schlanger alias Belsky or Schevek who was, it is alleged, Northern Hotel Victoria about April twenty-three. I anticipate no result but prompt inquiry is very important.[14]

The paper trail that began with the consulate general in Cape Town led directly to Washington and the Department of State. Murphy's cables and dispatches were forwarded by State to three other departments: the Department of Justice, which had jurisdiction over any legal questions and proceedings; the Department of Commerce, the parent agency of the Bureau of Navigation, which was responsible for the manning of U.S.-flag vessels and the licensing of officers of such vessels; and the Navy Department, whose Office of Naval Intelligence was called on to assist in investigating whether the crew had met with enemy agents in Seattle or British Columbia before the voyage and whether any of the crew had actually deposited money in various banks as was claimed in the confessions.

American consul general George Murphy was the point man during this investigation, which lasted several months. The Department of State was the conduit through which Murphy's reports and queries traveled to the proper government agencies for response. But these agencies all had higher priorities, and in the crush of activity connected with the war and its aftermath, weeks would pass before Murphy obtained answers to his cables, even though many were tagged "urgent."

On the afternoon of August 29, Murphy and Vice-Consul Charles J. Pisar, representing the Department of State, visited the detained men and began taking affidavits that focused on the deaths of Stewart and Hansen, the two men who had jumped or been driven overboard. By September 6, they had finished. The men's speech was articulate and in marked contrast to the repetitious, often incoherent and muddled language of the confessions they had signed aboard the *Puako*. When Jensen was questioned about Hansen, the second man to die during the voyage, he said that before Hansen went overboard, his "face was like jelly" from all the beatings. After hitting the water, Hansen grabbed the log line. When the second mate took hold of the line as if to pull Hansen in, Captain Pedersen ordered him to shake Hansen loose and let him go. Jack Joe recalled what he had witnessed.

> I heard him [Hansen] holler for help. The second mate called the master who came on the poop deck and looked in the direction where Hansen held to the log line, but I could see him no more. I heard the master laugh and then he ordered me to keep my course. The master struck me repeatedly and tried to force me to sign a statement, the

contents of which I did not know as I cannot read or write. One day the master pointed a revolver at me to force me to sign the statement. I refused and he then ordered the mates to tie my hands behind my back with a rope. They put me down a hatch where they left me for three days and nights—the master and the mates striking me repeatedly with a stick until I put my mark on a statement although I do not know what it contained.

L. A. Smithson, who also saw Stewart jump, said the cook had been ill-treated and had been repeatedly beaten by the master as well as by both mates. Smithson added, "Stewart was healthy when he boarded the vessel and was weak, beaten up and scarred from head to foot when he jumped overboard. When Stewart had sunk and was under the water, the second mate threw a rope to him. He was a good cook if the master gave him sufficient food, but the master only allowed him 49 pounds of flour to last seven days for all hands. The master cut food short all round."

The scale of provisions (see appendix 2), which was to be attached to all ship's articles and posted in the forecastle of all U.S.-flag ships, specified that each man was to receive 1.5 pounds of flour per week—19.5 pounds per week for the thirteen seamen. In addition, each man was to receive 10.5 pounds of fresh bread per week, or 136.5 pounds for the thirteen men. If Smithson is correct, and since flour is the basic component of bread, Pedersen was clearly in violation by issuing in total only 49 pounds of flour per week. Smithson continued:

> I was made to sign a statement at the point of a revolver that I and B. Olsen and F. Grielen were in a plot to kill the captain and destroy the ship. He accused me of receiving $1,000 for the purpose. I wrote it partly and the second mate wrote part of it. Before I signed I was several times struck with handcuffs and a club on the head. Three weeks ago I was put in the pump hold and a fire hose played on me to make me confess that I received $1,000, and to sign the statement, but it is all false.
>
> I do not know Schlanger nor none of the other names [Belsky and Schevek] in the statements. These names were all made up. I was in irons four times, the first time 12 hours, the second time 3 hours, the third time 3 days without anything to eat or drink. They let me out to work and put me back again. Every time I passed the master and mate, I was struck repeatedly. . . . One day Stewart asked me for a knife to cut some bacon for the master's breakfast. I told Stewart

Off Cape Town, August 27, 1918

the knife was in the drawer and he got it himself. Master accused me of giving him the knife in order to kill him. He beat me until I was forced to say that I had given him the knife. The master pointed a gun at me on four different occasions.

I saw the master and mates strike Reilly, Jones, Joe, Jensen, Jorgensen, Grielen, Campbell, and Olsen with blackball [a wooden ball attached to a strap], club, and ropes. I first saw Reilly working aboard about April 20th.

Other affidavits contained additional objects used as weapons: bare fists, feet, brass knuckles, the tiller stick, handcuffs, a slingshot, belaying pins, and a table board. The men were also repeatedly subjected to the "water cure" (described later in this narrative by John Walter Campbell). Jorgensen claimed, for instance, "I was given the water cure eleven times in seven days." Once men were put in irons, they were lowered either into the lazarette, which they usually called "the hold," or into the small boxlike storeroom, or into the pump hold. Sometimes days passed without their receiving so much as a cracker, bread, or a drink of water.

From these interviews, Consul General Murphy and Vice-Consul Pisar concluded that Stewart and Hansen had been "hounded to death." Murphy felt the men's statements were true and that Pedersen was directly guilty of murdering the Danish seaman Axel Hansen and at least indirectly guilty of the death of the cook John Henry Stewart, a United States citizen. He promised Washington that as soon as possible he would send copies of all the evidence and affidavits gathered to date. At the same time, because his own workload was so heavy and his staff so limited, he again requested authorization for the matter to be investigated locally "by trained and competent [British] judicial officers." To make his case, Murphy reiterated the difficulty that the war presented in trying to find transportation for Pedersen and any witnesses for a trial in the United States. In summing up the situation, Murphy stated: "The most charitable view which I can take of the master's plot charges is that he may be insane to the extent of being afflicted through drink or drugs with a form of persecution mania."[15]

CHAPTER 4

DIGESTING THE OFFICIAL LOGBOOK

Once the *Puako*'s official logbook was in police custody, Howe examined it and told Murphy he found it to be "a very confused record." Murphy said that "the dates of the entries were not in the sequence prescribed by American law."[1] Howe copied from the logbook selected entries that he felt might be pertinent to the investigation he had been asked by the consul general to make of the crew and ship's officers.[2] He later said that the entries he did not copy were all slop chest and cash accounts between the vessel and the crew. In reading the entries Howe copied, it appears from the spelling, grammar, and writing styles that the log was written up by at least two persons, the master and one or both of the mates—a common practice. Regardless of who wrote the log entries, it was stipulated by the Shipping Commissioners' Act of June 7, 1872, Section 59 that each day's entry "shall be signed by the master and by the mate, or some other one of the crew."

At this point in the investigation, Howe was not aware of the existence of a second logbook or diary, which had been kept by the mates and which was discovered in a later search of the ship.

The earliest items Howe copied were official logbook entries made before the *Puako* left Victoria. These revealed things one might expect to read in a ship's log of that period. For instance, men had been fined for refusing to do particular work or for using abusive or bad language. Even the entries regarding demotions once the ship reached open water on April 27 might have been expected with this green crew: Grielen, Jack Joe, and Jensen were all reduced to apprentice boy "on account of don't know anything regarding the vessel. Wages to be $40.00 per month."

April 28: "E. Riely [Reilly] has stowed away in fore peak, and came on deck 10 a.m. He was signed on ships articles as deck boy at $40.00 per month." According to Reilly's sworn statement earlier quoted, he was not a stowaway but was aboard by agreement with Pedersen, which Reilly claimed included the promise of a wage of $60 per month.

Bjarne Olsen's wages were also reduced to $60 per month, because Pedersen claimed the seaman was not able to perform the duties of boatswain.

An interesting aspect of the official logbook Pedersen surrendered at Cape Town is its irregularity. Under Section 58 of the Shipping Commissioners' Act, "Every vessel making voyages from a port in the United States to any foreign port, or, being of the burden of seventy-five tons or upward, from a port on the Atlantic to a port on the Pacific, or vice versa, shall have an official logbook; and every master of such vessel shall make, or cause to be made therein, entries of the following matters."

Section 58 specified eleven "matters" that a master was to log. Six of those have direct relevance to the *Puako* voyage of 1918:

> Second. Every offense committed by any member of his crew for which it is intended to prosecute, or to enforce a forfeiture, together with such statement concerning the reading over [of] such entry, and concerning the reply, if any, made to the charge, as is required by the provisions of section forty-five hundred and ninety-seven.
> Third. Every offense for which punishment is inflicted on board, and the punishment inflicted.
> Fifth. Every case of illness or injury happening to any member of the crew, with the nature thereof, and the medical treatment.
> Sixth. Every case of death happening on board, with the cause thereof.
> Tenth. The wages due to any seaman or apprentice who dies during the voyage, and the gross amount of all deductions to be made therefrom.
> Eleventh. The sale of the effects of any seaman or apprentice who dies during the voyage, including a statement of each article sold, and the sum received for it.

Section 59 of the same 1872 act mandated when the logbook entries were to be made.

> Every entry ... shall be made as soon as possible after the occurrence to which it relates, and if not made on the same day as the occurrence to which it relates, shall be made and dated so as to show the date of the occurrence, and of the entry respecting it; and in no case shall any entry therein, in respect of any occurrence happening previously to

the arrival of the vessel at her final port, be made more than twenty-four hours after such arrival.

In the case of an offense, Section 52 provided that "the offender, if still in the vessel, shall, before her next arrival at any port ... either be furnished with a copy of such entry or have the same read over distinctly and audibly to him and may thereupon make such reply thereto as he thinks fit; and a statement that a copy of the entry has been so furnished, or the same has been so read over, together with the reply, if any, made by the offender, shall likewise be entered and signed in the same manner."

The select logbook entries that Howe copied reveal time and again the reckless and irresponsible manner in which Pedersen maintained the *Puako*'s logbook.[3]

A week after departing Victoria and with the *Puako* off the Oregon coast at 45°15′ N, 127°29′ W (see her course on plate 5), Pedersen made note of a disciplinary problem: Frank Grielen was placed in irons around noon for being insubordinate. The next day Grielen apologized and was released. There is an eighteen-day gap before Howe's next copied entry.

"May 23: John Henry Stewart, cook, jumped overboard by fore rigging. The man aloft working reported cook overboard. Second mate A. E. Pedersen run forward and threw him a line, but to no good, he did not attempt to grab it, also hollered for him to take hold of the rope, but he sank and later came up to surface by mizzen rigging only for 2 or 3 seconds and sank and did not come up any more. The cause for his action is not known to anyone aboard." At the time, with a dead calm sea, the *Puako* was at 7°20′ N, 116°55′ W, some 2,200 nautical miles west-northwest of the Gulf of Panama, drifting in stays. The *Puako* thus was well to the east of the normal track of sailing ships en route to Cape Horn at that time of year.[4]

Following Stewart's death, the second mate wrote in the diary which he and older brother Leonard kept:

> John Henry Stewart took a notion to feed himself to the sharks, which he did in his own particular sort of way. He went to the fore rigging and looked up aloft and jumped into the sea backwards and feet first. He went down and came up with his hands over his eyes and he looked up at me but with no look of assistance, but sorrowful eyes, but I took pity on him and threw him the end of the foresail halyard, but he just opened his mouth and just swallowed two quarts of water and then he sank, but he did not want to see daylight any more so he did not stick his sunken mush up to Jesus any more.[5]

When a seaman dies, it is the duty of the master to take charge of all moneys, clothes, and effects that he leaves on board and either sell those effects at auction to another seamen or deliver them to the next of kin. Any deductions or fines are to be taken from the auction proceeds and wages due, with the balance sent to the deceased's next of kin as designated at the time of signing ship's articles. It is the master's duty to place in the official logbook a full accounting, witnessed by one of the mates and/or a crewman.

Loosely following the above stipulations, Stewart's effects were sold on May 26 to fellow shipmate Axel Hansen, who paid $13.00 for "1 suit case, 1 coat, 1 vest, 2 pants, 1 hat, 2 towels, 7 cotton shirts, 2 drawers, 3 aprons, 1 pair shoes, 2 union suits, 2 socks, 1 handkerchief, 1 pair garters, 1 white coat, 1 comb, 1 razor, 1 shaving brush, 9 collars, 2 neckties, 1 clock, 3 blankets, and a bundle of paper (mostly old rags)."

Up to this point, and in accordance with regulation, all of the official logbook entries had been signed "A. C. Pedersen, master" and were witnessed by either a mate or a crew member or sometimes by two individuals. But then came "May 20th and 23rd: John H. Stewart attempted to kill Master with a knife and is fined $50.00 each time. Amount total $100. A. C. Pedersen." This entry stands out for two reasons: It was inserted out of chronological order, at the end of a page dated April 17, and it was not witnessed by Stewart or anyone else, causing one to wonder whether the entry was actually written before Stewart died or after. Stewart was to have been paid $100 per month. By fining him a total of $100, was Pedersen planning to deduct the fine from the one month's wages due the dead cook's heirs and thus save the ship that month's wages, or was he planning perhaps to personally pocket the money?

The entry following the May 26 summary of items sold from Stewart's effects gives a small glimpse into life on board the *Puako*. "May 31: Bjarne Olsen fined $5.00 for not keeping his berth clean." Olsen had been told to "clean his room and air out his bed clothes as this was smelling sour, bad odor." The next two entries, dated May 25 and 26, are out of order, showing more irregularity. On the twenty-fifth, "Lester Jensen can perform the duties as cook and wages to be $75.00 per month from today." A day later, Pedersen had a change of heart. "Lester Jensen cannot perform duties as cook, don't know to make bread nor cook anything of salt food and his race [raise] of wages is canceled and to be same as deck boy." This second entry bringing Jensen back to his original wage of $40 per month was signed by Pedersen but was not witnessed by Jensen. Jensen would claim in a 1921 deposition that he never knew he had been demoted. He also would claim that Pedersen often complimented him on his bread, and well he might have, since Jensen had once worked ashore as a baker.

A gap of a month separates the next copied entry, dated June 25, 1918, when the *Puako* was at 41°31′ s, 117°32′ w, roughly west of Puerto Montt, Chile: "L. A. Smithson admit that I have been insubordinate to master on several occasions. I also have been taking things out of captain's slop chest to keep for myself and this morning placed poisonous milk on the master and mates table. I admit that I have done wrong and that you, Captain, has been better to me than my own father. L. A. Smithson was placed in irons until disobedience ceases 8 a.m." By 4 p.m., Smithson had been released after apologizing and stating that he would be faithful to the master and strictly attend to his duties.

An entry dated about a week later and only clipped within the logbook began "Explanation given by Lester Jensen about cabin boy L. A. Smithson putting tobacco in beans and starboard watch got sick."

> I [Jensen] received the beans last night and soaked them in clear water. I don't use tobacco myself and there was no tobacco slinging around in the galley when these beans were placed in the pot. I am sure they were thoroughly cleaned. These beans I put on the stove at six o'clock for boiling about 5 to 10 minutes before serving the meal. The boy [Smithson] came forward to get the food aft. As a rule I did not watch him what he was doing. The beans were served both for cabin and fo'c'sle. After seamen delivered dishes to galley they told me there was tobacco in the beans. They have been eating a good few of them. They also showed me the tobacco. I served other beans to them. It appears that cabin boy L. A. Smithson had dropped tobacco in the beans for some reason another as no one else had been in the galley during this time making breakfast and the boy uses tobacco. I live in the full belief that he has placed tobacco in the beans to get me in trouble. The result was we discovered a piece of tobacco cut off the plug that corresponded with the kind he uses.

In a second bean-related entry, this one part of the bound logbook and bearing the same date, Reilly "came to complain about the beans that was served for breakfast was not fit to eat on account of being mixed with tobacco. They are all sick on starboard watch." Despite all the fuss about the beans, Pedersen made no mention of anyone being disciplined.

By July 12 the *Puako* was at 55°3′ s, 88°59′ w, heading east toward Cape

Horn. Howe copied from the logbook a purported confession signed by the cabin boy "with oath by kissing the Bible." If Reilly quoted Pedersen correctly concerning Stewart's death—"I will fix it up so that nobody will know what happened"—then this "confession" signed by Smithson was the beginning of the master's scheme to "fix it up." Smithson stated that he and John H. Stewart and Frank Grielen had

> on May 2nd plotted to kill the master and second mate and sink the vessel and then commit suicide. I [Smithson] take a pair of handcuffs from drawer in the captain's bedroom; cook was to act friendly with second mate and persuade him to come down in the galley on a certain hour in the morning watch from 4 to 8 a.m. Then J. H. Stewart and L. A. Smithson were to place him in irons, by doing so the captain would soon inquire for him, as he would not be on the poop deck to look after the sailing of the vessel. Master would come forward and look for him. Then I and John H. Stewart and Frank Grielen was to kill the captain and the second mate and carry out plot. Somehow this failed because the second mate would not have anything to do with the cook. Between May 2nd and 20th Frank Grielen, John H. Stewart, and I, L. A. Smithson, planned again how to kill the captain by putting croton oil in his food as John Stewart had a small bottle.[6] This we did not do and I threw it overboard. On May 12th we still kept on talking about killing the master and put a hole in the ship and do away with ourselves. Then we planned to stab the captain with a French knife which was sharp and lying in a drawer in the pantry. On May 20th John H. Stewart was to come aft 9 a.m. and act as though he wanted something out of the store room and ask the captain some questions in order to get at him; then when the cook give me the signal for the knife I was to give it to him which I did and John H. Stewart take the knife with intent to kill the captain but was not smart enough. On May 23rd John H. Stewart jumped overboard and was drowned. On June 25th did I put poisoned milk on captain's table for him to eat, then was I placed in irons few hours, after was released by promised not to do this anymore. Captain did not know that we plotted to kill him. On July 4th did I put tobacco in this food for the captain to eat, but the sailors got this beans and they all got sick, by investigations found that I have put the tobacco in the beans then I confessed everything. The reason why I did this can I not explain any other way that they have talked in to me. The captain and mate have

been good to me and friendly toward me and therefore I confessed and told the truth as I have had no fault to find with the master officers and ship.

Ten days later, according to the mates' diary, the *Puako* was hit by a heavy gale. However, without mentioning the extreme weather, and in an apparent effort to make it appear that the crew was up to no good, the official logbook entry stated, "Lost fore sail and fore lower topsail on account of crew attempting mutiny. Is charging them for the sails lost [by] Frank Grielen, Axel Hansen, Lester Jensen, Bjarne Olsen which is implicated in the plot of sinking or distraining [perhaps he meant destroying?] the vessel."

While it is interesting that none of the four charged men witnessed Pedersen's logbook entry, even more curious is the absence of any mention of physical discipline. If these men were plotting to destroy Pedersen's ship, why did he not levy more than a fine? Certainly if the crew was about to stage a mutiny, the law was on the captain's side. At the very least it seems he would have put them in irons. In fact another ten days passed before he logged the application of any discipline against anyone, and then it involved only Grielen.

On July 24, when the *Puako* was at 51°13´ S, 48°40´ W, a position east and slightly north of the Falkland Islands,

> Frank Grielen was placed in irons and charged as follows: 1st Item: Plotting to kill the master; 2nd Item: Plotting to bore hole in vessel to sink her; 3rd Item: For safety of members of crew; 4th Item: Preventing him to stir up mutiny and revolt among the crew; 5th Item: For his own safety as he wants to commit suicide; 6th Item: For speaking against the United States Government. He said he [would] like to see the Germans win the war and lick them so bad that they would wipe the Americans and the English off the earth.

The next day, Grielen's alleged confession was written into the official logbook.

> I, Frank Grielen, confess and admit that I planned and wanted the master killed. Also influenced John H. Stewart to do so and thereby destroy the ship by running her ashore. I also admit sending the cabin boy into the captain's room to steal irons in order to lock up second mate and kill him after killing the captain, and having first mate navigate the ship also were to do away with the first mate if he refused to navigate the ship according to our directions and if John Campbell

would interfere we plotted to get rid of him also when the captain and mates were done for. This statement is the truth. By F. Grielen. Witnesses: Edward Reilly, L. A. Smithson, A. C. Pedersen, Master.

A few days later on the thirtieth, Pedersen logged problems he was having with Jensen, who seemingly was not happy to be in the galley.

> The crew were given their rations for one week for themselves to take care of and have L. Jensen cook for them what they wanted. This did not suit. L. Jensen acted contrary against them. Then one of crew came aft and explained matters to the master and it was decided for the ship to feed them as usual. Lester Jensen again began to act contrary. . . . Lester Jensen has also passed remarks he wished he was on deck again. In order to get on deck he began with his trick again such as dirty out everything in galley and this morning put soap in the hot cakes for us to eat, and is placed on deck to perform deck duties. The crew have to cook for theirselves on account of his dirty habits and acting stubborn and [in]subordinate and he has also said he wished he knowed where to bore a hole in the ship and he never expected to see Cape Town.

In the July 31 logbook entry Pedersen wrote, "Axel Hansen is charged and have admit that he has attempted to kill the captain and mates and destroy the ship and plotted and stirred up other members of the crew to mutinies." Pedersen charged Hansen with stirring up the crew, and although there is no mention of disciplinary action, there apparently was physical discipline. This may have been especially severe since Hansen was considered a union man. Pedersen detested seamen's unions and all they stood for. Axel Hansen could take no more. With a gale blowing, the ship traveling at 9 knots, and the second mate close behind Hansen trying to get in one more swing, the seaman ran to the side and jumped. The first mention in the logbook of Hansen's death is a statement signed by Grielen. Its intent was clearly to shift any blame away from the master and mates.

> He [Axel Hansen] has been in jail at Port McArthur, San Pedro Coy [County] as he said, "We blowed up one of the Standard Oil boats on the Pacific Coast." He has also had trouble with the Black Hands [a Sicilian underworld society] on shore and he didn't care a damned as he said he wanted to die as he was tired of living. He has said this several times in presence of others besides me, and he also said, "before I go I will take one of those bastards with me," meaning first

and second mates and master, he also said he received money from an Austrian count and had a good time, if he had saved it he would have money to last him his life time. It is no surprise to me that he did commit suicide by jumping overboard as he was afraid of the English and American authorities.

With the ship at 39°48′ s, 16°2′ w, a position roughly 1,500 miles west-southwest of Cape Town, Pedersen inserted his own entry for August 6:

"Axel Hansen jumped overboard by main rigging on starboard side at 6:15 clock a.m. break of day blowing a gale from NW, confused seas, ship running for all sails she could carry at the time going about 9 miles per hour.[7] Man aloft reported could not see him, ship was placed on course again as it was impossible to launch boat to get him."

Peter Jorgensen paid $6.00 for Hansen's effects, some of which Hansen had purchased after Stewart died: "4 story books, 11 cotton shirts, 6 drawers old, 3 undershirts old, 1 towel, 3 pair socks, 2 pants, 2 vests, 1 coat, 2 neck ties, 2 shoes brushes, 2 old blankets, 1 watch (nickel)." One small bag with unspecified papers was not sold. According to a statement given by Jorgensen, before Pedersen offered Hansen's effects to anyone, he picked through them like a vulture, keeping for his own use things like shaving gear and even Hansen's pipe.

Even though Bjarne Olsen had been named along with Hansen, Jensen, and Grielen in the logbook's July 14 entry concerning the loss of sails, and although Olsen was said to have been implicated in the plots, nearly a month passed before Pedersen's logbook individually addressed him: "Bjarne Olsen has been implicated in plots to kill the master and mates and to destroy the ship by giving L. A. Smithson tools to open drawers to get captain's revolver to shoot him with, also acted stubborn and contemptible and disobedient and stirred up other members of crew to mutiny also find fault with the American Government with regards to the present war. Placed in irons 5 p.m. August 11th."

On the same page, immediately after this August 11 entry, is one dated August 3.[8] "Lester Jensen is charged with plotting and stirred up other members of crew to mutinize. Also has attempted to poison the master and mates [and] John Campbell by putting glass in bread and small pieces of tin cut fine among fresh meat [canned meat] also put dirty dishwater in food. Also soap. Done all he could to get mates and master sick and died by ptomaine poisoning."

Pedersen made no mention of disciplining Jensen and logged nothing further of consequence for more than a week, after which there were several short entries. The wording is essentially the same in all, though the dates differ. The first, which involved Lester Jensen, was dated August 20. Three dated August 21 related separately to William Jones, Peter Jorgensen, and L. A. Smithson. Each entry was signed by the master, but none was witnessed. These August 20 and 21 entries claimed the involved crewmen were German spies and that they "Received money ($1,000) from Schevek for destroying the vessel, kill master and mates."[9] The four men were placed in irons. An entry on the twenty-second, which was also signed only by the master with no witness, involved James Campbell, who was "placed in irons, mutiny been plotting with the rest of crew as per statement from them in writing."

Although another week passed before the *Puako* reached Cape Town, Howe either found no more logbook entries or found none significant enough to copy.

CHAPTER 5

THE "PLOT" ENLARGES

In addition to the statements made by crewmen that were recorded in the official logbook, Pedersen had accumulated dozens of other statements and confessions which he alleged were made voluntarily by various members of the crew. These were bundled by Pedersen and turned over to Howe.[1] The earliest statement, a short one, was signed by Frank Grielen sometime following John Henry Stewart's death. Grielen referenced an alleged plot wherein Stewart was supposed to kill Pedersen. "On May 22, 1918, I asked John Henry [Stewart] the reason why he didn't get away [do away] with the captain, and he said 'I tried hard but couldn't do as I think captain [is] on to something going on,' and I said, 'let it go now. We will get him some other way.' I spoke to him [Stewart] that evening, he acted as though he got crazy over plotting because things didn't work the way we planned it."

Chronologically, the next several statements and confessions were signed by Smithson. The grammar seesaws as if coming at one moment from Smithson, then as if coming from someone else, and then back as if from Smithson. This is particularly evident in the first four numbered paragraphs. The earliest of these, dated June 25, is full of repetition.

1. On several occasions the master told me there is something wrong in the cabin, it smells and stinks sour. To this I replied I can't smell nothing. By investigating on April 30 in the tropics discovered one piece of fresh meat laying behind ice chest with a very slimy smell.
2. Was told to clean out water closet a whole week but with no attempt. Master had to clean out toilet and show him [Smithson] how and put effectives [disinfectant] in it.... I was told to clean the slop buckets out after every meal and in place of that I kept filling the two buckets up....

3. June 22, 1918, found two loaded buckets full of slops in the lower locker in pantry, dirty stinking rags and etc.
4. June 25, I admit that I placed on the master's table milk unfit for consumption, poisonous, and I was placed in irons until . . . [I] convince myself that I will not put on the captain's table any kind of poisonous food which I know I have done previously on several occasions, but he did not eat it nor the mates.

Smithson's July 10 confession is lengthier and rambling. In places it is so ridiculous it is humorous. On a more serious note, it seems to reflect coercion by Pedersen to blame Smithson for Stewart's suicide.

> I hereby confess to all I have done in disobedience. I signed on the ship on the fourth day of April. I left home in Vancouver and the last thing my father said was be careful of yourself and the same with my sister but in the place of that I have been doing everything wrong, first I had trouble with the cook [Stewart] and I thought I was smart and knew it all, and I used to give him a calling down, whenever there was one thing wrong till at last he couldn't cook at all. Then on the 23rd day of May he didn't have any breakfast ready, and I went down and helped him but I called him down and at half past ten he jumped overboard. The other cook [Jensen] came in and then I stole some stuff from the captain such as 2 pair white pants, 5 packages Bull Durham, 3 packages cigarette papers, 2 pair socks, 1 bar soap, 1 under shirt, 1 pair of hand cuffs which I was going to take home, but I got frightened and threw them overboard and I got chummy with the new cook and then we planned to run away in Cape Town, and then he started to talk IWW [This is the first mention in any transcript of the Industrial Workers of the World.] I fell out with him and then I told the captain and then the cook denied it. . . . Another thing I did was to put tobacco in the beans and tried to get the cook [Jensen] in trouble but the tobacco that I had proved that a piece had been cut [from it] which compared with that which was in the pot. . . . I admit that I told [Captain Pedersen] a lot of lies. One was that I told him that I was over twenty-one but I am only eighteen and will be nineteen on the 19th day of this month of July. And another thing I told him [was] that I worked for the C.P.R. [Canadian Pacific Railroad] for five months, but I only worked for a month and a half, and I don't know anything about this work as I never worked only on the farm for my father and at my trade as [a] dentist. . . . And another thing

I did, I drove the first cook over by growling at him and no one else did. The captain treated him like a gentleman and only told him what to do and what was right. . . . I hereby close and sign this paper this tenth day of July 1918.

On July 11 Smithson signed another statement. This one was headed "How planned, who implicated and who was implicated to kill the captain on May 20th for no cause whatever on his part but only to decide to get on shore." It is a monotonous repetition of earlier ones—all of them discussing the plot in which Smithson implicates Stewart, Grielen, and himself. In another statement on the same day, Smithson's confession focused solely on Grielen "who said to me that he was a pro-German and that he would like to see the Germans win the war. . . . I think that a man who will run down the country of the ship he works on is not fit to live for he is too low down to talk to. I asked him if there was any German [who he knew], and he said, 'Yes,' that his mother is a German and 'I'd like to see the Germans win the war.'"

According to Smithson's statements dated the eleventh, Jensen had talked often to Stewart and Grielen about the IWW, telling them that IWW leader Joe Hill was an innocent man and that shooting Hill had been an act of murder.[2]

Smithson's statements also alleged that William Jones told him he had never been treated better, that Reilly said the "captain and mates were the best men he ever worked for," and that similar sentiments were expressed by James Campbell.

In addition to a confession dated July 12 which was part of an official logbook entry, Smithson signed several separate statements dated July 12 which were mostly rehashing of earlier ones regarding the plot involving Grielen, Stewart, and Smithson. Smithson claimed here again that this plot had failed when the cook didn't carry through. In concluding the last of these July 12 statements, Smithson wrote, "And I am now glad that I did confess as I feel happier, and I am sure that I will not be tempted to do any acts of this kind any more aboard of any vessel."

William Jones also signed a brief statement dated July 12 saying that he had complained about the food but was now satisfied since the master had talked to the cook. Henceforth, he felt sure, the quantity and the quality of the food would improve. Jones signed a similar statement on July 23.[3]

On July 24 Smithson signed a very lengthy statement that had been started on July 23. Complex and convoluted, it not only repeated his earlier allegations about the plot, but it also included unrelated passages seemingly copied from previous logbook entries including one made as early as April. By July, Smithson had begun to shift blame for the plot to Grielen by saying that after Grielen was released from irons the first time in early May, he had told Stewart and Smithson that he "wouldn't think twice of killing the captain and mates that they were a no good bunch of sons of bitches. Then they [Grielen and Stewart] started to talk of killing themselves by jumping overboard. Then we got a little rough weather and as only about two of the crew had ever been to sea before, we all got sick, and I was so sick and despondent and wanted to get ashore again that Frank Grielen and the cook started to plan to kill the captain. Then they seen the state that I was in and got me implicated in it." Smithson confessed that it was then that Frank Grielen began to plot how to kill Pedersen. When Smithson was unable to get Pedersen's revolver for Grielen and Stewart because it was locked up, "John Henry went around like a mad man, hitting his head and then sit down and then get up and walk around." When Stewart failed to do his own work as cook, Smithson had to do it, giving Stewart a "balling out." As if taking the blame for Stewart's suicide, Smithson stated that it was his "growling" that had caused Stewart to go overboard.

Grielen's signature was the next chronologically to appear on statements—no fewer than thirty-five of them, the first dated in July, the last on August 24. In the early statements, Grielen said that Jensen had talked to him about socialism. In his two statements dated July 26, he alleged that Hansen was pro-German and that he used dope and that Olsen knew a lot about navigation and had a lot of navigation books. In statements made between the twenty-eighth and thirty-first of July, he began to implicate Hansen, Olsen, and Jensen in a new plan to mutiny, but it was not until August 1 that concrete details of the plot were finally put down on paper by the alleged mutineers in their signed confessions. By then there was no longer one plot but rather six separate ones. Each was a contingency if the other did not work.

Subsequent statements through August 12 were repetitive, and the same six crewmen were involved: Stewart, Grielen, Hansen, Olsen, Smithson, and Jensen.

By the middle of August, others were being dragged in by Grielen's statements, and now they, too, were confessing: Jones on August 14, 21, and 22, James Campbell and Jorgensen on August 24. Illiterate Jack Joe affixed his X on a confession dated the twenty-second. Typical of these is a string of confessions made on August 18 by Bjarne Olsen.

I, B. Olsen and Frank Grielen spoke about to get L. A Smithson, cabin boy, to get the captain's revolver, to kill the master and mates and if he could not get in the drawers I was going to give him tools to open the drawers with, if the cabin boy could not get the gun. I, B. Olsen, told him, "You watch your steps and watch where you walk, or else I'll dump you overboard, if you don't get that gun." Then I told Frank Grielen that I will get the gun myself the first chance I have. I told Frank Grielen on the morning of about May 29 that this afternoon would be a good chance to get the gun as we were going to re-bend lower and upper topsails. That afternoon around 4 p.m., while the captain and mates were forward, I tried the drawers in bureau and cracked the veneering. But I could not open them as they were locked, then I went back to my stateroom to get my tools, then I heard some one coming and I dropped my tools on the bench and started to brush my teeth. . . . [The intruder] proved to be the captain, and he asked me, "What are you doing around here. Why aren't you on deck bending those sails and get through with it?" Then I went forward and told Frank Grielen that the captain chased me forward and I couldn't get the gun. Then I told Frank Grielen, "We will get the sons a bitches some other way. He and me will destroy the ship." This is the truth.

We plotted then to change courses and not to steer straight in order to get the ship down further to the westward, closer to the Society Islands, in order to sight one of them. We were then going to overpower the officers and get away [do away] with the master some way, and lock up the rest of the crew that would not obey our orders. Those that were implicated were B. Olsen, Axel Hansen, F. Grielen, Lester Jensen [the same four who a month earlier had been charged for the loss of two sails]. We were then going to sail the ship ashore and destroy her some way. We were then going to take to the boats and pull ashore. This failed as the officers kept too good a watch on us at all times, therefore we did not sight any islands.

In another plot, which is full of detail about the weather and things that happened in the sinister "dark of night," the seamen planned to throw the master overboard. The mate's demise would come later.

I, B. Olsen came running from windward, down to leeward with full force and then shoved the mate with the intention of shoving him overboard, but this failed as the mate was too smart for me and flopped himself down on deck which saved him from going overboard. The mate asked me, "What are you trying to do." To this I answered, "It was not intentionally," three times. I was very excited at the time as I fully intended to shove him overboard.

The statement by Bjarne Olsen claimed he decided to bore a one-inch hole in the ship and sink her. This, of course, lacked rationality and would have been counterproductive to the seamen's alleged purpose, as everyone including Olsen could have gone to the bottom with the *Puako*—although, as Leonard Pedersen would learn years later, it is possible for a vessel loaded with lumber and timber to stay afloat and maneuver to a safe harbor.

In the final and perhaps most absurd plot, the seamen were, as a group, to take charge of the storeroom, starve the master and mates, and take over the ship. Olsen, who may or may not have known how to navigate, would sail the ship into some island or to the Chilean coast and dispose of her. According to Olsen, "This would enable us to get paid by the Austrian count. . . . Axel Hansen told me that the count would pay us well for destroying vessels, and he has received money from him before for doing the same; an oil tank steamer on Pacific Coast. She was blowed up down in Chile, Iquifue [Iquique]. For this he got one cheque for $2000 and may have got more but would not tell exact amount. This is all I know about the ransom."

In another statement Olsen disclosed more information concerning the money the *Puako* seamen allegedly would be paid for destroying the ship.

> I, B. Olsen, received from John Schlanger the sum of $1,000 which I have deposited in the Bank of Montreal, and after I accomplished to destroy the vessel and kill the master and mates and others of the crew I was to receive from him $4,000 more. John Schlanger is an agent for Count Von Aulsdorf, Minneapolis, Minnesota, 827 Washington Avenue. Then I went aboard the Barkentine *Puako* April 24, 1918, with the full intention to carry out my plots and kill the master and mates and destroy the ship and return to Victoria, B.C. and get my ransom. All of our plots we schemed on completely failed as we found the master too smart for us. The money I have deposited to my credit in the Bank of Montreal, do I willingly make it payable to Captain A. C. Pedersen of the Barkentine *Puako* for all the trouble that I have caused him. . . . He [Schlanger] also gave a check to Lester Jensen for $1,000 and also John Henry Stewart for $1,000 and this money is deposited in the Bank of Montreal. Also L. A. Smithson receive a

$1,000 from J. Schlanger "Deposit Check" which is deposited in the Bank of Montreal.

Accompanying this last confession by Olsen were two undated messages signed by Olsen and witnessed by James Campbell, John Campbell, and A. E. Pedersen.

> To the Proprietor of Hotel Occidental, Johnson Street, Victoria, BC.
>
> Please deliver on demand my suitcase with belongings to Captain A. C. Pedersen, master Barkentine *Puako*, on order given to anybody that he sends to get it.

> To Manager, Bank of Montreal, Victoria, B.C.
>
> This is to certify that I, Bjarne Olsen, has made the amount of $1000, one thousand dollars, payable and sign over to Captain A. C. Pedersen, master Barkentine *Puako* for him to receive that amount in full by signing his own name.

CHAPTER 6

THE SEARCH FOR THE TRUTH

By the end of the first week of September, every charged crewman had given affidavits to both the police and Vice-Consul Pisar. However, it was not until mid-September that any statements were taken under oath from Pedersen, the mates, the carpenter William Mattson, and ordinary seaman John Walter Campbell. In order to show impartiality and because he had been so closely involved with the crewmen, Captain Howe assigned Detective Sergeant R. Sowden of the South African Police to the task of taking the statements from the ship's officers and two potential defense witnesses, Mattson and Campbell.[1] The first of these were obtained on the twelfth from the second mate and the carpenter. The first mate and John Walter Campbell gave statements on the sixteenth. The statements of the mates, the carpenter, and Campbell add little, as they repeat logbook entries already discussed. Captain Pedersen's statement taken on September 23 has a few more details. For instance, he stated that at the start of the trip

> I found that the crew did not know much about sailing ships, they did not know the ropes and I told the mates to set to and teach them the names of ropes day and night. Hansen was the only man who knew anything.[2] We eventually got into choppy seas and the crew got seasick. The mates were kind to them and helped them with their work. I told the mates to be kind to them and teach them their work so that we should have a good crew when we reached Cape Horn. I also instructed the mates to teach them to steer the ship, and I took the wheel myself and showed them how to steer. In gales of wind I had to take the wheel and steer the ship as they did not know how to do it; it appeared to me that they did not want to learn anything; they appeared careless.
>
> I had plenty of fresh food and vegetables on board and I first had to complain to the cook about not putting vegetables on the table,

this was early in May. I told him that I knew there were plenty of vegetables and asked him what he was doing with them. I made an examination and found that a lot of vegetables and fresh meat had become decayed and rotten. I also drew his attention to a lot of bread and other food which I had seen floating past the ship. I showed him how to manage things and arrange the daily meals, and he seemed glad of my help and advice and said nothing to me. Finally one day he put some hash on the breakfast table which was not fit to eat, it actually stunk. I sent for him (Stewart) and asked him what was the matter with the hash, he replied that he did not know; I asked him if he ever tasted the food before we ate it and he said no. I then made him sit down and eat some of it, he ate a little and then said he was not hungry.

By the time the ship reached the tropics, Pedersen stated, the men had begun acting in a "funny manner." The mates complained that the men did not seem to want to learn and did not remember things they had been taught. Pedersen's version of Stewart's suicide generally followed the same story line as that within the logbook, and was in step with the logbook entries Howe had copied. He made no mention of any unusual events during the month following Stewart's death. In late June, when the first mate reported that Olsen had attempted to shove him overboard, Pedersen told the mate "to keep away from the side and let the men do the work." In his rambling discourse, Pedersen said that around the fourth of July, all of the crew were speaking amongst themselves about committing suicide.

Pedersen eventually came into possession of an IWW book, the so-called Little Red Songbook, which he claimed Smithson had put on his desk.[3] "I asked him [Smithson] what he meant by doing this, and he said he thought he would like me to know that there were I.W.W.'s on board the ship. He stated he had found the book forward. I kept the book and handed it over to the police at Cape Town. I afterward found out that this book belongs to Lester Jensen and that most of the crew were members of this Society."[4]

In this sweeping statement given to Sowden, Pedersen liberally tried to tar most of the crewmen as IWW members, but months later at trial in New York, he backed down and expressed doubt as to whether even Jensen was a member. Interestingly, during that examination in court, he claimed he had never heard the term "Wobbly" and did not know what it meant.

Near mid-July, Pedersen discovered that a pair of handcuffs was missing.

Knowing that no one entered my room but the cabin boy I questioned him, and he at first denied it; but on being pressed and after a slap or two he stated "I took the pair of handcuffs from the drawer in the captain's bedroom a few days after Frank Grielen was placed in irons the first time with the intention of putting the second mate in irons and detaining him in the galley so that the captain would miss him and look for him and go into the galley when he would hear him call out and they would kill the captain and the second mate." [After Smithson confessed] I made an entry in my logbook on pages 20 and 21 which Smithson, J. W. Campbell, and A. E. Pedersen signed.

Pedersen read into his statement various excerpts from his logbook as well as from statements signed by the crew concerning planned attempts that were to be made against his life and the lives of the mates. There were also, he claimed, plans to destroy the ship.

About this time [August 20 or 21] I got the anchors out to see what the crew would do. As a rule this is a sign that we are getting near to the end of the voyage and makes the crew happy, but these men acted crazy and acted as though they were going to do something they had not done, and seemed more desperate, and commenced to growl at one another as though they were angry at not having carried out their plots. . . . On August 21st I released B. Olsen from irons in order to have someone to work the vessel. I had to keep shifting them around to control them. . . . On August 23rd, I released Jones, Jensen, and Smithson from irons to perform ship's duties; that evening placed Smithson in irons again as he could not be trusted; he was told to clean up the cabin and he said to me "Yes, you bet your life."

For most of the voyage and for whatever reason, Reilly was the only fo'c'sle seaman not accused of involvement in the supposed and rapidly escalating plots. This may have been because Pedersen needed Reilly's word that he was a stowaway. But finally even Reilly was dragged in. Pedersen read from his log entry of August 23: "Reilly was placed in irons on suspicion of being implicated with others to destroy the vessel."

The same day, Pedersen claimed to have sighted a steamer bound south-southeast. He tried to solicit help from the ship by putting up the international flag signal Y-F, signifying his need for assistance in putting down a mutiny.

[The unidentified ship] slowed down and crossed our bow and then went ahead again—he [the other ship] did not hoist any signal. . . . The crew became more anxious to do us harm and on account of their statements I was more afraid of them and told them I would shoot them if they came too near; they were trying to crawl close to us. This is the time they got their black eyes, when they got crowding around us on the lee side. They would do anything to injure us. I don't deny hitting them because I had to in self defense. I had to have one or two on deck to work the ship. I could not let them all on deck at once or they would have overpowered us, the mates and myself.

When asked about the time the *Puako* was spotted by the SS *Magdalena* on August 27, Captain Pedersen stated:

> I hove to and the steamer stopped and put out a boat, and a signalman came on board and I explained that there was a mutiny on the ship and I asked him to wireless Cape Town for a tug to tow me in. He said he would do this and told me to keep my course right in—which I did. I kept steering in, but the man at the wheel kept changing the courses and I had to keep one of the mates at the wheel all the time. [Jack Joe and others had told Howe that Joe was at the wheel—in fact tied to the wheel—most of this time.] I saw the lights of Cape Town and the red light on the breakwater and gradually got sail in as we neared port, and came in between Robben Island and Green Point; it was thick and hazy at the time with squalls from N.W. I took soundings and dropped anchor in 6½ fathoms [39 feet] of water at 10:30 p.m. ship's time. I did not see anything of a tug boat through the mist and rain. . . . These are all the details I can think of at present as there was been [*sic*] such a lot of trouble every day, some of them minor ones, but all making up for more serious trouble as I later found out.
>
> I consider that the crew are nothing else but German spies and intended to destroy the vessel and kill the mates and myself and the carpenter; in fact all those who would not be on their side. This is borne out by their own statements which they gave quite freely and of their own accord. I consider that the action I took was necessary to bring the ship and cargo safely to port.

The ship's officers, carpenter, and John Walter Campbell made additional sworn statements on October 22 before Vice-Consul Charles J. Pisar, but like their earlier statements, these added nothing to what has already been covered.

Once it was determined by South African officials that the crewmen were probably not a threat to anyone and certainly were not enemy agents, they were moved to South Africa's immigration detention area located in Cape Town, where they had more freedom of movement. Soon after, Barney Olsen died. While the official medical cause was influenza, Barney's fellow sailors felt his death had been hastened, if not caused, by the almost inhuman treatment he had received at the hands of the Pedersens.

On October 9, George Murphy received the following letter:[5]

Dear Sir:
Word has just been received that Barney Olsen is dead. You have been previously informed that he has been continually complaining of pains in his back and kidneys caused by the horrible beatings received by the captain on board the ship.

We are positive that his untimely end has been caused by the ill-treatment he received by the captain.

We urgently hope that this matter will be carefully looked into if possible.

Yours respectfully,
Remaining crew of *Puako* in behalf of parents of deceased

Murphy followed up on this compelling request as soon as he could. On October 21, J. J. McGraph, secretary and treasurer of Somerset Hospital, Cape Town, replied:

American Consul General
African Life Buildings
Cape Town
Cause of Death of Seaman B. Olsen
Dear Sir:
In acknowledging your letter of the 14th Inst. and enclosure dated the 9th idem, I beg to advise you that Dr. A. W. Hauman, the Medical Attendant in the above case, states that the cause of death was Double Pneumonia arising, no doubt, from the prevailing epidemic. There were no marks of injuries on the body of the deceased.[6]

I am, Sir, Yours faithfully,
[signed] J. J. McGraph

About a month after the *Puako*'s arrival in Cape Town and after the ship had been unloaded, Murphy received orders directly from Secretary of State Robert Lansing to "detain the captain and the mates."

That Robert Lansing had become personally involved in the *Puako* matter is a measure of the importance the Department of State accorded the situation. Many of the dispatches Murphy received over the coming months were also signed personally by Lansing, indicating his continued concern and desire to see that the affair was properly handled. Lansing was not the only high official keeping a watchful eye. If the Department of State's *Puako* file DOS 196.3 is an indication, a great deal of correspondence between the departments of State, Justice, Commerce, and Navy concerning the *Puako* occurred at the highest levels. The *Puako* affair was not being taken lightly by anyone.

Lansing's order created for Murphy a quandary, because removing the ship's officers would leave no one on board to take responsibility for the vessel. The partners of Hind, Rolph & Co. of San Francisco—either not believing or not wanting to believe that their longtime employee had committed crimes serious enough for his removal—delayed responding for several weeks to cables sent by Murphy, the Department of State in Washington, or even their own shipping agent in Cape Town. Did they realize that under the recently passed Seamen's Act they, as the ship's owner, could be held responsible for Pedersen's actions? Or were they confused and in doubt because of a letter they had received?

Two days after the *Puako* reached Cape Town, Captain Pedersen had written a defensive letter to the ship's owners.[7] He enclosed a daily report of the voyage, asking that particular notice be taken of the distances sailed one day to the next.[8] Pedersen stated that throughout the trip wind conditions had been contrary and that he had continually experienced either squalls or calms. "The winds from the [normal] southeast trades on the Pacific . . . have been [instead] on the east and northerly quarter most all the time. That is one reason why it took me so long." Despite Pedersen's claim, when comparing the few known positions of the *Puako* against the British Admiralty chart *The World Sailing Ship Routes*, it is clear that the *Puako* generally followed closely in the analyzed wakes of hundreds of sailing ships that had made similar passages at that time of year. Unfortunately there is no way to compare the now-lost daily distances of the *Puako* against the other studied ships.

For a man in his mid-fifties who had spent nearly forty years at sea and who had made seven previous passages around the Horn, this voyage must have been among the most trying. Pedersen knew he would be negotiating Cape Horn at the worst time—July, dead of winter in those southern latitudes. He also knew when he left Victoria that his crew was inadequate and could not perform normal duty, as the men had had little if any time at sea and the mates were only boys with no experience in training and/or leading a group of men. To gain the approval of his employer and the ship's insurer to proceed to sea with such an unseaworthy crew, Pedersen must have stretched the truth considerably concerning the abilities of those he had hired, particularly his two sons. Pedersen devoted most of his letter to Hind, Rolph to the problems he had encountered with the "mutinous crew," and tried to bolster his position with his employer by writing of the valiant strides that had been taken by himself and his sons. "I must give the first and second mates great credit for standing by the ship the way they did, as their lives have also been in equal danger. Between the three of us, we have worked hard night and day and got the *Puako* into Cape Town in good condition." With a tone bordering on pride and self-satisfaction, Pedersen then informed the owners that the crew was in jail, that he had provided the authorities with full particulars, and that he had hopes they would all be hung, "as I know they all deserve to be hung, these German spies." Of interest, in the letter Pedersen does not mention the IWW, his theme consistently being that he had brought to Cape Town a shipload of enemy agents. However, that Pedersen's paranoia may have led him to think some or all of the men, the enemy agents, were also IWW members was important, as through this avenue they would have learned the tactics of murder and sabotage that, starting in July, became key parts of the plots to do in the ship's officers and destroy the ship.

Pedersen followed up his letter with a telegram to Hind, Rolph in late September. "Make inquiries to confirm statement of crew. Was there paid in to Bank of Montreal at Victoria during April one thousand dollars to credit of each Frank Grielen and Bjarne Olsen also in Seattle, State Bank, one thousand dollars in the joint names of Lester and Blanche Jensen. These are ransom money paid to crew destroy ship."[9] It seems obvious from the correspondence he sent to his employer that by the time the *Puako* reached Cape Town, Pedersen was convinced not only that the seamen were all German spies but that he could profit handsomely by turning them in to authorities.

When Lester Jensen asked Pedersen how he planned to prove he and the other crewmen were spies, the master crowed, "I have got all the proof; they will listen to me because I am captain; them black lime-juicers will line you up and shoot you like a dog."[10] As Jensen saw it, following Stewart's death and to remove any appearance of culpability in the cook's death, Pedersen devoted the remainder of the trip to brutalizing and assaulting the seamen until they individually signed statements that they were German spies.

When Hind, Rolph & Co. was finally made to understand the gravity of the situation by a personal letter from Secretary of State Robert Lansing, company president James Rolph Jr. cabled his approval for Murphy to ship a new master if he could find one. Even though Hind, Rolph did not like the arranged terms, Murphy found and shipped Eric Pearson, a British master and resident of Cape Town, who agreed to take the *Puako* at least to Sydney, Australia, where an American master might be located. Murphy also assisted Pearson in finding a new crew. The *Puako* crewmen were given the option of resailing under the new captain or waiting in Cape Town as detainees with the agreement that they would be returned to the United States at the government's expense to serve as government witnesses against the ship's officers. Two of the crew, L. A. Smithson and Peter Jorgensen, opted to sail with Pearson. The *Puako* was to sail in ballast from Cape Town. At Sydney she would load with copra and depart for Seattle.[11]

Once Murphy was confident that the *Puako* could be properly manned, he summoned Pedersen and his sons along with carpenter William Mattson and seaman John Walter Campbell on October 1, 1918—Adolph Eric Pedersen's eighteenth birthday—to his office where, after some considerable fuss, all five were formally discharged from the *Puako*. Murphy used the authority granted under Section 8 of the Seamen's Act to request that South African Immigration officials be on hand just outside of the United States Consulate General, where the five men were immediately detained and carted off to the Roeland Street Gaol (see plate 10).[12] Murphy cabled Washington on October 2:

> Discharged master exhibits a menacing attitude. Immigration authorities, considering him dangerous, holding him, others, jail as undesirable immigrants pending deportation. Unless I request their release, which I must refuse, the Department of State having ordered detention, Immigration officials arrange deport master, officers, shortly Boston; others later first opportunity. Urgently advise against sending by Puako any accused because of very great length of voyage, danger of escape islands, ports en route, not yet having owner's sailing orders. If the accused seamen sent [as] prisoners, there would be no room for crew.

Discharged from the _____ [censored] authorities are willing to assist, but they do not think it is possible British transport. The only hope, it seems to me, the Department to arrange British Government or to await rare opportunity transportation [on U.S.-flag vessel]. Accusations against the master, officers, Section 9, Act of Congress, 1915, evidence is considered complete. Witnesses: Reilly, Smithson, Jensen, Olsen, Grielen, Jack Joe, Jorgensen, Jones, James Campbell, John Campbell.[13] Against the master alone Section 11, Act of Congress, 1915, responsibility deaths seamen, violently forcing confessions now absolutely repudiated; unlawfully, knowingly, violating shipment laws by taking without any passport [to] sea, there shipping imperiled him, evidence logbook affidavits. Local authorities had been consulted; consider master is guilty. His attitude sullen, violent.[14]

Murphy incorrectly implied in the preceding paragraph that by taking Reilly to sea without proper papers, Pedersen had violated Section 11 of the Seamen's Act. That section refers to allotments and advances and thus had no relationship to Reilly's situation. Pedersen was instead in violation of Section 14 of the Shipping Commissioners' Act of June 7, 1872, which stated: "If any master ... of a vessel knowingly receives or accepts, to be entered on board of any merchant vessel, any seaman who has been engaged or supplied contrary to the provisions of this title, the vessel ... shall, for every such seaman, be liable to a penalty of not more than two hundred dollars."

CHAPTER 7

TRANSPORTATION SECURED

George Murphy's activities as consul general were guided over the coming weeks in part by Section 355, titled "Transportation of Persons Charged With Crime," of *Regulations Governing the Consular Service of the United States*.

> When, however, mutiny or other grave offense against the laws of the United States shall have been committed on board an American vessel on the high seas, and without the jurisdiction of any state, it is the duty of the consular officer into whose district the vessel may come to take the depositions necessary to establish the facts in the fullest manner possible. If the circumstances demand that the offenders should be sent to the United States for trial, he may apply to the local authorities for means to secure and detain them while they remain in port; and in all cases where the vessel is not bound for the United States, he is directed to procure at least two of the principal witnesses to be sent along with the prisoners. And he will, at the same time, promptly transmit certified copies of all the depositions, together with a carefully prepared report of all the facts and proceedings that may aid in establishing the guilt of the offenders, to the United States attorney for the district to which the prisoners are sent, and also a like report of the case to the Department of State. When practicable to do so, consuls should send the witnesses to the United States in the same ship with the accused, and in all cases should endeavor to get witnesses to the place of trial as soon as possible after the arrival of the accused.

While Murphy and his staff were working in Cape Town to fulfill their obligations under Section 355, the Navy Department's Office of Naval Intelligence (ONI), through its 13th Naval District, was carrying out an investigation on the U.S. west coast and in Canada at the joint request of the

Department of State and the Department of Justice.[1] Agent Claude Fortner of Seattle, working with a Major Jules of the British Military Intelligence Office at Victoria, determined that there was no validity to Pedersen's claims of the crew being German spies connected to any Austrian count. Nor was there any connection with various hotels in the Victoria-Vancouver area, or with accounts held in the Bank of Montreal. The report submitted to ONI director Rear Admiral Roger Welles indicated Pedersen was well known to United States and Canadian customs and immigration officials as well as to West Coast outfitters, all of whom shared basically the same opinion that Pedersen was "an expert seaman and navigator but that he is a very hard man with crews and considered rough with his men.... Fights between the skipper and crew continually occurred on his vessel."[2]

Investigators spoke with a Mr. Burford of U.S. Immigration who had personally had problems with Pedersen. Burford claimed that the master had once tried to smuggle a Chinese seaman into the United States. He cautioned that Pedersen "will bear watching as to his honesty, also that he would not hesitate to knock a man in the head with a belaying pin." To bolster his points, Burford related: "On April 21, 1916, one William King, a Negro, died aboard the captain's ship under peculiar circumstances."

R. M. Newcomb, the American vice-consul in Victoria who had signed Pedersen's clearance in April 1918, told naval investigators that on various occasions Pedersen had "tried to evade the regulations either through ignorance or intentionally." An examination of the records given to the investigators by Newcomb "showed that this man has had more trouble with his men and more mutineers on his boat than all of the others put together." The investigators determined Pedersen to be "a man of rather shady reputation concerning not only his dealings with officials at this port [Victoria] but also in the handling of his men."

A message wired from Victoria by American consul R. B. Mosher to the Secretary of State on September 19 and forwarded to Murphy stated, "No such person as Schlanger alias Belsky alias Schevek was at Northern Hotel Victoria about April 23, 1918. No valise was left at Occidental Hotel. One thousand dollars not deposited in bank Montreal by Frank Grielen or Bjarne Olsen."[3]

At the request of Murphy, Elliot Howe's police staff in Cape Town had made a search of the *Puako* in September while Pedersen was aboard. As anticipated, Pedersen had declined to give the police access to his cabin, and the police did not press the issue. Immediately after the master and mates were discharged from the ship and incarcerated in the Roeland Street Gaol,

Howe did a second, more thorough search of the ship in company with the older mate, Leonard. These two searches resulted in the discovery of an assortment of weaponry which eventually was sent to Washington along with signed depositions, the ship's official logbook, the mates' daily logbook [diary], and the large bundle of crew confessions that Pedersen had given to officials on the morning of August 28, just hours after the *Puako* arrived in Cape Town. The weapons turned up in the search included several illegal ones as well as three legal firearms that Pedersen had declared: a rifle, a shotgun, and a fully loaded pistol. In most references to Pedersen's pistol, it is called a "revolver"—even Pedersen uses that term—but it was actually a semiautomatic pistol. All of the weapons, legal and illegal, were shipped to Washington as part of the evidence package.

While he was collecting evidence, Murphy was also trying to locate a ship on which to transport the three *Puako* officers and those crewmen who had agreed to be transported to the United States to testify. The war and the resultant military takeovers of passenger ships had greatly reduced the amount of commercial shipping available to transport such a large group of detainees out of Cape Town directly to the United States. There was also very little opportunity to ship them via England. At one point Murphy thought he had a solution with the British merchantman *Hypatia*, but that fell through at the last moment because of the owner's excessive financial demands. On October 21, Murphy sent a lengthy dispatch to Washington in which, for the first and only time throughout the lengthy ordeal, he expressed his utter frustration.[4]

> At a time when my office [staff] was entirely insufficient to cope with the manifold work necessarily resulting from new war duties, and when I myself, as I had telegraphed the Department on several occasions, felt greatly weakened mentally and physically by a long continued strain without any opportunity for recuperation, the extremely trying work in connection with the *Puako* coincided with a deadly epidemic of influenza which caused the death of thousands of residents of Cape Town and temporarily deprived me of the assistance of five members of my small staff, including all of my typists.[5] Vice Consul Pisar and I were ourselves unwell, and we were alone in the office for about two weeks at a time when every ring of the telephone brought us some new duty—the sending of a seaman to hospital or his burial, important license matters, etc. etc.

Consequently, the taking of testimony in the *Puako* case was ex-

> tremely difficult and almost impossible, my nerves being in such a condition that I found difficulty in thinking and planning.... After it had been arranged for the master, mates, and one witness favorable to them [Mattson] to go on the *Hypatia*, the owners of that vessel became frightened for the safety of the ship by the unsavory reputation which Captain Pedersen had earned for himself here, and at the last moment these owners made such prohibitive conditions [demanding that the U.S. government assume full financial responsibility for the ship and her cargo] that all my carefully made plans came to nothing.

Murphy added that British Naval Control Officer Commander Delius at Cape Town had been in contact with the British Admiralty, and through that avenue he thought military transportation could eventually be secured to carry all of the men from Cape Town to England. Murphy was confident that from Europe, either a U.S. Army or U.S. Navy transport could bring them to the United States.

Although George Murphy was frustrated and tired, he continued to be optimistic that a ship could be located, as no one wanted Adolph Cornelius Pedersen out of Cape Town more than he. Murphy concluded his dispatch by reiterating:

> (a) that Captain Pedersen's violent and lawless behavior has caused much very unfavorable comment here, injurious to the good name of the American merchant marine;
>
> (b) that, in my opinion, this naturalized citizen lacks the law-abiding American attitude expected and required of the master of an American vessel, and is therefore unfit to hold a Master's Certificate; and
>
> (c) that the local authorities at Cape Town fully agree with me in believing that Captain A. C. Pedersen and his two mates, who are also his minor sons, are guilty of the crimes alleged against them by the crew of the *Puako*.

In a later dispatch dated October 28, Murphy used even stronger language concerning Pedersen.

> In my opinion, he is a very dangerous man, and the Reilly incident, as well as his spy fabrications against British subjects and American citizens, seem to warrant a suspicion that he is either insane or directly disloyal.... He is not a fit man to command an American ship

engaged in foreign trade and ... his visits to this port have tended to create an exceedingly bad impression among local officials and the population of Cape Town, for his behavior has been widely discussed here. For the protection of the good name of the American mercantile marine, he should not, in my opinion, ever be permitted to return to South Africa in command of an American ship.[6]

Even though World War I had ended November 11, 1918, demands on Allied merchant and military shipping continued to be heavy as troops were brought home from the battle fronts. In late November, Murphy wrote Washington that although transportation for the men had not yet been located, he had found a reliable means for sending the sealed parcel containing the weapons that the police searches had turned up: he had entrusted the parcel to the master of the SS *City of Bristol*, bound for New York, who was instructed to personally give it and a letter from Murphy to the customs boarding officer.[7] The letter instructed that the package be forwarded to Mr. I. P. Roosa, U.S. Dispatch Agent, 2 Rector Street, New York City, for transmission by him to the Department of State. In a separate dispatch sent the same day, Murphy forwarded additional affidavits including one of special interest from John Walter Campbell. While Campbell was held at the Roeland Street Gaol in company with the ship's officers and the carpenter, he spoke in defense of Pedersen and his sons; however, when he was finally moved into the immigration detention facility and reunited with the other crewmen, he crossed to the other side of the fence. He now said that the confessions of all of the men, including his own, had been given "under compulsion," and that for the most part, the men did not even know what they were signing, as their eyes were often almost closed from beatings and they were in a very cowed state.

It was at this point that officials obtained a description from John Walter Campbell of the "water cure" to which he and the others had been subjected. He began by explaining that the holds of the *Puako* were full of lumber. In addition, the ship carried lumber on her deck, where it was stacked ten to twelve feet high. A gasoline-operated bilge pump, fastened to the ship's deck (see plate 12), was surrounded by the stacked lumber to form an area known as the "pump hold." The pump was used to suck from the ship's bilges the considerable amount of water that continually seeped into the wooden ship through her seams, and a hose attached to the outlet side of the pump was run up over the lumber to allow the water to be pumped overboard. During the water cure applications, the hose was kept in the pump hold area. In one such application of the water cure, six of the seamen, including John Walter Campbell, were lowered into the pump hold. The mates chained the men together and water was "pumped on us with a gasoline engine. The carpenter started the engine and the hose was held by the two mates. The cold [bilge] water was sometimes forced on us for twenty minutes at a time ... to force us to confess. After this treatment, the victims invariably signed any statement the master dictated." The water cure was administered numerous times during the last three or four weeks of the voyage.[8]

In late December 1918, Murphy sent the last of the evidence, including statements written by Captain Howe and a Doctor Keet who had treated the men for their various injuries and illnesses. Keet made special note that he had hospitalized Lester Jensen, who was suffering from epilepsy which Keet felt had been brought on "by privations suffered on the voyage."[9]

A few weeks later, George Murphy cabled Washington with the news the Department of State had been waiting nearly three months to receive:

Cape Town, January 9, 1919, 5 p.m.

Secretary of State
Washington, DC
   URGENT. PUAKO matter. Three accused officers, ship's carpenter Mattson, seven other witnesses named my telegraph of October 2nd, except Smithson, Jorgensen ... sailed yesterday London or some other British port with two guards Tuohy and Keely. British transport Intaba. I have been able pay transportation thirteen men only as far as England, also advanced each guard thirty days' wages beginning eighth, agreement being twelve shillings per diem until return Cape Town provided they will return, concerning which Keely doubtful. Have also guaranteed guards' maintenance ashore England and United States. Return passage will be paid by the Department through the Embassy or otherwise. Request Department. [Request Department] immediately telegraph Embassy London take charge thirteen men on arrival in England, provide against their escape there, maintenance, and economical forwarding United States by an American transport or otherwise, as expenses long detention here and sending England very heavy.[10]

The Department of State immediately notified the Navy Department, which took charge of the men on their arrival in England. On 18 January, Josephus Daniels, Secretary of the Navy, alerted Admiral William Sims,

USN, to anticipate the arrival of the men in England and to make arrangements for their transport to the United States.[11] When the *Intaba* docked in Southampton on February 4, the Pedersens were immediately taken to a naval brig in Rockingham, where they were held. The location where the seamen witnesses were held was not specified. On February 10, now under naval guard, the Pedersens and all of the witnesses were put on the USS *Woolsey*, which took them to Brest, France. There they were all held in a naval brig until they were transferred to the USS *Rochester*.[12] A few days later, the USS *Rochester* left Brest en route to New York, where they arrived March 4, 1919.

HIND, ROLPH & CO.
SHIPPING AND COMMISSION MERCHANTS

ISLAND LINE

HR&Co.

HAWAIIAN ISLANDS
"Challenger"
"Defender"
"Emily Reed"
"G. W. Watson"
"Hawaii"
"Henry Villard"
"Honoipu"
"Homeward Bound"
"James Rolph"
"John G. North"

"JAMES ROLPH"

ISLAND LINE

HR&Co.

HAWAIIAN ISLANDS
"Kailua"
"Kohala"
"Kona"
"Koko Head"
"Lahaina"
"Mahukona"
"Makaweli"
"Muriel"
"Puako"
"Robert R. Hind"
"Wrestler"

302 CALIFORNIA ST., San Francisco, Cal.   212 MERCHANT ST., Honolulu, H. I.

Cable Address   AGENTS FOR
"ROLPH"   MESSRS. BLACK, MOORE & CO. - - - { 5 East India Ave., London, E. C.   CODES { A. 1.
          SEAHAM COLLIERY CO., LTD. - - -   { 28 Brunswick Street, Liverpool   { A. B. C.
                                            Sydney and Newcastle, N. S. W., Australia { SCOTTS'
                                                                                       { WATKINS'

1. By 1903 Hind, Rolph & Co. were shipping and commission merchants for twenty-one ships. Most of those were owned by Hind, Rolph or its subsidiary companies. Captain Pedersen would serve as master on both the *Challenger* and the *Puako*. Courtesy Captain Harold Huycke.

2. Captain Adolph Cornelius Pedersen and Gertrude Thornlun were married in 1890. Mrs. Pedersen and their three young sons were on board when the *Challenger* caught fire off the coast of Japan in 1905. Courtesy San Francisco Maritime NHP, Karl Kortum Collection, P89-085.004n.

3. Undated photo of *Puako* taken at San Pedro, California. When *Puako* left Victoria in April 1918, she had a similar appearance. At that time her deck load was ten to twelve feet high and consisted of logs sixty to eighty feet in length, squared off to a dimension of 24" x 24", with a top flooring of lumber 3" x 9". Courtesy San Francisco Maritime NHP, Phelps Collection, D1.9,758nl.

4. Most of the *Puako* seamen had no previous experience when they were ordered to unfurl the canvas off Cape Flattery at the start of her infamous voyage from British Columbia in April 1918. Under full sail, she could attain speeds in excess of 9 knots. Courtesy San Francisco Maritime NHP, Flora Buchanan Collection, J7.17,710n

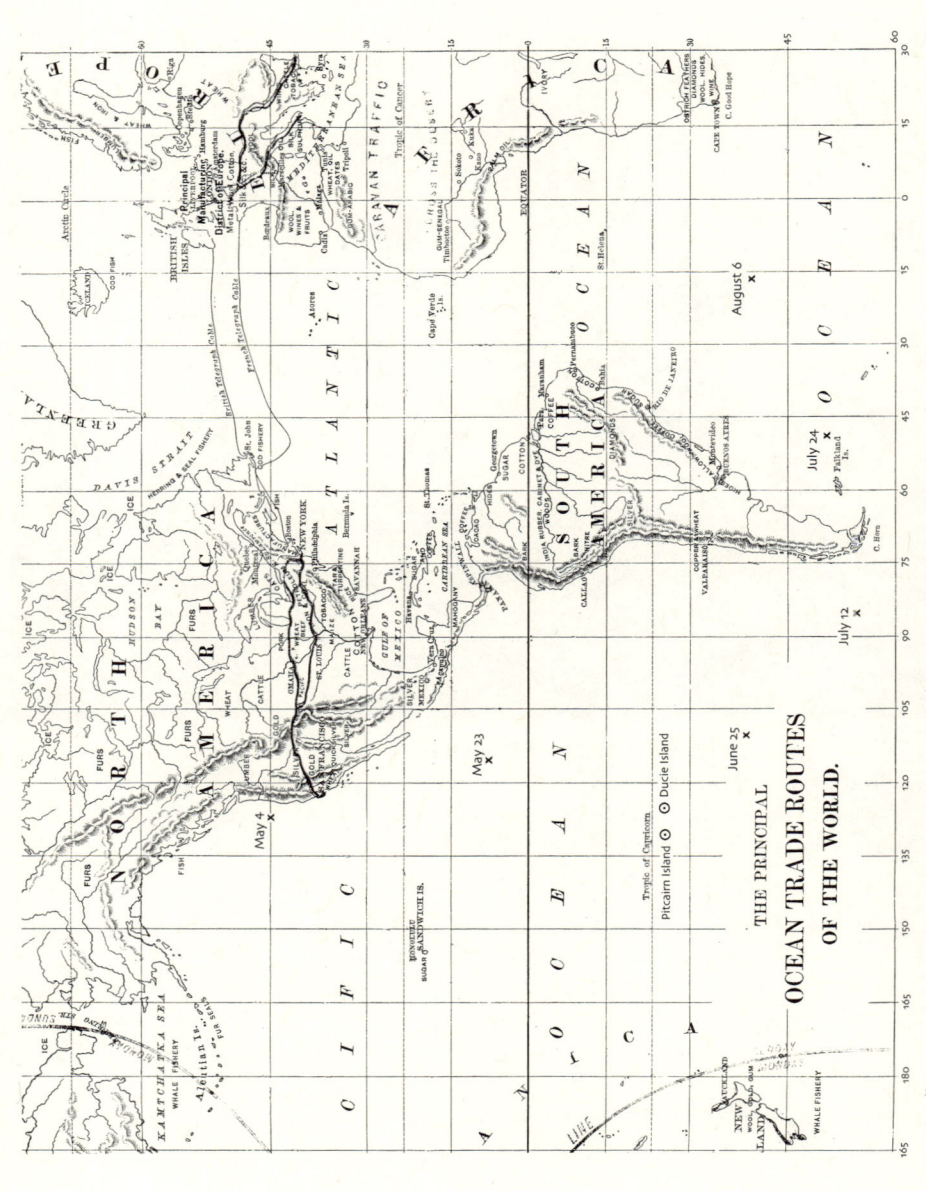

5. The six positions showing the track of the *Puako* are those that Police Captain Howe copied from the *Puako*'s logbook. The background map, which shows trade commodities circa 1900, is from *Harper's School Geography*, 120–21.

6. By 1917 the steamship was well on its way toward replacing the outmoded sailing ship, and young men with the desire to follow a seagoing career were looking unfavorably on the arduous life under sail. This wide-angle view of Cape Town's docks, circa 1920, which shows the Table Bay anchorage in the distance, is witness to that transition. Courtesy Cape Town Archives.

(Form No. 192—Consular.)
(Corrected November, 1910) DEC 12 AM 9 54

Consult General Instruction No. 338 when executing this form.

REPORT OF THE DEATH OF AN AMERICAN CITIZEN.

AMERICAN CONSULAR SERVICE.

101975

Cape Town, S.A., August 30, 1918.
[Place and date.]

Name in full: **John Henry Stewart** Age: **41**
[As nearly as can be ascertained.]

Native or naturalized: **Native. Born in San Francisco, Cal.**

Date of death: **May** 23 **1918.**
[Month.] [Day.] [Hour.] [Year.]

Place of death: **High Seas. Lat. 7 20' N. Long. 116 55' West.**
[Number and street] or [Hospital or hotel.] [City.] [Country.]

Cause of death: **Suicide by drowning on the high sea.**

Disposition of the remains: **Body not recovered.**

Local law as to disinterring remains: _____

Disposition of the effects: **Effects sold by Master of the Barkentine "Puako" to Seaman A.N.B. Hansen, for $13.00 — an entry of which was made in log book. Remainder of effects will be sent to the United States District Judge for Northern District of California at San Francisco, Cal.**

Person or official responsible for custody of effects and accounting therefor: **Master A.C. Pedersen, Bktn. "Puako."**

Accompanied by relatives or friends as follows:

NAME.	ADDRESS.	RELATIONSHIP.
----	---	---

Address of relatives (so far as known):

NAME.	ADDRESS.	RELATIONSHIP.
1. Mrs. W.F. Mosher	1203 Illinois Ave. Spokane, Washington.	
2. (The above name and address given in shipping articles as next of kin.)		

Notification sent to:

Dept. of State by **Mail** on **Sept. 5, 1918.**
[Name.] [Mail or telegraph.] [Date.]

Mrs. W.F. Mosher by **Mail** on " " "
[Name.] [Mail or telegraph.] [Date.]

This information, an inventory of the effects, accounts, etc., have been recorded in full in the Miscellaneous Record Book, pages **54**, and copies placed under File 330 in the correspondence of this office.

Remarks: **Deceased shipped as cook on the American Barkentine "Puako" at Vancouver, B.C. on April 2, 1918, at Seattle, Washington.**

Consul General of the United States of America.

[SEAL.]
No fee prescribed.

(To be sent *in duplicate* to the Department of State.)

---

7. The day after the *Puako* arrived at Cape Town, Consul General George Murphy prepared an official report of the death by suicide of John Henry Stewart. The information came from the ship's logbook, which Captain Pedersen turned over to the South African police. Records of the Department of State, file 196.3/107.

Copy-SDM

J.NO.03211 H.D.
1919 M.S.C.I

UNION OF SOUTH AFRICA

DEATH NOTICE.

Pursuant to the Provisions Contained in "The Administration of Estates Act, 1913".

1. Name of the deceased _____ BJARNE OLSEN

2. Birthplace and Nationality of the deceased _____ NORWAY

3. Names and addresses of the Parents of the deceased
   Father _____
   Mother _____

4. Age of the deceased _____ 27 _____ years _____ months.

5. Occupation in life of the deceased, or if a woman, of her husband _____ SEAMAN

6. Ordinary place of residence of the deceased, or, if a woman, of her husband _____ ex Detention Depot Docks, C. T.

7. Married or unmarried, widower or widow _____ UNKNOWN

   a - Name of surviving spouse (if any) and whether married in community of property or not

   b - Name or names and approximate date of death of predeceased spouse or spouses

   c - Place of last marriage

8. The day of the deceased: on _____ 8th OCTOBER _____ 1918.

9. Where the person died
   House _____ SOMERSET HOSPITAL
   Town or Place _____ CAPE TOWN
   District _____

10. Names of children of deceased and whether majors or minors

    State separately the children born of different marriages, and give the date of birth of each minor. Names must be in full. If there are no children, and either or both parents be dead then give the names and addresses of the brothers and sisters of deceased.

    CAUSE OF DEATH:
    DOUBLE PNEUMONIA

8. Seaman Bjarne Olsen died at Somerset Hospital in Cape Town. The official cause of death was pneumonia, but Olsen's shipmates were certain his death was hastened by massive internal injuries inflicted by Captain Pedersen and the mates, his teenaged sons. Records of the Department of State, file 196.3.

FOR THE DEPARTMENT'S FILES

J.No. 03211U.D.
1919

-Copy-SDM

CERTIFICATE OF DISCHARGE OF SEAMAN.

Consular Service, U. S. A.
September 27, 1918.

Name of ship........PUAKO.............................
Official number ...150973..K.S.D.J...................
Port of registry.....SAN FRANCISCO....................
Tonnage...1084 gross 1011 net........................
Description of voyage or employment, Lumber from.....
Victoria, British Columbia, for Cape Town............
Name of seaman............BJARNE OLSEN...............
Place of birth ....NORWAY.......................
Age........27...................................years.
Character......................................
Ability..
Capacity........BOATSWAIN............................
Date of entry April 23, 1918...Date of discharge 9/27/18
Place of discharge....CAPE TOWN......................
Cause of discharge....CRUEL TREATMENT................

I certify that the above particulars are correct, and that the above named seaman was discharged accordingly. The Master has refused to sign this certificate.

__BJARNE OLSEN__
Seaman   Master

Given to the above named seaman in my presence this____27 th_____day of September 1918 A. D

__GEORGE H. MURPHY__
Consul General of the U.S.

9. Once George Murphy, U.S. consul general at Cape Town, completed his investigation of the four-month voyage of the *Puako*, he issued a certificate of discharge to each of the injured seamen from the vessel. Records of the Department of State, file 196.3/133.

10. A modern view of Cape Town's Roeland Street Gaol, where the officers of the *Puako* were held for three months awaiting deportation to the United States. Courtesy Cape Town Archives.

11. George H. Murphy, consul general at the U.S. Consulate in Cape Town, was one of the first to recognize that the crewmen of the *Puako* were not mutineers but rather were victims of the master's brutality. Courtesy NARA, Suitland, Maryland, 059-250/47/32/01-Box 178.

12. The location of the bilge pump of the Hind, Rolph barkentine *Koko Head*, shown here on the occasion of her launching, was identical to that of the *Puako*, which was a sister ship. When timbers were loaded on the deck of the *Puako*, a space was left around the bilge pump, forming a roomlike chamber. It was in this chamber that several crewmen were subjected to the "water cure." Courtesy San Francisco Maritime NHP, Annie M. Rolph Collection, B9.129.

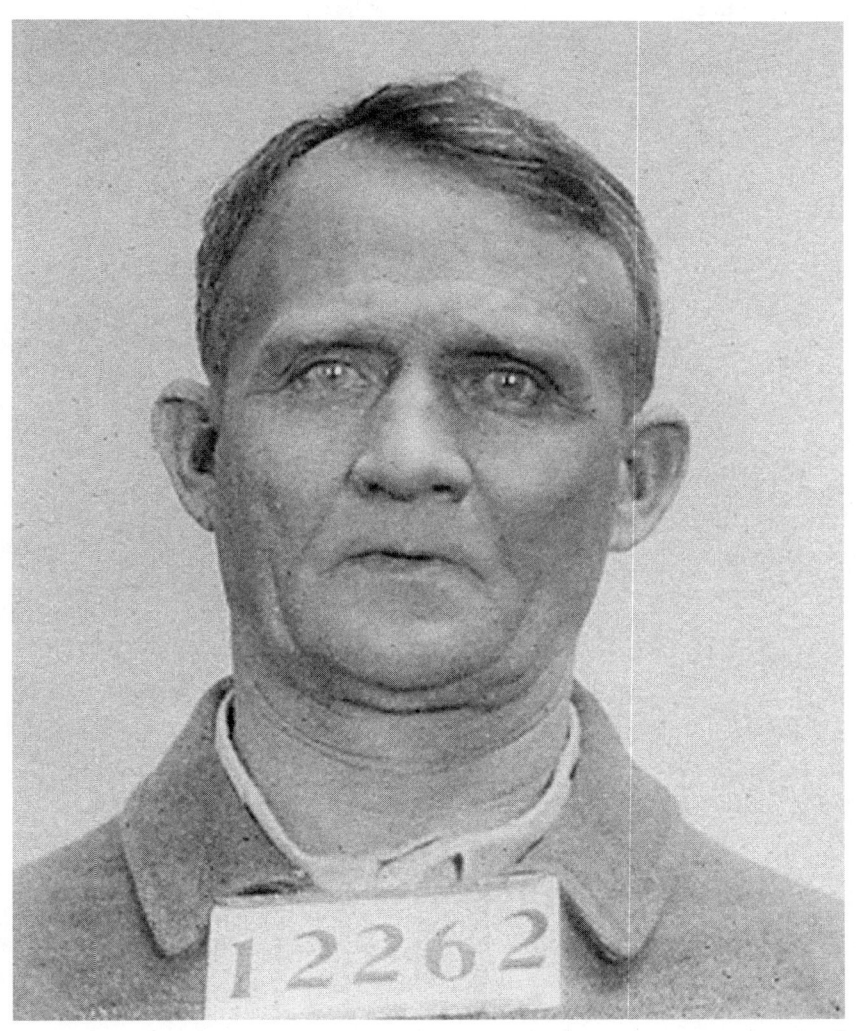

13. It was undoubtedly humiliating for Adolph Cornelius Pedersen, once the proud master of an American ship, to be processed at the United States Penitentiary, Atlanta, Georgia, where on April 1, 1921, he became just another number, 12262-131. Courtesy NARA, East Point, Georgia.

Department of Justice
United States Penitentiary
Atlanta, Georgia

Name	Adolph C. Pedersen	No.	12262
Alias	Adolph Cornelius Pedersen	Color	White
Received	APR 1 1921 3-9-21 Age 56	Apparent age	--------
From	S - N.Y., New York		
Crime	Mal-treatment of crew		
Term	Six, 18 month sentences concurrent. -------- Years 18 Months -------- Days		
Fine, $	None Costs, $ None Not to be held for fine and costs.		
Date of sentence	September 29, 1919 Commuted time 90 days		
Sentence commenced	January 1, 1921	To be given credit for three months served in jail, which time was served before date of sentence.	
Full term expires	June 30, 1922		
Short term expires	April 1, 1922 ✓		
Eligible for Parole	September 30, 1921 ✓		
Occupation	Master mariner		
Education	Common school	Religion	Lutheran
Nativity	Norway	Use drugs	No
Use tobacco	S.	Use liquor as a beverage	Yes
Parents living	Yes	Left home, age	16
Married	Yes	Number of children	4
Father born, where	Norway	Mother born, where	Norway
Where arrested	New York, N.Y.	When arrested	March 4, 1919
How long in jail before trial	3 months	Out on bond	Yes
How long in United States	36 years		
Citizen of United States	Yes	Speaks English	Yes

14. Pedersen's processing document indicates his sentence at Atlanta was to begin January 1, 1921. However, because of three months' time already served in New York before his trial, he did not report to Atlanta until April 1. Courtesy NARA, East Point, Georgia.

15. Frederick "Fighting" Hansen looked mild-mannered when he entered McNeil Island Federal Penitentiary on December 26, 1922, to begin serving his sentence of five years at hard labor for assaulting seaman Arne Arnesen. Courtesy NARA, Pacific Northwest Region (Seattle).

16. Leonard Roy Pedersen (1889–1992) talked freely in his old age about some of his early years as a young man at sea but had selective amnesia when questioned about the four months when he served as mate on the *Puako*. Courtesy Captain Harold Huycke.

17. When Adolph Eric Pedersen (1900–1991) retired from the San Francisco Bar Pilots Association, he moved to Ojai, California, to raise oranges. Those who knew him said he never talked about the voyage when as second mate he helped turn the *Puako* into a hellship. Courtesy Captain Harold Huycke.

THE RED RECORD.

Being a Bare Outline of Some of the Cases of Cruelty Perpetrated Upon American Seamen Between November, 1887, and the Present Date—"A Round Unvarnished Tale."

ECCE!

TYRANNUS.

18. "The Red Record," which first appeared on February 18, 1894, was for some time a regular feature in the *Coast Seamen's Journal*. Its motto "Ecce! Tyrannus" warned readers to beware of tyrants. Courtesy San Francisco Maritime NHP.

19. Andrew Furuseth devoted his life to making the seas a safer place for the common seaman. Following Furuseth's death on January 22, 1938, Secretary of Labor Frances Perkins allowed his body to lie in state in the Department of Labor, an honor never before accorded to any American labor leader. Author's collection.

CHAPTER 8

CAPTAIN AND SON INDICTED FOR MURDER

George Murphy and his consular staff had done a thorough job of gathering evidence and sworn statements. All of the material that Murphy had sent to the Department of State had been passed on to United States Attorney Francis G. Caffey in New York, who instructed United States Marshal Thomas D. McCarthy to arrest the Pedersens as soon as the USS *Rochester* arrived. McCarthy's men took the three ship's officers to the Tombs, a prison in downtown Manhattan. Bail was set at $25,000 for Captain Pedersen and $5,000 for each of his sons. The crewmen who had agreed to testify as government witnesses were all taken to the Ludlow Street Jail, where they were held as material witnesses.[1] Because Pedersen was still claiming that the seamen were pirates, they were initially held in lieu of $1,000 bail each; however, once their names were cleared, the men were free to move into hotels in the vicinity of the courthouse.

By mid-March, Assistant Attorney General Claude R. Porter was able to notify the Department of State that "the master and mates of the [*Puako*] have been held in the Southern District of New York in default of bail and all of the witnesses are also held in default of recognizance. The U.S. Attorney [Caffey] is engaged in an investigation of the case; part of the testimony has already been presented to the Grand Jury, and the remainder will be presented without delay. The U.S. Attorney promises a further detailed report in the case in due course."[2]

News of the misdeeds of Adolph C. Pedersen was quick to reach the attention of the fourth estate. Page 14 of the March 5 edition of the *New York Times* carried a long, reasonably accurate story that began with a headline and three subheads: "Captain and Mates Held for Flogging: Cruiser Brings Officers and Eight Seamen Off Barkentine *Puako* Under Arrest; Piracy

Charge Is Made; Tangled Tale of Events at Sea on Way to Cape Town Told to Authorities." A small unidentified clipping, which perhaps came from a Connecticut paper and which was saved by my late father-in-law, who was at the time attending Yale, began "Murder at Sea: Captain and Sons Locked Up in New York."

The Justice Department wasted no time in presenting its evidence against the ship's officers to a grand jury called into session by U.S. District Judge Learned Hand. The jury's lengthy indictment was read to the master and second mate at their April 1, 1919, arraignment. They were charged with killing "Axel Hansen, a human being, late able-bodied seaman and a member of the crew of the said vessel, by . . . causing him to cast, throw and plunge himself . . . from said vessel . . . causing him to sink in the said ocean, . . . drown and die."

A second count addressed the beatings Hansen had suffered, stating that it was the fear and apprehension of further beatings and violence against his body that drove him to "plunge himself" into the ocean where, despite his attempts to save himself and his cries for help, rescue attempts were denied to him by the defendants.

The same grand jury also indicted the master, the second mate, and the first mate for "felonious assault and maltreatment of the crew of the *Puako* during a trip from Victoria, British Columbia, to Cape Town which began April 27, and ended August 27, 1918."

The last item of the murder indictment as well as of the indictment for assault and maltreatment significantly stated that "the Southern District of New York, is the district in which the defendants were . . . first brought after the commission of the aforesaid offense." Pinpointing the place where the defendants were *first brought* became a point of argument. At the start of both the murder trial and a second trial on the assault charges, defense attorney Dudley Field Malone vehemently contested this jurisdiction and attempted to have the cases dismissed on the grounds that the Southern District of New York did not have jurisdiction over the defendants. He based his claim on the fact that the USS *Rochester*, had stopped for a period of time at a quarantine station located below the Narrows off Staten Island and in the Eastern District of the State of New York in order to allow a government physician on board to examine the ship and its passengers.[3] Malone claimed that it was there, in the Eastern District, that the government should have arrested the defendants; it was in that jurisdiction that any charges should have been filed; and it was in that jurisdiction that any trial should have been held. Instead, Malone argued, the government waited for the warship to come further into New York Harbor where it anchored in the North River, which was within the jurisdiction of the Southern District of New York. It was at this anchorage that the federal marshal arrested the defendants. In its counterargument, the government stated that it was the act of anchoring, or "touching land," that determined the jurisdiction for the trial.[4]

As they began to build their case in preparation for the murder trial, the team of U.S. attorneys headed by Francis G. Caffey felt that George Murphy and Captain Elliott Howe—men of solid reputation—would be valuable witnesses. When Acting Secretary of State Frank L. Polk wired George Murphy asking him to attend the trial, Murphy once again faced the task of locating transportation. The catch now was that time was of the essence. Murphy and Howe would have to reach New York within the next six weeks, a deadline they could not meet. The murder trial proceeded without them.

At their hearing presided over by Judge John Clark Knox, the indicted pleaded not guilty to all of the charges laid before them. Once Captain Pedersen and his son "Dolph" were arraigned, bail was denied and they continued to be held at the Tombs. Bail of $5,000 continued for Leonard Pedersen, who was charged only with the lesser crimes. Once that bail money had been paid, Leonard was released.[5] Potential jurors were summoned to appear May 26, 1919, with final selection scheduled for June 2, the date that Judge Charles Merrill Hough had set for the commencement of the trial.[6]

Even before the jury was seated, reporters with a ghoulish flair began to envision an extreme outcome. The *New York Times* wrote: "In the event of a first degree verdict, the Pedersens, under federal law, would suffer death by hanging. The place of execution probably would be the roof of the old Federal Building in City Hall Park, and the executioner would be United States Marshal Thomas F. McCarthy. So far as records show, this would be the first hanging by federal decree in the District Court of New York."[7]

Although all of the available *Puako* crewmen testified at the murder trial, the *New York Times* mentioned by name only two. One of those was Edward Reilly, who several times became so filled with emotion that he had to stop his testimony in order to recover. The other was John Walter Campbell, who gave clear details of the events before and after Axel Hansen's death. According to Campbell, at the moment he saw Hansen slip under the rail and jump, the second mate was closing in—only eight feet from the Danish seaman. Dolph then joined Jack Joe at the wheel in an effort to turn the ship more quickly and attempt to save Hansen, who was clutching the log line and begging to be rescued with smothered cries of "Oh, save me! Oh, save me!" But when the captain became aware of the situation, he shouted, "To hell with the man overboard. Put the vessel back on her course," and immediately ordered the men back to work. When Reilly did not react quickly enough, Campbell testified, "the captain picked up a tiller pin and started for him."[8]

The government rested its case after two days, and the defendants were called to testify on their own behalf. The second mate said the *Puako* had left Victoria with an inexperienced crew and that he and his brother Leonard had been told by their father to instruct the men, who were stubborn and did not want to learn anything. When asked about the water cure, the teenager said it had sometimes been necessary to turn the hose on members of the crew because they would not keep themselves clean.[9] When the defense attorney Malone began reading some of the detailed confessions signed by the crewmen, the gallery was piqued and attentive. There were audible signs of discontent when the court ruled the confessions inadmissible because they had no close relationship to the alleged crime of murder.

During cross-examination by Assistant U.S. Attorney S. Lawrence Miller, young Dolph attempted to paint Hansen as a confrontational, uncooperative seaman, a "sea lawyer." He said that Hansen had a book of rules which spelled out the duty of seamen to their officers and vice versa, and that he consulted it before obeying any order. From Hansen's book of rules Miller read an entry that had been written on the flyleaf: "This Dane is now a peaceful member of humanity. He won't preach the doctrines from the little green book inscribed *Sailor's Rule Book* again."[10] Dolph admitted that sometime following the seaman's death he had put that into Hansen's book.

The *New York Times* reporter that same day described Captain Pedersen as "shy and confused" when he took the stand. This was hardly the aggressive, profane man that the seamen and others such as Consul General Murphy had described. He spoke in so low a tone that his voice was scarcely audible, and much of his testimony was fragmented.

On June 7, the last day of the trial, Captain Pedersen was cross-examined by Assistant U.S. Attorney Ben A. Matthews, who assisted Miller. Pedersen admitted he had made no attempt to throw a life ring or anything to which Hansen might have clung, and that he never himself looked at the log line. When asked why he had not gone back to look for Hansen, Pedersen replied, "Because no man could live in water like that." Why was Pedersen so sure a man couldn't live in such a sea? Matthews asked, "Were you ever overboard?" Pedersen stated that years earlier he had fallen overboard and had saved himself by clinging to the log line for half an hour before he was rescued.

One of the last people to testify on behalf of the defendants was a Captain Charles Agar, a retired master, who said that the waters where Hansen lost his life were called by seamen the Roaring Forties or the Sailor's Grave, and that under the conditions described, it would have been dangerous to attempt to bring the ship about. It was a strange twist of fate that Captain Agar happened to be the same master who had rescued Pedersen when he fell overboard, albeit in calmer seas. Agar's opinion was countered by Captain John H. Cameron, also retired. Under the conditions described, said Cameron, "The risk would have been eliminated in bringing the ship around at a speed of 8 or 9 knots if the gallant yard had been dropped.... It would have taken about a minute to drop the gallant yard."[11]

The attorneys' summations were set for 10 a.m. on June 9. By afternoon the jury, which had been sequestered for the entire trial, was charged by Judge Hough to begin its deliberation. Hough said he would not entertain a verdict of murder in the first degree, since premeditation could not be proven. Nor would he accept more than one guilty verdict. In other words, if the master was guilty, the second mate was not, and vice versa.

It took the jury just sixteen minutes to acquit both men.[12] Father and son walked out of the courthouse to join their son and brother. All three were now freed on bail to await trial on the additional charges on which they had been indicted.

CHAPTER 9

THE GOVERNMENT'S SECOND ROUND

In the spring of 1919, after returning the murder indictment of which the master and second mate were acquitted, the grand jury also returned ten counts of assault and illegal imprisonment against Pedersen and both of his sons.[1] The first seven counts charged that the defendants "did with force and arms willfully, knowingly, unlawfully, and feloniously, without justifiable cause, beat and wound . . . on the head, face, and body . . ."

Count 1	Frank Grielen	July 24, 1918
Count 2	Frank Grielen	July 25, 1918
Count 3	Frank Grielen	July 26, 1918
Count 4	Jack Joe	August 2, 1918
Count 5	James Campbell	August 2, 1918
Count 6	William Jones	August 23, 1918
Count 7	Bjarne Olsen	August 23, 1918

Counts 8, 9, and 10 charged that James Campbell, William Jones, and Bjarne Olsen were unjustifiably imprisoned on August 23, 1918. At the end of the trial, before the jury deliberated, the third count was dropped by the government.

Assistant Attorney General Claude R. Porter notified Secretary of State Lansing on June 12, 1919, of the verdict in the murder trial:

> The United States Attorney [Caffey] states that the judge [Hough] who tried the case expressed the opinion that, while in his judgment the verdict as to murder was a proper one in view of all the testimony, yet he believed the master and mates should be put upon their trial upon the other indictments pending against them, charging assault and unlawful corporal punishment.

The United States Attorney is doubtful, in view of his experience on the murder trial, whether he can secure a conviction on these other indictments upon the testimony of the crew alone without corroborative outside testimony, although he believes that the story of the crew is true. The trouble is, as you are aware, that most of the members of the crew signed a statement implicating themselves in mutiny, etc. The United States Attorney suggests, therefore, that, with a view of these further prosecutions, the question be taken up again of securing testimony from Cape Town; that is, in effect, the testimony of the Consul General [Murphy] and of [Cape Town Police Sub-inspector] Howe.[2]

Acting Secretary of State Frank L. Polk immediately wired Murphy to again request his attendance at trial in New York.[3] A follow-up telegram asked if others from Cape Town such as Charles Pisar could also come to New York.

When Polk's wire reached Cape Town, George Murphy lost no time in securing passage for himself, Captain Howe, and Vice-Consul Pisar on the British steamship *Susquehanna*, scheduled to dock in Boston in mid-August. In the interim, presiding judge George Whitfield Jack delayed the trial proceedings from August until September 2, giving everyone ample time to prepare.[4]

As the trial began, the defendants pleaded not guilty to the seven counts of assault but admitted they had imprisoned the three plaintiffs named in counts 8, 9, and 10. They contended that such action had been necessary and justified because the three had been part of a plot or conspiracy to commit murder, mutiny, and piracy.

Assistant U.S. Attorney S. Lawrence Miller notified the court that he would call his witnesses in the following order: William Jones, Jack Joe, James Campbell, Jacob J. Goldfarb (a radiologist), Henry Ewing Hale (a New York physician), Frank Grielen, Edward Reilly, William Mattson, Captain Elliott Howe, Consul General George H. Murphy, and Vice-Consul Charles J. Pisar.[5] Miller had been a special assistant U.S. attorney under an appropriation for national security and defense until April 1, 1919, when he was transferred to work under the direction of U.S. Attorney Francis G. Caffey.[6]

Dudley Field Malone represented the defendants and stated he would call only Adolph C. Pedersen, master; Leonard R. Pedersen, first mate, and Adolph Eric Pedersen, second mate. From all indications, Malone was hired by Hind, Rolph & Co. Earlier in his career Malone, a formidable opponent, had served a short time under William Jennings Bryan as assistant secretary of state during the early years of the Wilson administration.[7] Of the two attorneys, Malone, who had a theatrical flair to his personality, was the more visible. At every opportunity he challenged Miller's questions, objected to witness answers, and argued incessantly with the court.

Miller, although less of a showman, was no less sharp, often cutting right to the quick to keep his points focused. As Miller addressed each of the seamen witnesses, his opening questions enabled the jurors to learn a little about each man's background—place of birth, past work experience, motivation for signing on the voyage. Then he immediately went to the heart of the matter, the specific assaults. These questions evoked forthright and disturbing answers which gave a clear portrayal of the violence that the seamen had witnessed.

William Jones (folios 76–386), the first witness called to the stand, was also one of the oldest and most articulate. With his wealth of life experience, he did not appear to be intimidated by any aspect of a court proceeding, especially the antics and verbal jousting of Malone. Jones testified that on August 23

> I was at the wheel when the captain came up and stood in front of me and kicked me in the shins, both shins, and called me a murdering son-of-a-bitch. He said, "You tried to kill me and my two boys," and he kept kicking me in the shins. Sometimes in the morning there were no watches; we were kept on deck from the 19th to the 20th, never were allowed in the forecastle at all. . . . That night [August 23], me and Jack Joe were called to the wheel. I was on the [weather] wheel and Jack Joe was on the lee wheel . . . and the first mate came up; he had a pair of brass knuckles on, and he put them right up to my face. After that he pounded me in the ribs, and on the arms, and after he had pounded me, he sent me around to the other side and put Jack Joe on the side I was on. He pounded him up the same way. And after he got through with him, he ran around and grabbed the tiller stick. . . . It is a stick sticking out on the wheel box to tell where the rudder is; it is about 2½ feet long. He grabbed that, and he beat me over the back and over the head, cut my head in two or three places, and raised welts on my back, from the neck all the way down; and he beat me at that time right up what was the poop deck. I got up on the deck load, and I fell back, and the captain called him back. Then I was sent forward

into the sail—they had an old foresail strung along under the main boom, and that is where we were put to sleep all the time.

On August 19 and 20 Jones was lowered into the pump hold:

> I was called aft and taken down in the cabin [with the master and mates] and the captain accused me when I got down in there of getting one thousand dollars from a German agent in Victoria to blow up the ship, and I denied this charge, and he fetched Frank Grielen in, a man that had been in irons for a month at this time—he fetched Frank Grielen in and he [Grielen] said "Yes, Jones and [James] Campbell got money in Victoria." Well, he never give me no chance to open my mouth at all. He just smashed me in the mouth. ... They beat me up until I was unconscious in the cabin, and the next thing ... when I came to I was going down in the pump hold; that is where I was locked up to Jensen; the water was pumped on us [by the carpenter and first mate] to make me confess to this. Cold water was pumped on us there on several occasions. I do not know how many; we were without a change of clothing, and we were made to stay there until along in the day of the 20th we were taken up on deck, taken forward of the mainmast, and Campbell and Edward Reilly, two of the crew, were compelled to beat us up there again. I was beat up that time until I don't remember going down into the pump hold again. ... When I came to, I was shackled up to Jorgensen, on the other side of the pump. On the next day when I was let out of there, I denied all these charges again. They took me up on deck. That was on the 21st, the day I was let out. I was taken out, taken forward of the mainmast, put on my things there, and the second mate came there with a paper and pencil, and he said, "This is all lies you told down there." I said "Yes, the whole thing is a frame-up right from start to finish." And he called me a lying Jew son-of-a-bitch, and hit me in the jaw and laid me over on the deck and from then on I got it right until the day I got out. Jim Campbell, the second day we were in there was taken down in the pump hold. He had a cut over his forehead at the time; he was bleeding; he was taken in there. I think the water was pumped on him once and then he was taken out. They made him climb up the ladder with his hands shackled; he got up nearly to the top and fell back on his side on the shafting of the pump. I never seen him [after that] only the day we were lined up [on deck under guard of the South Africa Police] with a shotgun on deck.

The Government's Second Round

The government's second witness was Jack Joe (folios 387–462, 912–21), a man referred to by some of the other crewmen as the "crippled Hawaiian." Jack Joe was a stark contrast to William Jones in that he lacked language skills and thus had a difficult time understanding many of the questions and court proceedings. Often Judge Jack interrupted the attorneys to ensure that Jack Joe really understood what was being asked of him. Despite his handicaps, Jack Joe was able to provide credible testimony that, when pieced together, provided the jury with an understanding of the vicious attacks made against him on August 21. "I was at the wheel when the captain tried to get me to tell who was in on the plot about which I knew nothing." When Joe gave him no names, Pedersen became angry.

> He punched me and called me goo goo and mongoose and son-of-a-bitch and German spy, and he hit me; and he kept in the chart room a ball on a rope, and he put in a 2-inch nut in a string, a line, and he hit me on the head.... The second mate, he hit me all over and the first mate he had the wheel with the one hand and kicked with the two feet, and the captain hit me all over with the tiller stick and knocked me down.... At that time I cried; he broke my head and my rib, and hit my hand and broke it.

Joe identified several items with which he had been beaten, including a belaying pin, marline spike, rope, and brass knuckles. After he fell, Joe said, the first mate

> took a 2-inch[-thick] rope and hit me; he tell me the son-of-a-bitch, black son-of-a-bitch, he no good, he die any way; we better throw him overboard. The captain said, "No. No." The captain said "What is the trouble?" The second mate told the captain the first mate want to throw Jack Joe overboard. The second mate said "No, I believe he come all right; he no die." The captain said "No, no, no; put him inside the hold [lazarette]." The second mate, he opened the hatch, and they got hold of me here and my legs, and I think eight or nine feet down they throw me down. Barney Olsen was in there with irons on his hands. All night I stayed inside; I cannot get up. I was all over blood, too.

James Campbell (folios 464–579, 3009–26) corroborated Jack Joe's testimony, stating that after Jack Joe was carried away, he had been told to help clean up the blood. "I drew water, and the carpenter brought it over and the captain said, 'Well, carpenter, we often had lots of dead men on our ship, but it is the first time I ever had to wash up blood myself from a black son-of-a-bitch.'"

Campbell testified that on the twenty-first or twenty-second he was getting galley supplies. "While I was getting some peas out of a sack in the supply bin, a shot rang out. I jumped up, turned around, and the captain had a revolver in his hand, and he said, 'Up with your hands.' I put my hands up. 'Put the handcuffs on him.' I don't know for sure which one it was put the handcuffs on me, but I believe it was the second mate.... Both mates were present." The master accused James Campbell of being in on the plot. When Campbell refused to confess and said he had no knowledge of any plot, Pedersen got a cup from the pantry, slung it, and split open Campbell's head. After a short time, "the mates took me down into the pump hold and pumped water on me. The first mate and the second mate had a celebration handling the hose, pulling it from one to the other." From then on, Campbell was kept in the pump hold almost continuously, undergoing several more water cures before the *Puako* reached Cape Town.

After describing the treatment he had personally received, James Campbell testified on behalf of Bjarne (Barney) Olsen, who died in Cape Town and who was named as the injured crewman in count 7. On August 23 James Campbell, Barney, and John Walter Campbell were in the after cabin with the master and both mates. Barney's hands were cuffed, and he refused to confess to the plot. Captain Pedersen ordered the mates to hit him. "They had a stick, a piece of table rack; they hit him over the head and shoulders, the both mates hitting him with their fists and with a stick, too. The captain had a gun in his hand, and he said to him 'I would just as soon shoot you as blow out a candle. Now, confess and confess quick.' I [James Campbell] went out of the cabin and I believe was sent forward to turn in. The next morning, the captain said to me 'We had a Helluva time last night. We made him squeal like a pig. Oh we give him a terrible beating; we made him squeal like a pig.'"

Frank Grielen (folios 623–909), who suffered torment and torture over a longer period than any other crewman, testified that during the night of July 24 he was told to go to Captain Pedersen's cabin. The master, both mates, John Campbell, and the cabin boy L. A. Smithson were there.

> Just as soon as I got down below they put my hands behind my back and handcuffs on me, and then the skipper accused me of plotting to kill him and sink the ship and kill the other members of the crew. He said the cabin boy confessed that; he said that I had plotted

with the cabin boy to do that. I denied the whole thing. I told him it was a frame-up. Then he snapped at me and said it was a lie; it was all true. Then he started clubbing me, he had one of them long clubs, him and his two sons, and the other two boys, they beat me until I could not see out of my eyes. Then he locked me up in the store room. It was about four feet; I could not stand up.[8] When he brought me in the second time, he said the same things all over again, and he said I was being paid for that by the German agents. I kept saying it was a lie. The next morning he brought me out of the hold again, and there was him and the cabin boy and sometimes one of his sons. My hands [were] tied around my back and a chain around my hands in addition to the handcuffs. . . . In the morning he took me down to the cabin. The cabin boy Smithson was there, and sometimes the second mate and sometimes the first. He started to explain to me that the cook—John Henry Stewart—the one that went overboard, he explained to me that the cook came down one time and tried to stab him with a knife, and he said I ordered the cook to go and do that. . . . I told him it was all a lie and I did not think the cook would do anything like that because he was a quiet man, and every time I said no, he said yes; he snapped at me; and every time he said to the cabin boy "Isn't that so!" and pointed at the cabin boy, and he said "Yes!" Every time. He had the cabin boy beaten up previous times. . . . After that . . . he says to me I been doing no work in Canada, all I been doing is blowing up bridges and factories and blowing up forests, putting the forests afire and all the likes of that.[9]

The night of the 25th, I was brought out of the hold, and the skipper was standing in the hallway between the cabin and the first mate's room with a long club in his hands. The cabin boy was standing there, his two sons, and John Campbell. The cabin boy had a scar on his left hand side, and he was telling me he was a detective and the skipper said he was a detective that he was put on the ship to follow me up by the company. I knew it was all a fake and then they said, they all said for me to confess and then they took me down in the cabin and started to beat me up. The skipper, the two sons, and the cabin boy all hit me. The captain told me that I said I was going to sink the ship and kill him and kill the cabin boy and two or three other members of the crew. . . . At that time I had my hands in front of me, handcuffed, and the cabin boy kept hitting me on the head and the skipper around the head and shoulders, and every once in a while he punched me in the stomach and told me to confess, and the second mate and the first mate also told me to confess, and the second mate was hitting me in the face as hard as he could, and the first mate was hitting me and the skipper told him to take something, to watch out for his finger, and then the first mate took a stick, and when he was all in, the second mate was going on, but they was tired beating me, and they held up. And the skipper said "Keep going, keep going!" They started going again, and the second mate took sort of a pocket flash light and started going around my face like this while the cabin boy kept hitting my head all the time, and they would not hold up until I said it was true, you see. Sometimes he told me I plotted to sink the ship, bore a hole in it; sometimes he said I was going to kill him, shove him over, and until I admitted it, every once in a while, the skipper jumped in with his club and punched me in the stomach. After that I said it was true. You see, I admitted it then and one of the mates, I guess it was the second mate, I'm not sure started writing down the statement.

Judge Jack interrupted and asked Grielen who had dictated the statement. "The skipper was there telling me all that stuff. It was dictated to me, four or five plots together, one right after the other." As the skipper dictated the statements, Grielen repeated them, and the second mate wrote them down.

After each plot, he [Pedersen] said this plot failed because the master and mate was too smart and after all the plots were over, he told me to sign my name. I objected at first, but he said "Wake him up!" and the second mate and cabin boy then jumped on me and started beating me in the face, and I told him I thought it best to sign, and I saw I could not get away from it, and I signed it any way to get out of the torture.... After I signed it, the skipper and the two sons started laughing and then he sent the whole rest of the men out and then he kept me in there all by himself, and he says to me then, he says, "You cannot go by yourself and sink me and kill my two boys. I will tell you who has been in those plots." And he named three or four fellows: Lester Jensen, Axel Hansen, Olsen. I guess that is about all. I did not say they was in it any more than I was. That night he locked me up in the hold. I did not get nothing to eat that night; the next morning, all I got to eat was a little bit of biscuit and some water.

Grielen stated that he was kept in the paint locker about four weeks.

The Government's Second Round

Before standing down, Grielen confirmed the earlier testimony given by James Campbell concerning Barney Olsen. He stated that on August 23 when Olsen told Pedersen that the talk about plots was all a lie, the master "jumped at him with a tool and hit him right in the face until he started bleeding like a pig. And the second mate punched him in the stomach and kicked him above the testicles. Then the second mate took a dishrag and wiped off the blood and hit him in the face with it." Grielen stated that he had been in the master's cabin, forced to witness the beating Olsen was given. "But then I was taken right away . . . into the hold."

Edward Reilly (folios 922–1039) was not named in the indictment of the Pedersens as an injured party; however, he was a valuable witness in that he was able to corroborate the testimony given by and about Frank Grielen and also the testimony concerning Barney Olsen. Around July 24 or 25, Reilly saw the mates each jump on Grielen and saw the master kick him and hit him. Reilly had been working on deck when the second mate told him to go down to the master's cabin. Grielen was there,

> in irons, and his face was all smashed up. . . . the captain, he was dictating a statement of Frank. The second mate was writing it down. So he would say, "Frank, is that right?" So Frank would say "No, I do not know what you are talking about." Then the captain would tell the second mate to go over and wake him up; wake him up. So the second mate would jump up and get hold of him and shake him. So when he was not coming through the way the captain wanted him to come, the captain had a pair of handcuffs in his hand, and he went like that (illustrating). So Grielen was all nervous and shaking, and he said, "Anything you want me to say or do, just tell me, and I will say it." So then the captain started in and was dictating a statement about different things that happened on the ship.

Reilly was in the cabin on the twenty-fourth for about an hour as the master wanted him to sign as a witness on some of the statements. He was again in the cabin on the twenty-fifth for the same reason and probably one other time as well. When asked if Grielen had signed his name voluntarily, Reilly said, "Well, he was afraid; he had to sign." Reilly also testified that he had seen Barney Olsen beaten by the defendants and hit between the eyes with a screwdriver by the master. Then Reilly was sent up on deck to take the wheel. He said he saw Olsen the next day and could hardly recognize him. He was all smashed up; his face was all swelled out, and his two eyes were almost closed.

Miller: Did he [Pedersen] ever threaten you?

Reilly: On several occasions after he let me out of the pump hold, he threatened me three or four times a day, and at night he would come out in back of me and say, "I will blow your head off; I will shoot you." I was so far gone I did not care nothing about it at the time. I said "Go ahead; I am bad enough now. I don't care what you do." At those times, he was wild looking. Awful wild looking. Then he would walk away and come back in a little while and talk nice.

William Mattson (folios 1040–1177, 1366–1440), the ship's carpenter and the oldest of the seamen, was the last crewman called as a government witness. He added more details concerning the night Barney Olsen was beaten so badly. Mattson had not actually witnessed the beating but had arrived later, drawn to the cabin by a "great deal of hollering. I saw this Olaf [Olsen] in the mate's room; he was lying there, dead to the world. . . . The mate was on top of him and the second mate was outside." Pedersen asked Mattson if he thought Olsen was dead.

> I went and looked, and I said he is out of his senses. I took hold of him by the legs, and the mate took hold of his body, and we carted him out on the deck load. I took my coat off and laid it under his head; my coat was all full of blood. And after that they put him in irons and put him down in the pump hold and pumped water on him that night. . . . The captain said he wanted him to confess where that money was. . . . He said they got a thousand dollars apiece and he wanted them to confess where it was.

It was about this time that Pedersen even accused Mattson of receiving money. Mattson laughed at Pedersen making a joke of the accusation, and the master never pursued the matter with the old carpenter, with whom he had been sailing for at least seven years.

The carpenter identified many of the weapons that the government had on display, pointing out the two clubs he had made for the master and the first mate. Mattson said that when Leonard wanted his own knuckle dusters, he showed him how to make a cement mold, which the mate filled with molten lead. Leonard's custom-made weapon was one of the exhibits that was unique and easily identifiable.

The earlier testimony of James Campbell corroborating Jack Joe's testimony indicated that Mattson had firsthand knowledge of the beating Jack Joe received on August 2. When Miller asked Mattson about the shipboard assault against Jack Joe, Mattson's testimony differed from what he had given in May before the grand jury, when he had affirmed the master's involvement in the assault. At the end of the court day, Miller saw Mattson huddled with Pedersen. When court resumed the next morning, before Mattson continued testifying, Jack Joe was briefly put back on the stand by Miller (folios 912–20). The jury's attention was directed to a new black eye Jack Joe had received sometime after court adjourned the previous day. Jack Joe explained that he had been returning to his hotel alone after dark when someone came up from behind and hit him. He was unable to say for sure who did it, but clearly Miller had a good idea. When Mattson was asked about Jack Joe's newest black eye, Mattson denied knowing anything about it, and perhaps he did not, although he and Jack Joe were staying at the same hotel. Mattson did admit, though, that the previous day he had spoken with the captain before leaving the courtroom.

Miller threatened to charge Mattson with perjury because of his waffling the previous day. Realizing he himself could be in serious trouble if he continued to change his grand jury testimony and now side with Pedersen by painting the crew as mutineers, Mattson finally acknowledged that he had never seen anyone attempt to hurt the master or mates; he had never witnessed anyone attempting to sabotage the ship; and he had never seen anyone commit mutiny. He also admitted that sworn statements he had made in Cape Town against the crewmen were false.

The testimony given by the crewmen who had lived through months of hell on board the *Puako* was almost too consistent, too grisly, and too graphic for a jury to accept unless it could be validated by credible witnesses of impeccable reputation—men such as Howe, Murphy, and Pisar. When Police Captain Elliott Howe was called by the government, he explained events as they unfolded in the first hours following *Puako*'s arrival at Cape Town. Pedersen had told him at the start that the crewmen were all German spies plotting to sink the ship and kill him and his sons. Because of the possibility that they were actually enemy agents, Howe decided to apply South Africa's immigration laws through which the crewmen could be removed from the ship and detained as prohibited immigrants. Pedersen had turned over to Howe the passports for those he was charging with mutiny as well as for Stewart and Hansen, who had died en route. He had no papers for Reilly, who Pedersen said was a stowaway. He also turned over to Howe the ship's logbook and the large bundle of papers identified by Pedersen as confessions. Pedersen told Howe that the confessions all related to the plots of espionage and mutiny. At Pedersen's insistence, before the crewmen were assembled on deck, the armed guard that had accompanied Howe to the

Puako was brought on board. Howe described the crewmen. "I went to have a look at them, and I must say I got a shock when I saw them. I expected to see a crowd of cut-throat desperadoes but instead saw the most miserable body of men I have ever seen in my life.... Of the nine men, eight had black eyes, some two, some one, and they had other marks on their faces" (folio 1190).

Howe specifically described the condition of certain men. William Jones's "eyes were black, his nose bruised, his back from about his kidneys up to his shoulders was one huge black and bruised patch which extended up in his ribs as well. It was swollen, and the man was evidently in great pain. His shins were also bruised" (folio 1197). Jones was very thin and was so weak that Howe could not take his statement that day. Jack Joe was in such pain he was practically doubled up. James Campbell had an open raw wound on his forehead extending between his eyebrows. He was "highly strung, nervous, and very emotional" (folio 1201). In order to let them rest and begin to recover, Howe said he did not take statements or have the other men physically examined for a few days.

Howe continued his testimony, stating that at Captain Pedersen's request, which was made around September 10 or 12, policemen from his contingent made a search of the *Puako* and brought back with them a few items including an IWW songbook which Howe described as a book of socialistic songs. At this time Captain Pedersen, the mates, the carpenter, and seamen John Walter Campbell were still aboard. Another police search was made of the *Puako* sometime after October 1. It was probably during this search that Howe found the diary that had been kept by the mates. This second search produced the weapons that the government placed on display at the trial as exhibits, including clubs, sheath knives, a rope end, and "knuckles." These had been found in the cabins that had been occupied by the master and the mates. Considering that Pedersen must have known that it would be damaging for such items as the brass knuckles to be found, it is curious that he never jettisoned them. Perhaps he never imagined that he would be removed from his ship.

Howe related that when he first went aboard the *Puako* just hours after she had arrived in Cape Town, Pedersen claimed that as part of their plots, some of the crew had stolen an auger from the carpenter. The master asserted to Howe that with this they had planned to bore a hole in the hull of the ship and thus sink her. During the second search, Howe discovered the auger in a drawer in the master's sleeping compartment. Leonard Pedersen, who accompanied the search party and was with Howe when the auger was discovered, told the police inspector that this was the auger the crew had planned to use to sink the ship. It evidently did not register with the first mate that finding the auger in the master's quarters might be considered incriminating. Howe said he put the auger back where he had found it, making a mental note but no outward comment in front of the mate (folios 1179–1247).

Consul General George Murphy, under Miller's questioning, provided to the jurors even more of a sense of what had transpired during the first hours after the *Puako*'s arrival in Cape Town. Defense attorney Malone, however, was more concerned about what had transpired later. He was specifically upset with the manner in which the Pedersens had been discharged from the ship by Murphy. Malone acknowledged to the court that, given cause, an American consul general had the authority to discharge not only crew members of an American vessel but also the ship's officers, including the master, but he aggressively argued that Murphy had misused his authority and that his discharge of the Pedersens had been capricious and without cause. Malone clearly attempted to establish that Murphy had a dislike for Pedersen and that he had therefore acted prejudicially in discharging the master and his sons. Murphy responded that Pedersen had been difficult and that on more than one occasion he had been sarcastic toward the staff at the consulate general, particularly the vice-consuls. Murphy stated emphatically that Pedersen's behavior had not influenced his actions, and explained that it was not he who made the decision to discharge Pedersen. That decision was made by his superiors in Washington. Since the circumstances in the case of the *Puako* were the most unusual Murphy had ever encountered in his thirty-three years in the consular service, he told the court, he had decided not to use the authority vested in him to discharge the ship's officers. Instead, he had filed a full report, accompanied by hundreds of pages of evidence, and then waited for Washington's instructions on how to proceed. Only when Washington's orders were received did Murphy act to discharge Pedersen. This revelation stopped Malone cold in his attempt to discredit the government's star witness, and his examination of Murphy ended abruptly.

The last government witness to appear was Charles J. Pisar, who had been a vice-consul at Cape Town in 1918. Miller and particularly Malone examined Pisar on the sequence of events as they had unfolded in Cape Town. Malone was especially intent on establishing when and how the master and mates had been taken into custody at the United States Consulate General by the South African Immigration officials. Pisar's testimony confirmed the testimony earlier given by both Howe and Murphy and reinforced the facts of the extraordinary difficulties under which George H. Murphy and his staff had labored.

"The conditions during the month of October, and especially during the second and third week, were appalling. Everything was disorganized there.[10] There were two hundred and fifty to three hundred deaths a day [from influenza], and every hospital was filled up. The telephone exchange was out of order; there was nobody there to make connections. The suburban railway service on which the city of Cape Town depends was absolutely demoralized, and all the banks were closed for two weeks; it was almost impossible to get anything done or have anything done" (folio 3063).

With this the prosecution rested. Malone immediately asked for a "dismissal of the indictments against the defendants on the grounds . . . that the Government has not adduced sufficient credible testimony to support its allegations of assault" (folio 1441). The court denied Malone's motion and asked him to proceed with the defense.

CHAPTER 10

THE DEFENSE

During defense attorney Malone's cross-examination of each of the government's witnesses, he had repeatedly attempted to ferret out any connection each man might have had to the Industrial Workers of the World (IWW), no doubt reasoning that if he could find even the slimmest connection, he could use it to bolster his claim that the crew had attempted to use terror tactics such as sabotage as well as work slowdowns against the ship and her officers. These were the tactics encouraged by the IWW, and these crewmen were, after all, potential IWW members, having come from the mines, lumber camps, and western wheat fields, all of which were industries targeted by the IWW for infiltration. One of the crew, Lester Jensen, had admitted that he brought aboard the IWW songbook.

Malone began his defense by introducing as exhibits more than two dozen of the statements Pedersen had given to the police in Cape Town. This was a long, tedious process with considerable repetition. His reasoning may have been that if jurors heard the same story often enough, they would begin to believe it. With a few carefully chosen statements, Malone implied the men had confessed to using IWW-type tactics against industries ashore and to plotting against the *Puako* and her officers. Malone told the jury that it was for them to decide whether statements by crew members were the literary creations of Adolph Cornelius Pedersen and his sons or, as Malone asserted, true confessions signed by men who had been intent on committing murder, mutiny, and mayhem. In an attempt to sway the jury in his direction, Malone remarked that if these were the creations of Pedersen, then he would advise him "to quit shipping and go into the writing of best sellers" (folio 3079). Malone then called to the stand the Pedersens, whom he had undoubtedly coached in hopes of making their best side shine.

First to testify was the fifty-four-year-old master. At 5'7" and 160 pounds, quiet-spoken Captain Adolph Cornelius Pedersen hardly appeared the brute a juror might have envisioned after hearing the testimony of the government's witnesses. Under Malone's direct examination, Pedersen appeared patient and kindly, even fatherly—a man who neither could nor would do any wrongful act against another.

In his cross-examination, the government's attorney took the offensive. By using the words "bully" and "coward," Miller attempted to bring out Pedersen's other side. Under Miller's questioning, Pedersen stated that while some men he had sailed with in the past were truthful, it was his opinion that all the members of this crew had lied and that even Police Sub-inspector Captain Howe had lied on the witness stand. The cross-examination of Pedersen was lengthy and often tedious, with Malone interrupting and challenging nearly every question put by Miller. Almost without exception the court allowed Miller to continue, but not without controversy between the attorneys. Regardless of how long and hard Malone debated a point—and some of his challenging arguments were extremely lengthy—in the end the government usually was able to question the witness on the particular point, albeit some of the questions had to be reworded to make them more acceptable to Malone.

One aspect of Miller's questioning concerned Reilly, a topic Malone had not covered in his direct examination. This may have thrown Pedersen somewhat off balance. Was Edward Reilly a stowaway? Pedersen's initial response was "Yes, I looked upon him as a stowaway." When Pedersen continued to state that Reilly was a stowaway, Judge Jack showed concern that perhaps Pedersen did not understand the legal meaning of the word, so he intervened. Pedersen finally admitted with some air of authority that he knew what a stowaway was. When Miller resumed, Pedersen would not back away from the statement he had made in Cape Town concerning Reilly.

> Miller: And yet at Cape Town, to support your charges against this crew, you made the statement he was a stowaway, didn't you?
> Pedersen's earlier quiet, calm demeanor now changed. He became arrogant, defiant. Yes, I can call him a stowaway.
> Miller: You can call him a stowaway?
> Pedersen: Yes, sir, Mr. Miller. I am the master of an American ship. (folio 1796)

After that exchange, which undoubtedly raised an eyebrow or two, Pedersen was pushed until he finally admitted that he had made no attempt to obtain a pass for Reilly from the British authorities in Victoria. If Reilly had, as claimed, been turned down by British military authorities because of having a hernia, obtaining a pass would have been but a simple matter to make things right. After all, Pedersen had earlier obtained a similar pass for James Campbell, who was also a British subject. As Miller continued to prod in areas where the captain did not seem to have been well coached by Malone, Pedersen was evasive, elusive, and at times uncooperative. His reply to the prosecution concerning the weather of July 14, when the ship encountered the worst storm of the trip, is a case in point. The captain had tried to give the impression that the sails were lost because the crew failed to obey orders, but as it was brought out, the primary factor in the loss of the sails was the severe weather. With prompting from entries read by Miller from the mates' logbook, Pedersen grudgingly had to admit that at the time the sails were torn away, the ship was in the throes of a heavy gale with seas at least as high as 45 or 50 feet, and that a covering of ice and snow made everything on board slippery. The weather conditions were compounded by incorrect orders given by the mates, who had little experience in handling a ship on their own during such adverse conditions.

When Miller's questioning changed to address acts of corporal punishment committed against the crew, Malone's challenges became even more vigorous and argumentative. During these exchanges, Pedersen became vague and even feigned forgetfulness, although occasional probing and prodding by Judge Jack seemed to have a restorative effect on both his memory and his willingness to square a bit closer with the truth. Miller picked at issues gleaned from Pedersen's statement made in Cape Town and also from the logbook, wherein the master had stated that men had not done their jobs or that they had been insubordinate and mutinous. Pedersen was free to consult those documents when replying and did occasionally read from the logbook when it was to his advantage. Over and over, Pedersen cited statements by the teenaged cabin boy, L. A. Smithson—the youngest of the crewmen—who, according to statements given in Cape Town, had been terrorized by Pedersen. Miller was quick to point out that Pedersen had labeled Smithson "tricky" and "sneaky." Yet Pedersen's alleged single source that the crew planned to mutiny was Smithson. Based on that dubious information brutally coerced out of Smithson, Pedersen had ordered men to be variously beaten and tortured.

When asked to demonstrate or describe a few of the occasions when Pedersen said he had felt threatened by the men, particularly by Stewart, Grielen, Hansen, and Olsen, the master ended up looking foolish, as again Malone had apparently not prepared his client for this line of questioning.

Miller put forth the obvious fact that, had these men intended to do in Pedersen or his sons, they had ample opportunity. Pedersen admitted that members of the crew could easily have pushed or thrown any one or all of them overboard, but said neither he nor his sons were ever hit or otherwise physically assaulted by anyone.

When questioned about Stewart's suicide, Pedersen claimed that he had attempted to learn from each of the crewmen why Stewart had jumped over the side. "Some said he was crazy; he had leprosy, a venereal disease...some said he had sores all over his body; there were cuts in his hands with his knife; some said he could put his hands on a hot stove and hold hot knives and irons; he never had no feeling." At first he could not recall who had told him these tales, but Miller kept pushing him. Finally Pedersen named the cabin boy Smithson, a convenient scapegoat who was not available to counter Pedersen's claims (folios 1872–74).[1]

Miller became particularly persistent in his questioning of Pedersen concerning the master's charges that the crew had attempted to poison him by putting such things in the food as dishwater, Lysol, soap, and tobacco. While these items could have unpleasant aftereffects, Miller noted that they were not poisons. Had someone in the crew really wanted to poison Pedersen, Miller suggested, they might have used items considered to be poisonous such as strychnine or Rough on Rats. Finally Pedersen had to back down and acknowledge that he had no idea if anyone had tried to poison him despite the very serious and specific charges he had leveled against the men upon arrival at Cape Town. What he did know was that at some point toward the end of the voyage he had become very sick with diarrhea. Since in the past twelve years he had never been sick like that on his ship, he could only assume that the source of his illness was a substance the crew had put in the food. When the crew began vomiting with intestinal illness, Pedersen blamed it on the juice from the small piece of tobacco that had somehow found its way into the bean pot. Miller in a somewhat sarcastic tone asked Pedersen if he really believed that the juice from such a small piece of tobacco could have sickened the crew. Pedersen made no response. For a man accustomed to being in charge, especially someone with Pedersen's personality, the many hours of cross-examination by a sharp government attorney had to have been extremely difficult. It was undoubtedly with relief that he was able to step down.

Leonard Roy Pedersen, now twenty, was the first of the two mates to take the stand (folios 2342–2638). He had been going to sea with his father since childhood except for a few years spent ashore while attending a grammar school in Oakland, California. Although he had made trips to Australia, South America, and Japan, the voyage that had commenced in the spring of 1918 was his first 'round the Horn. When his father had difficulty locating officers for the trip, Leonard was examined for purposes of insurance by S. Cullinghole, surveyor, who certified him on March 8, 1918, as qualified to sail as acting mate. Cullinghole worked at the time out of the Vancouver harbor commissioner's Office of Port Warden. Considering Leonard's young age, his lack of experience, and the position he was to assume as second in command of a large oceangoing vessel, one wonders about the comprehensiveness of Cullinghole's examination.

In response to a question by Miller, Leonard said that prior to the start of the trial he had met a number of times with defense attorney Malone. The two appeared to have developed an almost scripted testimony, starting with an accusation Leonard made against Peter Jorgensen. Leonard alleged that sometime in March 1918 while the *Puako* was being loaded in Vancouver, Peter Jorgensen "dumped a hatch down on my hands." At the time, Leonard's fingers were on the coaming of the hatch as he was lowering himself into the lazarette. When the heavy hatch cover came down, the tips of his fingers were nearly severed. "I didn't feel anything just then; but when I was going up I saw my fingers and saw the ends of them were hanging down.... The first thing I did was to shove them back on" (folio 2355). His brother and John Campbell took Leonard ashore to a doctor for treatment. Leonard claimed that his left hand remained bandaged for most of the trip. He also maintained that he was left-handed. Malone's intent here is clear. By starting off with this incident, he was seeking to invoke the jury's sympathy. But more important, if Leonard's working hand had been bandaged, Malone could try to paint a scenario making it impossible for Leonard to be the tough person that was alleged in the indictment. The ploy did not work. At intervals during cross-examination, the government's attorney asked Leonard to take hold of an object or to point at this or that. Instead of using his left hand, as a left-handed person would do, Leonard used his right. Miller noted that during the previous day, while being examined by defense attorney Malone, Leonard had also shown a preference for using his right hand. It seemed pretty clear that Leonard's "working hand" had not been injured and that he would have been quite able to use it to issue any sort of blows against the crew.

Adolph Eric "Dolph" Pedersen next took the stand (folios 2639–3004). Under Malone's almost fatherly guidance, he stated he had completed grammar school and on turning sixteen had begun sailing with his father in a paid capacity. His first voyage as ordinary seaman had been aboard the *Puako* in 1917 when the ship sailed from Victoria to Cape Town and thence to Australia, Manila, and back to the U.S. West Coast. During that voyage Dolph was promoted to able seaman and finally, while the *Puako* was in Manila, to acting mate. Because of this past experience, Pedersen had received permission from Hind, Rolph & Co. to carry Dolph in 1918 as second mate.

In his questioning of both Dolph and Leonard, Malone inquired as to the problems each had experienced with the crew during June 1918 when the ship was in the South Pacific in the vicinity of the Society Islands and the Pitcairn Island group. Both boys claimed the men often steered the ship off course by two or three points and sometimes as much as four points. If in fact the men were steering that erratically, these were large errors, as one point of a compass is 11¼ degrees. During some men's two-hour wheel watches, the mates claimed, they sometimes had to correct the helmsman as much as eight or nine times. Although their father had stated under cross-examination that the ship when well south of the Equator was steered sometimes to the east and sometimes to the west, both Leonard and Dolph claimed the steering errors were always to the west—their implication being that the men were trying to reach one of the islands in the South Pacific. Dolph said this had exposed them unnecessarily to squall conditions and unsteady winds when they passed through the Pitcairn Island group. This may have been intended to give the jurors the impression that the principal islands of that group, Pitcairn and Ducie, are almost within sight of one another. Perhaps he himself did not know better. Ducie, which in 1902 became part of the Pitcairn Island group, is in fact 325 miles east of Pitcairn Island. The *Puako* had passed well clear of both of them. Under cross-examination, Dolph said he was aware of Pitcairn Island's connection to the HMS *Bounty* mutineers, but interestingly enough, at least outwardly, that famous mutiny was never introduced as a possible influence on events as they transpired aboard the *Puako*.[2]

The allegation had been made by Pedersen and the mates in their sworn statements that the ship had been deliberately steered toward land where the crew would kill the master and the second mate and sink the ship. While Captain Pedersen's testimony left the impression that Barney Olsen was behind this and may have known something about navigation, Dolph was only certain that Olsen knew how to steer. Since Olsen had died months earlier in Cape Town, there was no way for the prosecution or the defense to prove whether or not he had knowledge of navigation. Despite this, in his summation Malone stated emphatically, "Olsen knew navigation, and was reading books on navigation. He could navigate a ship, and when he was in there disobeying orders between those two islands, Barney Olsen knew just exactly where he was trying to bring that ship" (folios 3106–07). This was an inane statement by Malone, as Olsen had neither access to the ship's charts nor navigational instruments with which to take sights and establish the ship's position.

In their separate sworn statements given in Cape Town, the mates had each made serious allegations against the crew claiming their actions—or lack thereof—had been mutinous. The strongest of these was their assertion that the loss of two sails as the ship neared Cape Horn was the result of the men not pulling hard enough to properly adjust the sails and the bracings when the ship was hit by a squall. While the impression was given by the mates that the full crew had been involved in that dereliction, the fact was brought out that the sails had parted even before the mates had called all hands to help (folios 2606–8, 2841–42). Leonard and Dolph said that on another occasion the men would not pull on the sheets and that they did not sing out in answer to their orders. Using the fully rigged ship's model that Leonard had constructed for use at the trial and a fan to represent the wind, Dolph positioned the sails and explained the situation. Miller, who appeared to have a working knowledge of sailing ships, quickly pointed out that with the wind filling the sails, putting an excessive strain on the sails and sheets during such high winds, it would have been all but impossible for that small group of men to adjust the sails. Finally, in their frustration because the men had not done as they had been ordered, the boys called their father in hopes that he could force the men to pull harder. Seeing the situation, the seasoned master ordered that the ship be turned up into the wind. This action took some of the strain off the sails so they could be readjusted. Had the crewmen committed mutiny in this case? The boys had no alternative but to back away from that accusation.

A good portion of the direct and cross-examinations concerned the injuries the crewmen experienced during the voyage. Leonard recalled only that some had small bruises or facial marks which he attributed to their falling on the timber. In answer to a juror's inquiry as to whether Leonard was talking about milled lumber or round logs, Leonard explained that the deck load consisted of logs squared off to 24" x 24", sixty to eighty feet in length, with a top flooring of lumber 3" x 9". Leonard referred to the huge squared-off logs as "sticks." The flat lumber became very slippery when it was wet, and especially so when the ship was in the freezing temperatures near Cape

Horn. It was in these latitudes that the *Puako* encountered the worst storms, which regularly deposited sleet, snow, and ice on her. Leonard said everyone was falling—even he had fallen. He distinctly recalled that twenty or thirty times he had seen William Jones fall while on the deck load. This was the man who Police Sub-inspector Captain Howe noted was especially bruised on arrival at Cape Town. Leonard claimed that Jones seemed to be more prone to falling than the others, insinuating that these falls had caused the ridged welts on Jones's back described by Howe. But another question from a juror to Leonard confirmed that the top layer of the deck load consisted of flat boards. The juror obviously wondered how a fall on flat boards could cause bruising in the form of ridged welts.

Before he stepped down, Leonard admitted to once striking Reilly in what he called self-defense, but he claimed definitely that he had never hit anyone else. Nor did he know anything about a particularly unique lead knuckle-duster marked Exhibit 14. No matter that Mattson had identified it and had testified that he had shown Leonard how to make it (folio 2392).

Even though Captain Howe had testified as to what a congenial, compatible group the crewmen were, especially under the trying circumstances of their detention in Cape Town, each of the mates alleged there had been a number of fights on board the ship between crew members. Leonard recalled three: Grielen vs John Campbell, Jorgensen vs Hansen, and Jorgensen vs Reilly. Dolph recalled three others: Reilly vs John Walter Campbell, Reilly vs Jensen, and Grielen vs Smithson. From depositions and earlier crew testimony, Miller knew something about the so-called fight between Grielen and Smithson and asserted that it seemed to him more like a beating, noting that it had been carried out in the master's cabin with at least Dolph and the master present and that neither ship's officer had taken action to stop Smithson from throwing seven or eight punches at Grielen, who probably was in irons and unable to defend himself.

Under Malone's questioning in what seemed to be an effort to show malevolence among the men, Dolph alleged that the fight between Reilly and John Walter Campbell had erupted after Reilly called Campbell a "damned Yankee." As Campbell took a swing, he in turn had called Reilly a "God damned Irishman"—epithets repeated until they were separated by Dolph.

Malone's interest in a possible connection of the crewmen to the Industrial Workers of the World was again brought to the forefront. Leonard indicated that he had sometimes heard the men singing certain IWW songs but offered nothing more specific. Dolph was far more forthcoming in that regard. He recalled some of the titles and said that the words he had heard were from the little IWW songbook Pedersen had turned over to Captain Howe. Although the words of the songs Dolph mentioned were not read in court, they were entered into the trial record for the jury's benefit (folios 2795–2811).[3]

Under both direct and cross-examination, Leonard initially said he never saw anyone with a black eye, although one morning following an altercation he had seen Grielen with a "darkened eye."

> Judge Jack interrupted: You heard the Consul General testify the other day that when the vessel reached Cape Town, and the crew was mustered on deck, that eight or nine men had one or more black eyes.
>
> The Witness [Leonard]: I heard him testify that, yes, sir.
>
> The Court: Is that correct?
>
> Leonard: No, sir; not eight or nine of them had black eyes; there was Edward Reilly and Peter Jorgensen, and Jack Joe. That is the only ones I ever saw with swollen eyes.
>
> The Court: At the time they arrived, then, Reilly, Jorgensen, and Jack Joe?
>
> Leonard: And Jensen.
>
> The Court: Did either one of those four have two black eyes?
>
> Leonard: I think Jensen did; I am not sure, though.

Despite the direct participation of Judge Jack, Leonard continued to claim that many of the black eyes the men had on arrival in Cape Town were the results of either fights or falls that had occurred as much as three weeks before arrival (folios 2617–38).

> The Court: And it stayed black for three weeks?
>
> Leonard: It didn't stay black; but there was a mark.

The judge then asked that a portion of Captain Howe's testimony be re-read. "I saw Jack Joe. He was practically doubled up. I did not examine him carefully. In fact, I could not get much out of Joe that day. But he was also obviously in pain, and he had to lay down when he was in the cell" (folios 2630–31). Following that reading, Leonard was asked to describe Jack Joe's appearance on the day the *Puako* arrived in Cape Town. Said Leonard, "Oh, he looked an old worried man when I saw him that day."

Of the two boys, Dolph under questioning seemed the quicker, brighter, feistier, and certainly more responsive. In contrast to Leonard, whose testimony had to practically be dragged out of him, Dolph quickly recalled seeing black eyes on all but John Walter Campbell, Mattson, and William Jones. In describing the crew of the *Puako* in general terms on their arrival in Cape Town, Dolph claimed they were "dirty; had beards. Grielen had one of those Van Dyke like [beards]." Dolph described his father as being sick and weak during the trip. Leonard was so ill he had to go to the hospital, and Dolph himself was a little sick with dysentery (folios 2774–75, 2859).

A lot of Dolph's testimony was related to the level of cleanliness on board. Although he personally took a bath every two weeks, he said he was not aware of the men ever bathing (folios 2717–19). In fact Jorgensen, Dolph claimed, was so disgustingly filthy that it had been necessary to pump water on him.

> Dolph: The carpenter came to me and told me that Jorgensen was stinking down there [in the pump hold], and he had mussed in his pants, and he had mussed in his pants before that and put it away under the forecastle head, and the whole place was stinking; he would not change his clothes right away.
> The Court: Jorgensen would not?
> Dolph: Yes, sir; and this time I pumped water on him in order to make him change his clothes. He was stinking and the whole hold was stinking. (folios 2924–25)

Dolph was equally colorful in his depiction of the galley at some point after Jensen took over as cook.

> Well, Jensen, after he was put in the galley to cook, he had the whole place down there just smelling something awful, sour; he used to wash his galley out with his dishwater, what he had. And he used to go barefooted in the galley there, and when he would come on deck his toes would be all filled with kind of mushy stuff. Filth. He may have cleaned it up a little bit, but it never smelled better or looked better. So we had to get all the sailors down there and take all the pots and pans out of the galley and clean it, and all the woodwork around, and scrub the pots with sand and canvas.[4] (folios 2691–92)

Dudley Field Malone took the stand after the mates stood down and the testimony of the defendants closed. Once sworn in as a witness, he assumed the roles of both examiner and witness. His purpose in going through this exercise was to put into the record the attempts the defense had made to locate Smithson for appearance at the trial. "I communicated with the firm of Hind, Rolph & Co., the owners of the *Puako*, for the presence at the previous trial, and I again communicated with them for the presence at this trial of the cabin boy Smithson. I received word from Hind, Rolph & Co. that whereas Smithson had shipped back on the *Puako*, he had deserted at Australia, and was not available for subpoena or presence at the trial." The government's attempts to locate Smithson had also been unsuccessful.

At the end of the testimony phase of the trial, court adjourned early to give the attorneys time to polish their summations and the jury a well-deserved break.

CHAPTER 11

SUMMATIONS

On September 19, 1919, each attorney presented his summation to the jury. Defense attorney Dudley Field Malone (folios 3070–3218) began by asserting that this had been the most extraordinary case of his career. Then, after a few pleasantries directed to Judge Jack, Malone wasted no time in reacquainting the jury with some of the crew. Grielen was "a square-jawed, hard-fisted radical economic person." Jack Joe was repeatedly referred to in a degrading manner as "Black Joe." Malone twice described the deceased Barney Olsen as "the big fellow, the one-hundred ninety pound man." He questioned how "these boys . . . these youngsters" could possibly have assaulted such a huge hulk of a man, of course making no mention of the crew's testimony which had set the scene for the uneven matchup between Olsen, whose hands were bound, and the freewheeling mates.

According to testimony by members of the crew, by the time Olsen was so viciously attacked, he and others of the crew had already been on the receiving end of numerous beatings and other tortures. Many of those attacks and beatings took place in the master's cabin and were very one-sided—usually one crewman, often in cuffs, against the master, the mates, the cabin boy, and sometimes also the deck boy John Walter Campbell. A minimum of three to one, but often four or five to one. Additionally, the crewmen claimed they had been starved into a weakened condition.

Malone was not ready to believe any of the testimony from the seamen. He put forth that all of the witnesses were liars as well as enemy collaborators, asserting that to a man the crewmen were un-American, intent on doing in Pedersen and his sons—three patriotic Americans, citizens of a country at war against Germany. Malone reminded the jury that "the old captain"—Pedersen was by then fifty-four years of age—had worked for the same firm for seventeen years, and that "the youngsters" were but teenagers during the voyage. He painted the three as quite remarkable individuals, especially Dolph, the youngest, lauding his impressive knowledge of sailing and the art of navigation, over and over emphasizing that it was these three against "the bad gang." Malone even enfolded into that gang the master's old friend and shipmate William Mattson.

Launching into the body of his lengthy summation, Malone stated to the jury: "If at any time, gentlemen, your recollection of the testimony in this case differs from mine, I know you will take yours; I expect you will take yours." He then presented a chronology of the case with rapid-fire oratory aimed so as to gain the jury's acceptance of his own version of the facts and events. He jumped from witness to witness, issue to issue, keeping his audience off guard by misstating, misquoting, and misallocating. Over Miller's objections, Malone insisted on labeling Grielen and Reilly as draft dodgers, creating an illusion that did not exist in the background of either man. After giving his spin on Reilly's situation in Victoria and during the first days of the voyage, Malone, himself an Irishman, added, "Gentlemen, I appreciated Reilly, I suppose, because I know the line of demarcation between fact and Celtic imagination."

Before Pedersen cleared out of Canada, the collector of customs in Victoria had cautioned the master about enemy raiders thought by the U.S. Navy to be operating off the west coast of Mexico and possibly in the South Atlantic, where there were also thought to be minefields. While the navy's warning would have related to enemy surface raiders, it was more to the defense attorney's purpose to depict them as submarines, and thus Dudley Malone made the warning more dramatic, stating: "All the dangers of the submarine warfare in the war days were the things through which Captain Pedersen brought this little ship with this green crew" (folio 3105). Later, to reinforce his point, Malone remarked of Pedersen, "He had a ship with a valuable cargo worth $120,000 to take from Victoria to Cape Town in war days, through mines, the submarine zone, and raiders"[1] (folio 3132). Malone's explosive delivery did not give the twelve men of the jury, all residents of the North Atlantic seaboard who were surely familiar with the World War I submarine menace in that area, time to consider that Malone was rewriting naval history when he alleged that German submarine activity had extended into the South Atlantic and Pacific Oceans. Germany had no submarine operations in the South Atlantic or Pacific during World War I. German submarine activity in the Atlantic was clustered in the North Atlantic from the British Isles into the Mediterranean and along the eastern seaboard of the United States and Canada.

The remainder of Malone's summation dealt in one way or another with the confessions the crew had signed, which the seamen claimed had been the imaginative creations of the ship's officers. Concerning one confession in particular that had been signed by Jensen, Malone theatrically pondered whether it could have come from the master, and then unequivocally, hardly taking a breath, told the jury:

> It didn't come out of the captain for two reasons: First, because it is not true, and secondly, he didn't write it because if it were true, you don't suppose the captain would be such a fool as to set down or write in a statement to hand to the authorities that he had the worst ship on the Pacific coast, do you? I leave this to your reason.
>
> This statement is a statement of one of the crew, composed by another member of the crew. The statements belong to the crew, and they came out of the crew, and when one was caught and squealed on the other, the second and the third squealed on the fourth; the jig was up, and they all confessed and got under cover as quickly as they could. That is my theory of the case. (folio 3099)

Malone then tried to explain why the *Puako* ended up transiting the Pitcairn Island group, claiming that it was this crew and not the winds that caused the *Puako* to be between the islands. "And the point is they got that ship over between those two islands [Pitcairn and Ducie] when they should not have been near the islands at all. That is the uncontradicted testimony in this case, that the ship was taken so far off course that she was over in that group of islands and had to be steered between two of them" (folio 3107).

According to the comprehensive study chart *The World Sailing Ship Routes*, which illustrates the routings of sailing ships over a hundred-year period encompassing the early 1900s, there was nothing unusual about the *Puako*'s track. Historically, the summer winds and resultant currents in the eastern Pacific usually carried sailing ships through the Pitcairn Island group between Pitcairn Island, position 25°04´ s, 130°05´ w, and Ducie, position 24°40´ s, 124°48´ w, which are separated by more than three hundred miles.[2]

The defense attorney saved his last act and best showmanship for George Murphy and Charles Pisar when he contended that the staff of the United States Consulate General at Cape Town had acted prejudicially toward Pedersen. Malone went so far as to accuse Murphy of "conniving" with British officials. Malone pointed to the defendants—again reminding the jury of their citizenship. The Pedersens had not only been betrayed by the crew, "these I.W.W.'s, this gang, these nomads," but even by the American consul general, his vice-consuls, and British officials—Malone repeatedly accusing them all of malice.

> When I speak of these things, gentlemen, I tell you of knowledge—if you will pardon the allusion, when I was Assistant Secretary of State in Washington for a year, I was Chief of the Consular Service of the United States and had complete charge of the Consular Service.[3] I know what the duties of consular officers are. If there was no other way excepting this technical way of handing over American citizens to the British authorities, the American Consul [General] could have permitted the captain and his two boys to take the *Puako* back to the United States. They would have taken it back to the United States; they had to bring a return cargo. They would have brought it back.

Without giving the jurors a chance to reflect on the unreasonableness of that remark, Malone moved quickly on to other issues, never mentioning Section 355 of the Consular Regulations, previously reproduced, which specifically governed the orders from the Department of State to Murphy as well as the independent actions of Murphy and his staff.[4] Malone also either overlooked or was unaware of Section 8 of the Seamen's Act, which allowed consuls to enlist, as Murphy had done, the aid of local authorities "in the most effectual manner."

Malone closed his lengthy summation most graciously, as he had begun it, starting with an apology to the jury.

> You are all men of responsibility; you all have your homes and your businesses, and I very much regret if at any time during the course of the trial I have delayed the case by bringing out testimony that you considered repetition or needless. But yet, gentlemen, the responsibility on a lawyer who feels his responsibility, who must protect the reputation and the liberty of an old man like this sea captain, thirty-eight years at sea, and these two youngsters, who have their careers before them on American ships, is a real responsibility. It is a responsibility that has worn on my nerves during these three weeks, and at times I have not been in the best of temper. At times I have clashed with my distinguished opponent. I know you will hold none of those things against my clients, and that any mistakes I have made in the trial of the case, or any omissions, I know you will not charge against them.
>
> My responsibility is ended, and with firm confidence in the spirit of fair play and justice of a New York jury to this father and his two

sons, four thousand miles away from home, I hand my responsibility over to you.

Following the noon recess, the prosecution's case was summated (folios 3219–93) by S. Lawrence Miller, who led off with a somewhat tongue-in-cheek critique of Malone's performance, which he called a gift of elocution and a command of argument. "I believe if I had a dollar and he talked to me about it long enough, I would think it was ten dollars." Feeling he had the jury's attention, Miller then turned serious, addressing the issues of truth and witness credibility, noting to the jurors that Malone had not only attempted "to raise a smoke screen between you and the truth," but perhaps had thrown "a little mud on some very honorable gentlemen who have appeared here from Cape Town." Speaking primarily of the crewmen who had testified, Miller asked,

> Were they frank? Were they straight forward? Did they look you in the eye? Did they look counsel in the eye? . . . Gentlemen, they are ignorant men. Can you conceive of any chorus of ignorant men inventing a tale like this and not being contradicted in some particular and caught in some particular on cross-examination?
>
> Now, compare the attitude of the defendants when they took the stand. Would they look you in the eye? Did they hesitate? Didn't they become embarrassed? . . . If they have been trained, and they are of a higher mentality than the witnesses for the Government, one of them [Pedersen] forgot his cues when it slipped out that he hit Barney Olsen with the screwdriver. You can't train witnesses and have them stand up under cross-examination. It can't be done; and that you have seen.

This lengthy discussion on truth set the tone for the remainder of Miller's remarks. He repeatedly struck out at the credibility of the defendants. "I do not see halos of truth around their heads."

Miller said that for the first three months of the trip, there was no talk of a plot or mutiny, the first mention coming in July from L. A. Smithson, a boy whom the master himself had described as "a dirty, tricky, sneaky, disobedient boy." In making that claim, Miller was off by several weeks, the first logbook mention of a plot occurring soon after Stewart committed suicide, and it was not until July after the IWW songbook was found that the single plot exploded into six separate but overlapping plots.

According to Miller's version of events, it was after the master "slapped"

Smithson for stealing a set of handcuffs that Smithson not only purportedly confessed that he stole the handcuffs but said to the master that he took them to give to Frank Grielen and Barney Olsen "so they could lock you up." Miller questioned whether Smithson had volunteered this information to Pedersen after being given only a gentle slap, of the type that had been exampled by Pedersen under oath, or whether this "disobedient boy" had been hit a pretty good blow. To avoid further abuse, did Smithson make up the story and voluntarily implicate Grielen and Olsen with little or no persuasion? Or did Smithson receive the "third degree" and then implicate Grielen and Olsen after the words were put on paper for him to sign? Miller theorized to the jury that it was through the evolving nature of the confessions signed by Smithson and then by Grielen and others that the plot became more and more complex. If some of the crew had wanted to kill the master, it would have been easy for them to pick him up and throw him overboard. After all, he was often on deck, moving among the men. If the men were intent on sinking the *Puako*, Miller pondered, why had they not come on board armed, perhaps with bombs? If the Germans wanted to sink the ship, why would they pay $40,000 to these ignorant amateur crewmen to do the job when one German agent in harbor could have accomplished the task in much less time for less money? Miller labeled all of the aspects of the plots "figments of the imagination," asking the jurors, "Isn't it absurd?"

Miller then expressed his own theory as to how the master was able to get all of these men—Smithson included—to repeatedly sign their names on confessions that were far-fetched and untrue. "I think if I took that big club in there that belongs to the captain and handcuffed him and had him in this room alone for about five minutes, I could make him confess that he was the devil himself without much trouble, and he would be glad to sign his name to the document. . . . And I don't need two or three men to help me, either. That is easy."

Miller next reviewed the beatings administered to Jack Joe that had resulted in dislocating his hand and breaking his ribs. Citing the way William Jones had been beaten and knocked about, Miller described Jones as "the human rubber ball," questioning the defendants' claims that the mass of welts on Jones's back had come from a fall. How, Miller wondered, could someone fall on the deck load of flat lumber and end up with bruising in a pattern of black and blue stripes?

Miller had his own slant as to what had motivated Pedersen. He viewed Pedersen as a coward and a bully who had an underlying fear of people around him—a man who would go to any extremes to protect himself. He reminded the jurors that the master had admitted during questioning that he had been afraid of most of the crew—even crippled Jack Joe. Emphasizing this point to the jury, Miller said:

> When a man is afraid, he is going to take desperate measures. . . . [He claimed to be] scared to death, in spite of the fact he had a rifle, shotgun, revolver, and several clubs and weapons; and he had himself, the two mates, Mattson, John Walter Campbell, and Smithson. Six of them against these eight poor fellows up forward [who were] half-starved the whole trip. . . . Of course he was afraid. Any man who is a coward will start at his own shadow if he sees it at night. Any man whose conscience is bad will do the same thing. But does that justify him in beating up men who say they are innocent and imprisoning men who have done against him no act whatsoever?

Miller's second theory that he put to the jury concerned the deaths of Stewart and Hansen, which Pedersen must have known would provoke interest from the authorities in Cape Town. Did Pedersen speculate that the authorities would be less interested in two dead men and more interested in a ship's crew if it were made up of German spies, mutineers, and pirates? If so, while authorities were dealing with the crew, Pedersen and his sons could skip. To make the whole thing work, Pedersen would need proof in the form of the confessions. Without giving the jurors time to wonder how this second theory might have played out, Miller launched into a third explanation with the three words, "They liked it! Yes, they liked it! . . . There is a certain element in human nature that is savage. . . . We have a little second mate here who had never been in much authority before. It is a great thing to see these older men jump about at the snap of your fingers, and if they don't do it quick enough, hit them a crack."

After addressing the character of the master, whom he called "yellow," and the mates, especially the second mate, for whom the attorney seemed to have a particular dislike, Miller reviewed the sufferings the crew had experienced at the hands of the defendants. He stressed the point that the worst punishment the law could bestow would not compare to the suffering the crew had experienced. He encouraged not only that the master be punished but that the mates be punished as well. "They have been under a master who is a teacher of very questionable ability . . . a master whose instincts are brutal. . . . They are growing up. They have committed offenses. If they are going to be allowed to feel that the acts they have done are going to be allowed, to feel that the acts they have done to their fellow beings are justifiable and excusable without blame, they are going to practice it on more."

To reinforce his plea for punishment, Miller pondered: "How many members of the crew have been beaten and often killed by those in authority we will not know until the sea gives up its dead. The master on a ship has complete command of them. They have to do everything he says. They are his slaves. That is what it comes down to."

Miller then explained to the jury that the Seamen's Act passed in 1915 had been necessary to protect seamen from masters and bucko mates who had taken advantage of their position. "If this captain had wanted to preserve himself from any plots, all he had to do was . . . put them in irons. Those are the punishments provided here by the law.[5] He could put them in irons and bring them home to the authorities that would try them. But he was a prosecutor, judge, and executioner, all at once."

Miller told the jury that the crew was powerless under the law to strike the master. Although he did not cite the law to the jury, Miller was referring to the Act of April 30, 1790, Section 8: "Every seaman who lays violent hands upon his commander, thereby to hinder and prevent his fighting in defense of his vessel or the goods entrusted to him, is a pirate and shall suffer death." Miller stated that the seamen's only course was "to stand up under that kind of punishment and that kind of abuse and that kind of torture until the captain himself said every one of them wanted to jump overboard.[6] It takes a brave man to suffer. . . . Put yourself in their position. What can they do? Stay there and suffer and that is what they did."

Miller reinforced time and again his contention that the defendants had repeatedly lied to the court.

> You [the jurors] know when they are lying. You are men of discernment. You can tell. Gentlemen, evil does come home to roost. You cannot do anything like this and not pay the penalty some day. . . . When you judge these men, give them justice and give them mercy. . . . Give them justice; the kind which they dealt out. . . . Give them the mercy they showed this crew, because the great God works through human agencies toward the end of justice and humanity.

CHAPTER 12

JUDGE JACK'S CHARGE OF THE COURT

At the end of summations, the jury was presented with the "charge of the court" (folios 3298–3341). Judge George Whitfield Jack began by giving the jurors some basic guidance, then turned to the specifics of the trial, reviewing the first seven charges of assault and delineating which defendants should be judged on each of the charges. He prefaced this discussion by stating that under Section 291 of the Federal Penal Code, it was

> a crime for a master or officer of a vessel of the United States, on the high seas, to beat, wound, or, without justifiable cause, to imprison any of the crew of such vessel, or to withhold from them suitable food and nourishment, or inflict upon them any cruel and unusual punishment. ... The master is vested, by law, with almost military authority over his crew, but with this great authority goes an equal responsibility. He may punish members of the crew for insubordination, refusal to obey orders, mutiny, and other offenses, but he may do so only in the manner authorized by law. ... The law does not tolerate beating a member of a crew as a method of discipline or coercion. ... The government of the United States, while giving masters of vessels great authority over their crew, will protect the crew against improper treatment by the master, against the indignity and physical pain of a beating, unless it is necessary under the circumstances I have just narrated.

In reviewing the three counts concerning the charge of illegal imprisonment of James Campbell, William Jones, and Barney Olsen, Judge Jack stated:

> Only the second mate had any part in the placing of the men in irons, and he acted under the orders of his superior officer. Consequently,

you cannot find either the first or second mate guilty on these three counts, and your inquiry as to such counts will be confined to the guilt or innocence of the captain of the vessel.

Pedersen's defense for such imprisonment had been the claimed existence of a plot to destroy the ship and kill the ship's officers. Judge Jack continued:

If you find from all of the evidence that there was such a plot on the part of those imprisoned, or if you find that, under all of the circumstances, a reasonable man might have thought there was, even though in fact there was not, and that acting under such belief the captain imprisoned the men named in the last three counts of the indictment to prevent a mutiny, the killing of the officers or the destruction of the vessel, then I charge you that the imprisonment alleged would have been justified. Otherwise it would not. When you retire to the jury room, you should take up the indictment count by count and determine the guilt or innocence of the accused under each count.

Once the matter of guilt or innocence was in the hands of the jury, it took the body of twelve men only two hours and fifteen minutes to return its findings. On the charge "did with force and arms willfully knowingly, unlawfully, and feloniously, without justifiable cause, beat and wound ... on the head, face, and body," the verdicts were:

Count 1	Grielen	July 24, 1918	Not guilty
Count 2	Grielen	July 25, 1918	Master, mates, guilty
Count 3	Grielen	July 26, 1918	Dismissed
Count 4	Joe	Aug. 2, 1918	Master, mates, guilty
Count 5	Campbell	Aug. 2, 1918	Master, guilty
Count 6	Jones	Aug. 23, 1918	Master, guilty
Count 7	Olsen	Aug. 23, 1918	Master, guilty

and on the charges of unlawful imprisonment:

Count 8	Campbell	Aug. 23, 1918	Master, guilty
Count 9	Jones	Aug. 23, 1918	Not guilty
Count 10	Olsen	Aug. 23, 1918	Not guilty

In rendering its verdicts against the two Pedersen boys, the jury requested that the court "exercise such clemency as you consistently can in the case of the two mates, on account of their age."

Adolph Cornelius Pedersen was sentenced to eighteen months on each of the six counts, the sentences to run concurrently, with a credit of three months applied at the beginning for time already served. While Judge Jack's eighteen-month sentence might seem insufficient considering the crimes, it was in line with the punishment guidelines contained in Section 9 of the Seamen's Act, which in part states, "No form of corporal punishment on board of any vessel shall be deemed justifiable, and any master or other officer thereof who shall violate the aforesaid provisions of this section . . . shall be deemed guilty of a misdemeanor, punishable by imprisonment for not less than three months nor more than two years."

Leonard and Dolph were both sentenced to six months on each of two counts, the sentences to run concurrently. Like their father, they received three months' credits for time served.

And so it was that in September 1919 one of the most abusive chapters in the twentieth century's history of the sea came to an end.

Or had it?

CHAPTER 13

APPEAL DENIED

As might have been expected, immediately after the trial, Dudley Field Malone filed an appeal of the convictions. In his brief, Malone again argued that the venue of the trial should not have been the Southern District of New York. He next argued that the court erred in permitting the government's attorney to threaten to impeach the credibility of the government's witness William Mattson; that the U.S. attorney erred in disclosing testimony that had been heard before the grand jury; that the court's admission of a club as evidence (Exhibit 13) was prejudicial without proof of its connection to a particular assault; that the U.S. attorney's use of the mates' diary, also referred to as the mates' logbook, constituted an unreasonable seizure and resulted in a violation of the Fourth and Fifth Amendments; that the captain did have the authority to punish a crewmember if this was done "by way of correction . . . to preserve the good order and discipline of the ship"; and that the verdict of the jury was not justified by the evidence.

While waiting for the scheduling of the appeal, and since Malone's charges made against Murphy during the trial were so serious, the Department of Justice launched an immediate investigation of what had transpired during the fall of 1918 in Cape Town. Following that investigation, R. P. Stewart, assistant attorney general, sent a report to Secretary of State Robert Lansing stating that his office had thoroughly reviewed all of the records concerning the *Puako* matter and that the Department of Justice "is convinced that Mr. Murphy not only acted conscientiously but also conducted himself with good judgment and with a proper sense of his official duties."[1]

On October 6, 1919, Wilbur J. Carr, writing for Secretary Lansing, advised Murphy: "The Assistant Attorney General says that your testimony and that of Vice Consul Pisar and Captain Howe corroborated the testimony of the crew and was most helpful in the trial. In view of the difficulties experienced in this case and the amount of time and careful attention given to it, the Department desires to express to you and to Vice Consul Pisar and Captain Howe the appreciation of this Government for the assistance rendered in connection with this matter."[2]

Those must have been welcome words, which should have enabled the consul general to put Pedersen and the *Puako* out of his thoughts. But it was not to be. On January 23, 1920, George Murphy reported to Secretary Lansing:

> I have the honor to quote from a personal letter today received by me from Mr. W. W. Masterson, American Consul at Durban, regarding statements made to him orally by Captain Albert C. Wilvers, Master of the American steamship *Westport* which is in that port.
>
> [Masterson wrote:] I have just had a talk with the captain of the *Westport* that has just arrived, and according to him there is an association or federation of captains of American steam and sailing ships, and these captains have banded themselves together to secure the release of Pedersen and his sons of the *Puako* from their terms of imprisonment; and to do you all the harm possible. It seems that this boat [*Westport*] was due to sail some two weeks before she did, but the other captain refused to bring the ship out here because you were still the official at Cape Town, and that these captains are trying to get all the captains to enter into an agreement to refuse to bring any ship out to Cape Town as long as you are in charge there. Now I am possibly telling you something you knew of; but if you have not, it seems to me that you should put the Department on the guard in the matter. ... The captain [Wilvers] said that the firm of Hind, Rolph of San Francisco, are helping these captains in the matter.[3]

The Department of State thought the matter of enough concern to forward Murphy's letter to both the attorney general and the Department of Commerce. On March 26, 1920, State received the following response from E. F. Sweet, assistant secretary of commerce:

> The papers which have been submitted to this Department in connection with this case indicate a proper attention to duty on the part of the Consul General and unless you have information to the contrary, it is the opinion of this Department that he should be sustained in this matter in every particular. The action of the court was conclusive so far as this Department is concerned, and should any master

licensed by the Steamboat Inspection Service of this Department decline to proceed to Cape Town because of the conviction of Captain Pedersen and his sons, it will be a proper matter for consideration by that service in connection with the revocation of the license of such officers.[4]

So far as could be determined, the attempted boycott never went beyond the talking stage. In light of the disclosure, Murphy offered to be moved to another post—perhaps one inland so as to spare the Department of State any embarrassment or inconvenience—but at least for the time being, he was kept on at Cape Town.

The appeal that Malone had filed was finally heard during the October 1920 term of the United States Circuit Court of Appeals, Second Circuit. United States Attorney Francis G. Caffey prepared the brief for the government.

While Malone was waiting for the appeal to be scheduled, he had become active in political endeavors. In mid-July 1920 a short-lived party called the Farmer-Labor Party held its one and only presidential convention in Chicago. The delegates' first choice was Robert M. LaFollette, the same Senator LaFollette who had been instrumental in ushering through passage of the Seamen's Act in 1915. When LaFollette declined to accept the nomination, several lesser-known candidates agreed to have their names placed in contention.[5] The two top contenders after the first ballot were Parley P. Christensen, an attorney from Salt Lake City, and Dudley Field Malone. Christensen took the vote, solidifying his support on the second ballot, but placed a distant fourth in a four-man field in the general election which was won handily by Warren G. Harding.[6]

On the West Coast, while the appeal process was under way in New York, a libel cause brought by six of the *Puako*'s former crewmen against the ship's owner, the Barkentine Puako Company, was slowly working its way through the federal court system. It had its beginnings some months earlier in New York when on May 31, 1919—two days before any of the *Puako* officers were first put on trial for murder—Silas Blake Axtell, proctor for the libellants, prepared an initial libel on behalf of seaman Lester A. Jensen in "a cause of action, civil and maritime, for personal injuries, neglect to treat, etc., against the Barkentine Puako Company." Since the Barkentine Puako Company was a corporation existing under the laws of the State of California with its principal place of business San Francisco, the seaman's cause would eventually be tried in that city in the Southern Division of the

United States District Court in and for the Northern District of California, First Division, in Admiralty. The decision to try the libels in San Francisco was founded in the Act of March 3, 1911, Section 43, under which all pecuniary penalties and forfeitures may be sued for and recovered either in the district where they accrue or in the district where the offender is found. Axtell, who had offices at 1 Broadway, New York City, would work with the San Francisco firm of Wallace and Ames.

Axtell, a colleague of Andrew Furuseth,[7] had for years worked tirelessly for the passage of the Seamen's Act of 1915 and later the defense of Section 9 of that act, which provided that the owners of a vessel could be held fiscally liable for damages resulting from the actions of the vessel's officers. The goal of that section had been to encourage shipowners to take more care and responsibility in hiring their ships' officers. At a time when shipping profits, especially profits from sailing ships, were marginal, many provisions of the legislation seem to have been more or less ignored by many—but not by Andrew Furuseth and Silas Axtell. By the mid-twenties, Axtell's activities on behalf of seamen became a thorn in the side of many shipowners, who for some five years attempted, albeit unsuccessfully, to have him disbarred.

When Axtell had first learned of the events on board the *Puako*, he wrote the Department of State asking for information concerning the vessel, the voyage, and the seamen. On January 19, 1919, he requested the names of the defendants who were to be tried for murder and the names of those the government would call as witnesses. On the twenty-first, he wrote yet again, stating that he had in his possession a letter from *Puako* seaman Frank Grielen, and offered the letter to the government if it might be of value. The Department of State referred Axtell to the Department of Justice.[8]

Soon after the *Puako* seamen were returned to the United States, Axtell made direct contact with Lester Jensen. During his first meetings with Jensen, the groundwork was laid for a libel suit which would ask fiscal remuneration for the pain and suffering Jensen had endured both on the ship and since the arrival of the *Puako* in Cape Town. The first paperwork for that civil suit was drawn on May 31, 1919.

That a libel on behalf of Lester Jensen was prepared and ready for filing so quickly after the seamen arrived in New York indicates Axtell's keen interest in the welfare of the *Puako* seamen. This is not a surprising development considering Axtell's background and his fierce activity in court in defense of various sections of the Seamen's Act. Jensen's cause, *Lester A. Jensen vs Barkentine Puako Company*, was made under the provisions of the Act of July 1, 1916, recodified July 1, 1918 (Section 1, Judicial), which stated "that courts of the United States, including appellate courts, shall be open to seamen, without furnishing bonds or prepayment of or making deposit to secure fees or costs, for the purpose of entering and prosecuting suits in their own name and for their own benefit for wages or salvage and to enforce laws made for their health and safety."

In introducing the case, Axtell stated that it was "a tale of a series of most outrageous abuses of the libellants who were seamen on board the Barkentine *Puako* at the hands of the master and the two mates." The first three paragraphs of the brief summarized the voyage, named the parties on board, identified the two seamen who had been driven to suicide, and noted the death in Cape Town of Bjarne Olsen. Paragraphs 4 through 6 stated:

> After the commencement of the voyage and about three days before the arrival of said Barkentine in Cape Town, while libellant was in the performance of his duties and without just cause or reason, he was unlawfully and wrongfully beaten up, assaulted and injured by the master and mates of said vessel and was struck over his head with a heavy and loaded club and his face was punched in and several of his teeth knocked out. That he was otherwise hit with sticks about his head, face, and body; that he was struck with several iron rods which were subsequently jabbed into his sides and body. That he was otherwise inhumanly and brutally treated, and was caused to suffer fits [epilepsy] and has been and still is suffering from hemorrhages of the brain.
>
> Fifth: That by reason thereof, libellant became sick, sore, lamed and disabled; that he has suffered pain and agony; that his face, head and body have been mutilated; that he has been and will be prevented from working; has suffered and will suffer great pain; has lost and will lose large sums of money which he otherwise would have earned; all to his damage in the sum of $5,000.
>
> Sixth: That said injuries were not caused by any want of care and disregard by libellant of any lawful commands of the master and other persons in authority of the said Barkentine *Puako*, but wholly and solely by reason of the negligence of the respondents in that they failed to exercise reasonable care in engaging as master of said Barkentine a competent, proper, and law-abiding person. That it was known or should have been known to the respondents that said master was incompetent, and by reason of his notorious bad character, was not a fit

person to command the said Barkentine, thereby rendering the said Barkentine unseaworthy.

Paragraph 7 of the brief stated that the libellant had been denied prompt and proper medical care and attention and that even though severely injured and in great pain and agony he had still been forced to perform his duties. This had greatly aggravated his injuries, rendering them permanent. For this additional damages of $5,000 were asked.

Five other *Puako* seamen would submit similar libels on August 5, 1920. These six libels were collectively filed and by February 1, 1921, had been assigned case numbers: 17068 through 17073. For purposes of streamlining, a stipulation filed November 13, 1922, joined together the six cases under case 17068 titled *James Campbell, Libellant vs The Barkentine Puako Company*. The notice of motion filed on March 8, 1921, summarizes the claims of all the seamen: James Campbell, Frank Grielen, William Jones, Jack Joe, Lester Jensen, and Edward Reilly. Collectively, the six men asked for a judgment of $40,000—a princely sum in the early 1920s.

James Campbell's claim was for $3,000 in damages and stated that he was "beaten up, assaulted, and injured by the Master and mates on various occasions; hit over the head with a large, heavy club; handcuffed with heavy chains, and confined in the pump hold, and drenched with water; compelled to climb the ladder with hands handcuffed and as a result fell down the ladder and broke his ribs and injured his fist; his clothes were ripped from his body and [he was] otherwise brutally treated."

Frank Grielen's cause asking for $3,000 stated that he had been "assaulted, beaten up and injured by the Master and mates; placed in irons and otherwise brutally treated."

William Jones's cause asking for $3,000 stated that he had been "assaulted and injured by the Master of the vessel on several occasions, and beaten about the face, head, and body; handcuffed with chains and confined in the pump hold, and given no food, and other brutal treatment."

Jack Joe asked for damages of $3,000 for having been "assaulted and injured by Master and mates of vessel. Tied with ropes around his body in awkward and cruel positions. Kicked and beaten by Master; a heavy stick broken over his side, fracturing one or more of his ribs, and his scalp opened up with a heavy instrument."

Edward Reilly's claim for $3,000 in damages stated that "about five days before the vessel arrived at Cape Town, [he was] assaulted and beaten up by

Master and mates; hit over the head, face, and body with a heavy instrument and otherwise brutally treated."

Each man asked for an additional award of $3,000 for lack of medical care and attention.

Part of the moneys the seamen were asking was to cover wages they had earned but had not received. At the time the seamen were discharged by Consul General Murphy in Cape Town (see plate 9), Murphy had paid them off—but the payments were based on what Pedersen said was due, which meant the man's monthly wage less any deductions Pedersen felt disposed to make, whether or not they were legitimate. Since for most of the trip, regardless of weather and sea conditions, the men had worked longer days than required under Section 2 of the Seamen's Act, their calculations of wages due may have factored in what we today call overtime.

At the start of the cause, all of the libellants either were considered seafarers by occupation or had become widely dispersed. It therefore was deemed impossible to have them all present on any given date. Accordingly, the case was to be submitted to the court almost entirely upon deposition. Proctor Silas Axtell would be assisted by his brother and law partner, L. V. Axtell, as well as by San Francisco attorney Alden Ames of the firm Wallace and Ames. In the end, the proctors for the libellants could produce depositions from only four of the six libellants: Lester Jensen, James Campbell, Jack Joe, and William Jones.

In making their claims against the owners of the *Puako*, the libellants stated that liability against the Barkentine Puako Company arose "by reason of the negligence or failure on the part of the owner to employ competent servants, here the master and mates of the vessel, [and] by reason of the relationship of principal and agent [Pedersen], [and] for the torts of the agent committed in the course of his employment."

Ira S. Lillick, a San Francisco proctor in admiralty, represented the respondents.[9] Lillick, who was assisted by his partner J. A. Olson, began the challenge to the cause by notifying on March 8, 1921, that in the courtroom of the Southern Division of the U.S. District Court for the Northern District of California on March 12, a Saturday, the respondents would "move the above entitled court for an order of dismissal of the above entitled action."

In asking for a dismissal, Lillick stated that the demand was stale and asked the court to follow the lead of courts of equity. Lillick gave by example one or two cases wherein courts of admiralty had followed courts of equity and had instituted a statute of limitations. Axtell had anticipated such an

Brutality on Trial

argument, which is why he had filed Jensen's libel in 1919, early in the game. In rebuttal to Lillick, Alden Ames, writing for the libellants, pointed out the extreme differences between those cited cases—a main point being that the involved injurious treatment addressed in the cited cases had occurred while the vessel was in safe port in the United States. In the *Puako* seamen's cause, the seamen's injuries occurred during a voyage that had lasted many months and had carried the seamen thousands of miles from the United States. Alden Ames concluded his argument by stating, "Seamen are not able to perfect their rights with the rapidity of others as they have no settled place of abode and are compelled to be away from this country for long periods of time. It is perhaps with such an idea in mind that the law has grown up in admiralty which grants leniency to seamen in this regard."

In concluding his brief of libellants upon exceptions, Ames quoted from *Gabrielsen vs Waydell*, 67 Fed 342. "If in any case an agent could represent the principal about the treatment of a servant, a shipmaster would seem to represent the owners about the treatment of seamen." He followed this by citing a decision rendered May 3, 1916, in *The Blakeley*, 234 Fed 959, a suit brought by Avgot Sjorberg, a seaman, against the schooner *Blakeley* and J. W. Hanka, master, for injuries inflicted by the schooner's second mate. The court had held that under Section 9 of the Seamen's Act, "the owner is liable as well as either the master or the vessel."

Lillick began to prepare the defense on behalf of the Barkentine Puako Company. Beginning on March 9, 1921, less than a month before the Pedersens would begin serving sentences resulting from the trial in New York, Adolph Cornelius Pedersen and Leonard Roy Pedersen, witnesses for the respondents, were examined. Their testimony was taken "de bene esse"—in advance of trial for use at trial in the event the witness could not appear in person. The depositions were recorded in the San Francisco offices of Ira S. Lillick by Alden Ames, proctor for the libellants, and J. A. Olson, proctor for the respondents. The process of deposing Captain Pedersen and his son Leonard lasted a number of days. From the captain's deposition, there is an indication that Dolph may have been ill at that time. Except for listing him as a witness, the record I obtained makes no mention of Dolph's deposition, leading me to wonder if the circumstances of illness prevented his ever being deposed. With the appeal pending from the previous trial and now a new trial beginning against his employer, Adolph Cornelius Pedersen was under considerable strain and often exhibited signs of irritation and anxiety during the direct and cross-examinations.

On March 21, 1921, the circuit court of appeals in New York issued a mandate affirming the district court's judgment against the Pedersens. They were ordered to present themselves to U.S. Marshal Thomas D. McCarthy in the Southern District of New York not later than March 30. The elder Pedersen was taken to Georgia, where McCarthy delivered him to Warden Fred G. Zerbst at the United States Penitentiary in Atlanta. When the once authoritative ship's master awoke on April 1, 1921, he was just another number, 12262-131 (see plates 13 and 14).

The Pedersen boys served their three months' time at the Essex County Jail in Newark, New Jersey, where the federal government had leased beds for the housing of short-term federal prisoners.

On April 2, Charles P. Sweeney of the law offices of Dudley Field Malone wrote Warden Zerbst requesting instructions on how mail was to be forwarded to Captain Pedersen.[10] In an attempt to assist Pedersen as he entered the prison system, Sweeney closed with the comment, "I might say that this office has been greatly impressed by the character of Captain Pedersen and that we regard him as a man of unusual personal qualities."[11] Although there is nothing in Pedersen's prison file to indicate his conduct during the months of his incarceration, it was probably not unusual that when he first came up for parole in October 1921 he was denied. He was released from Atlanta on April 1, 1922. With the three-month credit for time already served, his normal term would have ended June 30, 1922.

Long before Pedersen had arrived at the federal penitentiary in Atlanta, attorneys were busy gathering evidence and preparing arguments for another round, this the collective suit for damages brought by the *Puako* seamen. Depositions were taken "de bene esse" of three of the seamen at the New York offices of Dudley Field Malone. Lester A. Jensen was deposed May 24 and 31, 1921, Jack Joe on November 15, 1921, and James Campbell on January 23, 1922. William Jones was deposed before the American consul in Cardiff, Wales, on May 2, 1923. The proctor for the libellants also took a deposition from Dr. Henry Hale, who had examined Joe, Campbell, and Jones in 1919 upon their arrival in New York. As in his testimony at the 1919 trial, Hale could only confirm that various injuries had occurred; he naturally could not provide any definitive information as to when or exactly how the men were injured. Harry Ohlsen, secretary and agent of the San Pedro Branch of the Sailors' Union of the Pacific, was a witness as to Pedersen's character. He had known Adolph C. Pedersen personally for about twenty years but by reputation for many more, and he stated that Pedersen's reputation "is bad." Ohlsen, who was deposed in Los Angeles on March 30, 1923, claimed that over a period of many years, his union had received a number of complaints against the captain, whom he described as a "bucko." Joseph Ward, agent for the Eastern Gulf Sailors' Union at Port Arthur, Texas, who had met Pedersen in 1918, was deposed in Texas on May 24, 1922. He, too, stated that Pedersen's reputation was "bad." Neither man's statement was challenged by the proctors for the respondents.

Before Consul General George H. Murphy, now living in Zurich, Switzerland, was deposed, lengthy interrogatories and cross-interrogatories were drawn up by both sides and filed on June 30, 1922, under the title "Stipulation for Taking Testimony of George H. Murphy, Witness for Libellants Upon Deposition." The interrogatories were translated into German so they could be presented to Murphy by members of the Division 4 District Court in Zurich. Murphy's answers, given in German on May 11, 1923, were then translated into English for use in the American court. This resulted in a number of errors, which Murphy noted to the court and which were corrected before the transcript was forwarded for use in the seamen's causes.

George Murphy was as usual clear and concise in answering the direct and cross-interrogatories. He stated that in Cape Town Pedersen's reputation among various officials and businessmen was "not good," but volunteered no specifics. Even though it does not appear that he had reference to any files, as they had been left in Cape Town when he moved to his new post in Zurich, he exhibited an impressive memory with detailed answers that conformed closely to the initial record he had forward to Washington more than four years earlier. Throughout, although George Murphy seems to have handled his relationship with Captain Pedersen in a most professional manner for which he had received high praise from his superiors at the Department of State, the respondents still felt compelled to ask in cross-interrogatory if Murphy had personal animosity against Pedersen. The simple reply was, "No, I had only official dealings with him." His only critical remark was directed more to Hind, Rolph & Co. than to the *Puako*'s officers. Murphy stated that he felt the mates were both too young to have been given such positions of responsibility.

Although a George Larsen and an Edward Anderson were listed in trial documents as witnesses on behalf of the libellants and C. O. Andersen, Edward Nelson, and Adolph Eric Pedersen (Dolph) were to appear as witnesses for the respondents, I could locate none of their testimony in the trial record held at the National Archives at San Bruno, California. George U. Hind did apparently sign a lengthy statement on behalf of the respondents, and it is perhaps that document that is discussed both in the respondents' brief dated January 21, 1924, and in the libellants' reply filed January 28, 1924.

Appeal Denied

It was not located either. Referring to that statement, Lillick in the respondents' brief stated, "Mr. Hind has testified that he heard of no complaint against the Master during the long number of years he was in the service of the Hind, Rolph Company, the agents of the vessel." To this the libellants replied, "The bad reputation of Captain Pedersen has been established by testimony of men in different localities [including San Francisco] who are in a position to know that reputation. Mr. Hind, in claiming that he did not know that reputation, is either displaying colossal ignorance or gross carelessness in not finding out a fact of vital importance in connection with his business."

On February 20, 1924, the Honorable Frank H. Rudkin, circuit court judge, issued a memorandum addressed to "James Campbell, Libellant, No. 17068 and consolidated cases 17069, 17070, 10771, 17072, 17073." This memorandum contained his "Final Decree" for the collective libellants:

> These several libels were filed to recover damages for personal injuries and for lack of medical treatment. The libellants were employed as members of the crew of the Barkentine *Puako*, which sailed from Victoria, B. C., in the latter part of April 1918 and arrived at Cape Town in the latter part of August, after a voyage of 122 days. The cruelties complained of, occurred principally within the last two weeks, before the arrival of the vessel at Cape Town.
>
> The testimony in the case is voluminous and extremely conflicting. The witnesses agreed only upon the fact that the different libellants were handcuffed and confined on different parts of the ship for periods varying from a few hours in some cases, to several days in others. In addition to this confinement, the libellants claim that they were brutally assaulted from time to time, and that they were denied proper food and medical attention. A review of the testimony would serve no purpose.
>
> In justification of his act in handcuffing and confining the libellants, the Master claimed that the crew was mutinous, and planned the destruction of the vessel, and the killing of the ship's officers. But the size of the crew, the sources from which the members were gathered, their conduct toward each other, and all the surrounding circumstances, satisfy me that the suspicions of the Master, in this regard, were without foundation. I am of opinion, however, that the conduct of the Master was inspired by fear, rather than by malice. Doubtless there has been more or less exaggeration and withholding of facts on

both sides, and neither party was entirely free from blame, but a careful review of the testimony convinces me that the several libellants are entitled to damages in the following sums. Campbell, $2,000; Jensen, $2,000; Jones, $1,500; Joe, $1,500; Reilly, $250; Grielen, $500. The latter two did not take sufficient interest in the case to appear as witnesses in their own behalf, although the libels have been pending for a period of about three years.

Let Decrees be entered accordingly.

CHAPTER 14

"FIGHTING" HANSEN

Following her infamous voyage, the *Puako* sailed in ballast to Sydney, Australia, under the command of Eric Pearson, the master recruited by Consul General George Murphy in Cape Town to replace Adolph Cornelius Pedersen. Sailing with Pearson was his wife Louie and their 3-year-old daughter Lulu. Shortly after the *Puako* arrived back in the United States on May 20, 1919, Captain Pearson, a resident of Cape Town and British subject, was replaced by Captain Charles Emil Helms, a naturalized American citizen. On June 6, 1919, the *Puako* left San Francisco for Astoria, Oregon, from where she was towed upriver to Portland. At Portland the barkentine was loaded with lumber consigned for Port Natal (Durban), South Africa. She arrived in Durban on 29 November. From Durban her routing took her to Hobart in Tasmania, to Newcastle in New South Wales, and then to Honolulu. Before she departed Honolulu on June 29, 1920, Captain Helms hired a new first mate, one Frederick Hansen.

Hansen, a native of Denmark, was a hardened, well-muscled man of thirty-seven years, nearly six feet tall, weighing 285 pounds.[1] In addition to his close-cropped brown hair, bushy mustache, gray eyes, and unusual bulk, Hansen had several unique distinguishing features, the most noticeable being his tattoos. A depiction of the Statue of Liberty covered much of his right forearm. On the left forearm was the word "Friends," flanked by Danish and American flags. The back of each thumb had a star. Three years before Hansen signed on the *Puako*, he was convicted of murdering a seaman, Raoul Tourice, while aboard the *H. K. Hall*. The details of that murder, taken from the trial transcript of *U.S. vs Frederick Hansen*, Case 2112, Criminal, USDC, Northern District of California, Second Division, were published in the *Coast Seamen's Journal* under the headline "The Bucko Again." It appears from that account that on September 1, 1916, while serving as first mate, Hansen "beat a young mulatto, Raoul Tourice about the head with a spanker—a sheet at the end of which he had tied a knot, until Tourice fell down on deck, the blood streaming from him; whereupon the mate jumped upon the prostrate man and kicked him to death."[2] In connection with Tourice's death, U.S. District Attorney J. B. Preston conducted a preliminary investigation of both Hansen and the *H. K. Hall*'s master, Daniel O. Killman, but only Hansen was indicted. Convicted on February 10, 1917, he served but ten months for the crime. Less than a year after his release, Hansen was under investigation again, this time for the death of Charles Hannen, second mate on the schooner *Edward R. West*, C. W. Brasting master. A preliminary inquiry was conducted by William W. Masterson, American consul at Durban, following the *Edward R. West*'s arrival at that port on September 3, 1918. This, coincidentally, was less than a week after Consul General George Murphy had begun his investigation in Cape Town of Captain Pedersen and the battered *Puako* seamen.

On the twenty-third of September, after hearing of Hansen's detention in Durban, Murphy wired Washington from Cape Town: "Hansen, mate American vessel, Edward R. West similar origin [as Pedersen] accused Durban similar offenses, brutal murder while at sea. Is it possible Germany using Norwegians, Danes, Swedes to cause trouble to delay American vessels?"[3]

After the attorneys at the Department of Justice in Washington examined the evidence Consul Masterson had forwarded to them from Durban concerning events on the *Edward R. West*, officials at Justice decided to file charges. That plan was abandoned, however, when witnesses willing to testify against Hansen could not be found.

There is no evidence that Helms knew Hansen's background when he hired him at Honolulu, but after spending some time with Hansen en route to the West Coast, it is a good guess that Helms was glad to see him leave the ship once it arrived at Victoria on August 9, 1920.

"Fighting" Hansen's next employment would be as first mate on the four-masted barkentine *Rolph*. The 1,386-ton, 231-foot *Rolph* had been built at a cost in excess of $250,000 at the Rolph Shipyard in Rolph, California—a place with an interesting history dating back to the mid-1800s, when it was founded and given the pleasant name Fairhaven. In 1874 Hans Bendixsen had settled there and opened a shipyard, which he operated into the early 1900s. The shipyard changed hands at least once before it was purchased in 1917 by James Rolph Jr. By that time Rolph, then forty-eight years of age, had been serving as mayor of San Francisco for five years while still wearing the hat of president of Hind, Rolph & Co. With the growing demand for ships—including sail vessels—to meet wartime needs, Rolph saw with his purchase of the shipyard an opportunity to become an even larger player in the West Coast shipping community. He quickly enlarged the shipyard, which was soon employing four hundred men. Soon after buying the yard and not being shy at self-aggrandizement, he took steps to have the community renamed Rolph. To educate the children of his employees, he built a new school for the town, the Rolph School. The school's dedication on February 22, 1918, coincided with the launching of the shipyard's first four-masted barkentine, the *Conqueror*.[4]

The *Rolph*, launched seventeen months later in July 1919, would carry a total of sixteen: master, two mates, carpenter, cook, cabin boy, and ten seamen. Albert Henry Sorensen, a seasoned captain, was given command. Sorensen, born October 4, 1869, in Aalborg, Denmark, had become a naturalized United States citizen at the age of twenty-four. He was first issued a license as master of sail vessels over 700 gross tons, on October 13, 1911. With the vision to recognize that a career in sail would be short-lived, in 1918 he obtained dual licenses as master of sail vessels and master of steam ships, both licenses being for any tonnage, any ocean.

In mid-September Hansen was signed on as first mate of the *Rolph*. While the ship was being loaded with lumber at the Dollarton Mill in Vancouver, Sorensen was putting together the rest of the crew. One of those was Frank Fredette, who was signed on as carpenter. A conversation Fredette had nearly fifty years later in 1967 with a reporter named Cecil Clark gives a glimpse of what life was like from the very start on board the *Rolph*.[5]

On Fredette's first meeting with Hansen, the mate ordered him to remove two nail kegs from the launch and bring them to his cabin. While Fredette was putting the kegs down, Hansen "pulled a .38 revolver from his hip pocket and threw it on the bunk." Fredette was then ordered to get a hammer to open the kegs, each of which contained eight bottles of rum. "Hansen promptly pulled the cork on one of the bottles and poured himself a hefty slug." When Fredette asked why he had the gun, Hansen said he always carried one. Then he proceeded to tell Fredette a somewhat rambling story concerning a Japanese seaman he had recently escorted from the *Puako* to the immigration shed. Hansen had hoped the man would try to escape so he could "drop him, just to see him fall." Hansen then boasted of fights he had with assorted policemen, producing as evidence a large array of buttons, badges, and belt buckles he had collected as trophies from these encounters.

A day or so later, when an intoxicated Hansen decided to speed up the longshoremen loading the *Rolph*, Fredette saw the mate come on deck armed with a cutlass. "After a few wild injunctions and wilder waves of the weapon, the longshoremen quit in a body." The mill's manager telephoned police, and shortly thereafter motorcycles bearing North Vancouver policemen were headed for the wharf. Meanwhile, Hansen had passed out on deck. When the police arrived and woke up the mate, Hansen was "mild as a lamb," leaving quietly with the policemen, who locked him up. Fredette said that after Hansen was taken off, life was easier, and in a few days' time the ship was loaded and ready for sea. As the last man was signing his name before the U.S. shipping commissioner, a launch came alongside. Up the rope ladder came none other than Hansen. Within hours the *Rolph* was under tow to the headland of Cape Flattery, where her sails were set to begin a nonstop voyage to Melbourne, Australia. Shortly after she was under way, Hansen gathered the crew on deck and gave them an idea of what the next weeks would be like. "You lime-juice sons-of-bitches, I've got youse where I want you. Your happy days are over now. You are with Fighting Hansen now." Throughout the voyage, Hansen abused the seamen, calling the men foul names and kicking and striking them with whatever was at hand. In a deposition given months later against Hansen, *Rolph* seaman Eric Harrison said the mate barked, "I will show you _____ [expletive deleted]. I will show you that I have sailed on the *Puako*."[6] By this time, thanks in part to embellished newspaper stories that had appeared in various West Coast papers including the *San Francisco Chronicle* and the *San Francisco Bulletin* in May 1919, the *Puako*'s reputation as a hellship was pretty widely known and talked about in ports like Vancouver where most of the *Rolph*'s seamen had been recruited. Several of them had regularly sailed in and out of San Francisco and undoubtedly had read or at least heard the stories. Harrison said that Hansen—assuming, probably correctly, that the men would not know the difference—bragged that he had been on the *Puako* in 1918 on the trip to Cape Town, claiming that it was he who had made two of the seamen jump over the side.

According to Harrison, Hansen would make it "a special business of rapping and hitting us over the back while we were pulling on the braces and knocked us down with his fist." During one of his fits of rage, Hansen threatened that "if anyone went out on the jib boom and fell off he would throw him a grindstone, and he could grind his way to Hell."

Hansen was especially rough on the second mate, a man named Gilmour. According to the depositions that would be given by crewmen James McQueen and Frank Fredette, Hansen repeatedly "hammered" the second mate on the ears. When the mate's left ear swelled until it was "half the size of his head," Gilmour begged Hansen not to hit him any longer, but Hansen kept at it until the left ear was pretty well beat up. Then he moved to the right one, which he also turned into a cauliflower.

Hansen often chased the men around deck using various pieces of rope to hit them when he caught them. Fredette recalled being struck by "the widow and her four daughters," a reduced version of a cat-o'-nine-tails. At one point, while being chased by Hansen, Fredette fell on an adze and severely cut his leg, which was slow to heal after infection set in. No wonder, as the only medical aid he received from Captain Sorensen was an old rag with which to wrap the wound.

When the ship arrived in Melbourne, most of the crewmen, including the badly battered second mate, left the *Rolph* and made their way to the American consul, who granted them discharges based on the ill-treatment they had received. The consul sent Gilmour to the hospital, where he remained for a couple of weeks.

Fredette had tried to quit the ship with the rest of the crew, but Sorensen refused to release him, claiming it would be impossible to find another carpenter. In desperation, the night before the *Rolph* was to sail for Newcastle, New South Wales, Fredette jumped ship and found his way to the U.S. consul. Much of what the carpenter had to tell the consul about Hansen confirmed the stories of the other seamen. It also confirmed something else. According to Fredette, Sorensen not only knew that Hansen was mistreating the men but by his demeanor seemed to condone it. He perhaps even encouraged it by smiling and occasionally laughing as Hansen dealt out his choice punishments. Fredette said independently that the captain and mate were frequently seen drinking together and that often when Hansen was giving it to the men, the captain would just turn around, never saying anything. While there is no way to know why Sorensen was never motivated to stop Hansen, some of the men suggested that he, like the men, was afraid of the mate. Because of Sorensen's actions—or lack thereof—few ever complained to him, feeling it would do no good and might even make a bad situation worse.

By the time Fredette made his report to the consul, Sorensen had found some replacement crewmen and, although shorthanded, had sailed from Melbourne for Newcastle, where the *Rolph* was to load coal for Mejillones, Chile. Fredette, who needed treatment for his leg as well as an illness (syphilis), was sent to the hospital in Melbourne and remained under treatment for six weeks.

When Sorensen left Newcastle in February of 1921, the *Rolph* again had a complete crew, which included two Americans and a number of foreign seamen, most of whom had considerable sailing experience. Among the roster were Lawrence Heinrich, American; Demetrius Kohilas, Greek; John Kaptein, Russian; Adolph Seppinen, Finnish; Charles Noling, Swedish; a German named Snyder; and Arne Mikel Arnesen, a naturalized U.S. citizen. George Stephens, nationality unknown, had been part of the original crew signed on in Vancouver. Although Stephens had left the ship at Melbourne, he rejoined the *Rolph* at Newcastle and remained on board until the ship returned to the United States. He was the only seaman Hansen ever left alone. Some of the men referred to Stephens as "Hansen's pet"; others seemed to suggest that Hansen viewed Stephens as a younger brother.

Within hours of leaving the docks of Newcastle, Hansen was up to his old tricks. It was the worst of voyages, from what both Hansen and Mother Nature would dish out. For fifty days of the sixty-one-day trip, the weather was extremely bad—so bad, in fact, that one man, Snyder, was washed overboard. In the heavy seas the ship's bow "dove down twenty feet" into the sea and then lifted. "It was not fit for any man. Men were scared," Arnesen testified. At one point when the men tried to move to a safer area, Hansen threw belaying pins at them. One pin hit Snyder and knocked him off balance at the moment the ship's bow buried itself. When the ship recovered, Snyder was seen overboard, thrashing and hollering, begging to be helped. As the *Rolph* moved farther and farther away, Sorensen threw a rope over the side, but it was too short to reach even halfway to the water. To no avail, Snyder yelled out again and again, begging to be rescued. According to Arnesen, even before Snyder's last cries were heard, Sorensen had gone below and Hansen was bragging, "There is one Dutchman gone." When Arnesen angrily told the mate that more could have been done to save Snyder, Hansen threatened, "Look out, you bastard. You will be going over the side, too." Hansen purportedly told one of the other seamen, "I am scared that fellow [Arnesen] might tell something about what happened on this trip if he lives. I think he has got too much of a mouth . . . knows too much." Arnesen said the ship had by this time turned into a madhouse. In his eighteen years of going to sea, he had never seen the likes of it.

In a lengthy letter written later by Arnesen and published in the June 15, 1921, edition of the *Seamen's Journal* under the title "A Tale of Terrorism: Victim Relates Facts of Frightful Experience on Board Hell Ship," Arnesen vividly recounted his days on the *Rolph* with Hansen. He ended the letter asking the whereabouts of Hansen as well as Hellfire Pedersen. "Hansen has been tried before. Where are they at present? Are they still on board ships using their brutal tactics?"

According to trial testimony, another seaman Hansen knocked around was Adolph Seppinen. For him the closest call came when Hansen grabbed his throat and shoved him down a hatch. Luckily for Seppinen, there was no permanent injury or ill effect from that encounter. John Kaptein and Demetrius Kohilas were not so fortunate. In addition to feeling the pain from the mate's usual "tools," which included belaying pins, fists, ropes, and even his boot, Kaptein recalled being hit across the kidneys with a big razor strop. More seriously, Hansen decided to work over the seaman's head. By the time he was through, Kaptein was permanently deaf in the left ear. Of all the seamen, it was Kohilas who suffered the greatest loss. From being repeatedly struck on the face by a rope wielded by Hansen, Kohilas was virtually blind. For the remaining forty or so days of the trip, Kohilas found his way around the ship, even into the rigging, by groping.

Like the seamen who had made the first leg of the trip from Vancouver, Arnesen and his shipmates often saw the mate and captain drunk and knew from the cabin boy that the two officers frequently imbibed together. During some of Hansen's more congenial moments, the mate even offered his rum to some of the seamen, particularly to his alleged "pet," George Stephens.

When the *Rolph* arrived in Mejillones, Chile, on April 30, 1921, six of the eight seamen who had signed on in Newcastle received permission from Sorensen to go ashore. (Of the other two, Snyder was dead and Stephens stayed on board with Hansen.) From local police and port authorities the seamen learned that the closest American consul was some sixty miles distant in Antofagasta. Two days later the men were at the consulate telling their story to Consul Thomas W. Voetter, who had been alerted by authorities in Mejillones and who had accordingly summoned the seamen. As a group, the seamen agreed to return to the *Rolph*, but only on the condition that the mate be removed. Captain Sorensen was summoned by Voetter, told the situation, and told to produce the mate. At this time Voetter read to Sorensen the statements from the six crewmen. The master "did not make any reply under oath, but said that he 'could not truthfully declare that he did not know something was going on.'"[7]

The following day, Hansen appeared. Using money obtained from Sorensen—nearly $900 cash in U.S. currency—Voetter paid off Hansen and told him he was being sent back to the United States as a passenger on the *Del Rosa* to face charges that had been made against him. Voetter wanted to use the same authority George Murphy had earlier used to detain the *Puako* offenders in Cape Town, namely Section 355 of *Regulations Governing the Consular Service of the United States* as well as the Seamen's Act, Section 8. This would have allowed local authority to take custody of Hansen, hold him, and escort him to the ship for transport back to the United States. But Chilean authorities, not wanting to get involved in what they saw as a matter for the United States to handle on its own, refused the request for assistance. As a result, while Voetter was preparing the paperwork, Hansen got up and walked out of the consul's office. Voetter had no way to stop him.

As might have been expected, Hansen never showed up at the *Del Rosa*. The ship sailed with only two seamen passengers from the *Rolph*, the Americans Arnesen and Heinrich. Both were returned to the United States under provisions of the Act of February 28, 1803, which stated in part: "It shall be the duty of the consuls, vice-consuls, commercial agents, and vice-commercial agents, from time to time, to provide for the seamen of the United States, who may be found destitute within their districts ... sufficient subsistence and passages to some port in the United States, in the most reasonable manner, at the expense of the United States."

Kohilas was sent to a local Chilean doctor, who did what he could over a period of a few weeks to help the near-blind seaman. When he could do no more, Kohilas was advised to go to the United States where trained specialists might be able to restore more of his eyesight. Soon after, Voetter arranged for the man's passage to San Francisco.

John Kaptein and Adolph Seppinen were true to their word. Without Hansen on board, they did return to the ship and were on board the *Rolph* when the barkentine arrived in San Francisco after making stops at Caleta Coloso, Chile, and Honolulu. The remaining seaman, the Swede Charles Noling, had found employment on another ship.

In making his final report to the Department of State, Consul Voetter concluded, "I would recommend that the license of Frederick Hansen be canceled." The consul's memos were distributed to the Bureau of Navigation's Steamboat Inspection Service, but Voetter's recommendation was never acted on—which is odd, given that Hansen did have a current license as master of sail vessels over 700 gross tons, any ocean. Is it any wonder that, despite the passage of the Seamen's Act in 1915, officers like Hansen were still, six years later, getting away with murder?

CHAPTER 15

FOUR DAVIDS TAKE ON GOLIATH

In his "Opening Brief on Behalf of Libellants" for the *Puako* seamen's libels, proctor Alden Ames had told the court that incidents of abuse of seamen had been numerous following passage of the Seamen's Act. He pointed to the battered seamen from one ship in particular, the barkentine *Rolph*, who had recently found redress through the courts. Not only were their arguments similar to those Ames was putting forth on behalf of the *Puako* seamen, but the *Rolph* seamen libels involved as respondents some of the same principals—one in particular being James Rolph Jr. That libel to which Ames referred, *Kohilas vs Barkentine Rolph Company*, 293 Fed 269, which was heard in April 1923, did not have the sensational qualities of the *Puako* criminal trials in New York. However, because it involved San Francisco's popular mayor, James "Sunny Jim" Rolph Jr., it did attract considerable attention among the public. One of its interesting aspects was that a Greek seaman, Kohilas, with but little command of the English language was willing to pit himself against Rolph's enterprise—especially considering that the suit was filed in the mayor's hometown. Through some fortunate means, probably union effort, Kohilas had been placed in the most able hands of admiralty proctor H. W. Hutton. Over a period of several months, either in person or by deposition, Hutton would parade an impressive field of witnesses before presiding judges Maurice T. Dooling and John S. Partridge. In all probability, Hutton anticipated that a successful outcome for his client would generate profitable publicity, as Jimmy Rolph's interests were represented by the powerful firm of Sullivan and Sullivan and Theodore J. Roche. Wilfred Tully and an attorney named Barry were assigned by the firm to represent Rolph's enterprise in court.

On behalf of seaman Kohilas, Hutton filed two actions in 1921 against the Barkentine Rolph Company and its parent corporation, Rolph Navigation and Coal Company. In the first action, case 17349, he had sued for wages and maintenance. The decree in favor of the seaman in the amount of $632.17 was issued March 23, 1922, and satisfied April 10, 1922.[1]

The second, more complex action, case 17350 for damages, was filed almost simultaneously by Hutton, again on behalf of Kohilas. Three other *Rolph* seamen were joined to the Kohilas case as intervenors: John Kaptein, Arne Mikel Arnesen, and Adolph Seppinen. Kohilas asked for $20,000, and Kaptein and Arnesen each asked for $10,000, while Seppinen asked only for $1,000.

The earliest points-and-authorities filed by Hutton stated that Hansen had a "worldwide reputation" for assaulting seamen while employed as first mate aboard various vessels. He said this was a "matter of common knowledge among seafaring men on the Pacific Coast of the United States of America where the master and owner of said vessel resided." Hutton then graphically described the manner in which Hansen had viciously attacked and injured each of the four libellants using various weapons which included ropes, belaying pins, pieces of wood, and his own feet and fists.

Summarizing their cases, Kohilas and Kaptein each claimed damages for permanent injuries and for failure of the vessel and its owners to provide medical treatment. Arnesen sued for continued abusive treatment, and Seppinen sued for being beaten and choked.

The libellants claimed collectively that there had been lack of due care by the respondents in hiring Hansen in the first place; that once on board there was lack of due care in restraining him; that so long as Hansen was on board and unrestrained in his actions, the vessel was unseaworthy; that the seamen had a contractual right to good treatment; that the master allowed Hansen to escape; and that Kohilas had an absolute right to medical treatment while in Chile—treatment for which the Barkentine Rolph Company had refused to pay.

The points-and-authorities noted that it would have been impossible for the master not to have known of Hansen's abusive treatment of the seamen on board his ship, and that Hansen's treatment of the stevedores which led to his detention by North Vancouver police should have been adequate reason for the captain to discharge him before the voyage started.

Hutton pointed out that if anything had happened to Captain Sorensen during the voyage, Hansen would have succeeded him. Whenever hiring a mate, Hutton submitted, unusual and extreme care should always be exercised, as the man might at some point be charged with the care of the lives of all on board and with the care and safeguarding of the owner's property.

Hutton cited a portion of the decision in *Baltimore and Ohio RR Co vs Henthorne*, 73 Fed 634: "It is manifest from the foregoing passage that the duty of the master to select fit and competent persons is viewed by the Supreme Court in the same light as the duty of the master to provide reasonably safe machinery, and that neither duty can be so delegated as to relieve the master from liability for a failure on the part of his subordinate to whom the duty is delegated to exercise proper care in its discharge."

Hutton also quoted Section 1079 of Charles Bagot Labatt's *Commentaries on the Law of Master and Servant: Including the Modern Laws on Workmen's Compensation, Arbitration, Employer's Liability, etc, etc.*: "The obligations of a master to see that the servants hired by him possess the qualifications, mental, moral, and physical, which will enable them to perform their duties without exposing themselves and their co-employees to greater danger than the work necessarily entails, are, in their broad bearings, similar to the obligations which are incumbent upon him with regard to other agencies of the business." As for the hiring of Hansen at Vancouver, Hutton stated, "It is idle for the defense to claim the master knew nothing about it. It does not take a master of a vessel long to size up a man. If he cannot do that he is incompetent."

Sorensen testified that he had used extreme care in hiring Hansen, claiming that Hansen's previous employer, Captain Helms of the *Puako*, had "highly recommended" Hansen to him. Sorensen stated that Helms had even written a letter of recommendation, although he was unable to produce it when asked. "No one," Hutton charged, "hires a man for a responsible position on the word of only one man."

After stating that he knew nothing unfavorable about Hansen prior to hiring him, Sorensen also asserted that he did not know Hansen had been removed from the *Rolph* and detained by police in Vancouver in the days before the *Rolph* sailed. This last seems to have been a blatant lie, since Sorensen had just testified that he was on board the ship for the entire period of her loading.

In response to Hutton's suggestion that he should have asked the company to do an investigation of Hansen, Sorensen said that it was the policy of the company, in this case Rolph Navigation and Coal Company, to take a hands-off approach to crew hiring whenever their ships were away from San Francisco. He stated that he never notified Rolph company officials as to whom he had hired and that the company learned the names of crewmen only after he had discharged them. If this was the policy concerning one Rolph ship, one would think it the policy toward all of them. Yet Captain Pedersen of the *Puako* during his own trial in New York during 1919 had indicated that wherever the *Puako* was, be it Vancouver, Cape Town, or Australia, he kept his company abreast of all his actions, including information about the crew he signed on. Indeed, when the parents of a *Puako* seaman were concerned about the whereabouts of their son, they wrote to Hind, Rolph & Co. The company knew exactly what ship their son was on, when he had signed on, and all other particulars. Without question, they could not have known this unless Pedersen had given a copy of the crew list to the company's agent in Victoria for submission to the company, or had himself sent it directly to the company prior to departing Victoria.

The original crew of the *Rolph* were mostly residents of British Columbia who had signed articles for a round-trip voyage. Yet they all left the ship half a world away at Melbourne, Australia. Hutton questioned Sorensen as to why crewmen who lived in British Columbia would leave a ship in Melbourne and take their chances of ever getting home rather than fulfill the terms of the round-trip articles they had signed. Sorensen stated that the men had all left the ship in accord with "private agreements" he had made with them prior to leaving Vancouver.[2]

Hutton next explored whether the *Rolph* was seaworthy with Hansen on board. Safety being a test of seaworthiness, Hutton asked whether Sorensen and the ship's owner had provided reasonably a safe premise for the seamen. Hutton said they had not. Quoting from a Court of Appeals decision (*Hamilton vs US*, CCA 268 Fed 21), Hutton stated that "inherent in the shipping articles was *the absolute obligation* [Hutton's emphasis] of the owner and operator to see that the vessel was seaworthy. . . . To render a vessel seaworthy with respect to her crew, she must be reasonably safe."

In countering the libellants' claims that Hansen's actions had been the cause of Kohilas's loss of sight, the respondents' attorney stated that Kohilas had been near blind when he was hired. He asserted that Kohilas had been hired at the last moment and that it was not until after the ship was at sea that Sorensen noticed a defect in Kohilas's eyes, one in particular, which led him to realize that Kohilas could not see.[3]

To try to substantiate the claims of the master, the best the respondents' attorney offered was the testimony taken by deposition in Australia of one Oswell Frank Healy, superintendent of a seamen's boardinghouse in Newcastle where Kohilas had been living prior to signing on the *Rolph*.[4]

Healy testified that he distinctly remembered seeing a "white spot" in one of Kohilas's eyes. He further stated that one of his eyes was "cast with a kind of glazed expression." The other eye was "peculiar." Despite his claim that Kohilas had those optical defects, Healy said he had often seen the seaman reading or at least looking at books and newspapers and said he did not seem to have any trouble getting around. Toward the end of the interrogatory, when asked whether anyone from the Seaham Collieries had contacted him, Healy answered affirmatively. That question was no doubt asked to help discredit Healy's testimony, since the Seaham Collieries served as agent for Rolph Navigation and Coal Company in all of its dealings in Newcastle.

Following the introduction of Healy's deposition, H. W. Hutton put to rest the question of Kohilas's eye by producing a close-up passport photograph taken just a day or two before the *Rolph* sailed from Newcastle. In the photograph, Kohilas's eyes appeared perfectly normal. Hutton also produced the seaman's passport, which had a section for "distinguishing features." The only entry therein was a remark concerning missing fingers. Hutton argued that certainly if the man had an eye with a noticeable white spot, such a defect would have been mentioned.

The key witness for the respondents was Captain Sorensen. During his tenure as a master of sailing ships out of West Coast ports for the past eighteen years, he had made numerous runs to South Africa, Australia, and South America. He had also made regular coastal runs between San Francisco and Tacoma. Despite the fact that Frederick Hansen's reputation was well known along the West Coast, Sorensen claimed that he had not heard of the man until he hired him in Vancouver. After his initial interrogation, Sorensen was recalled to give further testimony at least two other times over a period of several months. During these, Sorensen kept to the middle of the road, never saying anything too laudatory about Hansen but never being too derogatory either. What was most noticeable about the master's testimony was how ignorant he tried to appear about activities that had taken place on the *Rolph*, practically under his nose, during the four months of the voyage. This was in contrast to the statement he had made in Chile to American consul Voetter, albeit that statement had not been made under oath.

Hutton called a host of witnesses as well as the libellants themselves. The *Rolph* seamen did their best to be clear and forthright during what must have been unfamiliar and perhaps intimidating circumstances. Because of language difficulties, receiving some of their testimony became a laborious task, especially in the case of the most injured man, Kohilas. After a few one-on-one attempts, the court determined that it could be sure of Kohilas's responses only if the interrogations were channeled through an interpreter arranged by the Greek consulate.

A number of doctors gave expert and detailed testimony concerning the injuries to Kohilas's eyes and to Kaptein's ear. Those doctors—eye, ear, nose, and throat specialists—were U. S. Public Health Service physicians from the Marine Hospital in San Francisco. One testified that Kohilas had scarring connected to damage to his cornea and iris. One eye also had a detached retina. Barry, one of the respondents' attorneys, attempted to make a case that the problem with Kohilas's eyes, particularly the scarring, was caused not by trauma but rather by syphilis. Although Barry spent considerable time discussing blood tests, particularly Wassermann tests, his attempts to connect the scarring with syphilis proved unsuccessful. Both doctors, W. Alexander and Ralph Barnard, said that while syphilis could cause scarring, it certainly could not cause a detached retina. Furthermore, none of the blood tests that had been administered to Kohilas had tested positive for syphilis in the first place. The cause of his condition was to them clearly trauma, a severe blow to Kohilas's head in the vicinity of his eyes. In their opinion, Kohilas would be permanently blind in one eye and, after their surgical procedures, could expect to have no more than "navigational use" of the other eye.

Doctors J. L. Spear and W. J. Pettus addressed the condition of Kaptein's ear. From examination they had determined that the drum was slightly inflamed and that air and bone conduction was obliterated. This was irreversible damage that could only have been caused by trauma to the head. The doctors both agreed that the thirty-six-year-old Russian was permanently deaf in that one ear.

The last witnesses Hutton called were four men who either knew or knew of Frederick Hansen. One of them, Alfred Knitzer, had been working on sailing vessels for thirty-five years in every position but master. For most of those years he had sailed as mate. He had known Hansen slightly for the past fifteen years and described his reputation as "bad, very very bad." George Larsen, assistant secretary of the Sailors' Union of the Pacific (SUP) did not know Hansen personally but had heard a lot about him and considered him a "bucko" mate. He claimed that anyone who had sailed for more than two or three years on the West Coast would have known of Hansen's reputation. Eric L. Erickson, agent for the SUP, was a "first patrolman," a job that involved visiting ships in order to represent the crews. He had held that position for about twenty years and had known Hansen for about ten years. "Hansen's reputation has been a common discussion on the city waterfront right along about the ill-treatment seamen received at his hands," Erickson stated, and spoke specifically of two ships from which seamen had lodged complaints against Hansen, the *Charles F. Crocker* and the *Edward Lavidst*. Erickson was probably referring to the *Edward R. West*. Perhaps at some point in the questioning he confused the ship's name, or perhaps he spoke with a heavy Scandinavian accent, causing the court stenographer to hear *Edward R. West* as *Edward Lavidst*.

The last witness for the libellants was Walter Macarthur, whose career along the waterfront had begun years earlier when he worked with Andrew Furuseth. Later he was employed by the Coast Seamen's Union as editor of the union's weekly paper, the *Coast Seamen's Journal*.[5] Currently Macarthur held the position of United States Shipping Commissioner for the Port of San Francisco. While all of the testimony that was given on behalf of the libellants was reasonably persuasive, Macarthur's was perhaps the most damaging to the respondents. Commissioner Macarthur, who had gone aboard the *Rolph* at some point after her return to San Francisco and talked at length with Sorensen, described a roomlike structure at the break of the poop which had large windows facing forward. While standing inside the structure, Macarthur said, he remarked to Sorensen that "he commanded a complete view of the deck from those windows." The master agreed and told the commissioner that from those windows he used to see the mate, Hansen, beating the seamen. This agreed with what Sorensen had told Consul Voetter, but it was a contradiction of Sorensen's statements given under oath. When the respondents' attorney Barry questioned the accuracy of the commissioner's testimony, Macarthur curtly replied, "My memory is quite clear."

Barry next tried to discredit Macarthur by bringing up the question of licensing. Seemingly under the impression that Hansen was licensed, Barry had asked the commissioner why Hansen's license had not been pulled if he was as bad as Macarthur and others had claimed. Macarthur replied that mates of sail vessels, even those over 700 tons, were no longer required to have a license.[6] He explained that a mate "is an unlicensed man in the same category as any other seaman. . . . No one would have any official right to intervene, for or against." According to Macarthur, the best you could do with mates like Hansen was to catch them, charge them, convict them, and hope others would not hire them.

While Macarthur was correct in his discussion of mates' licensing, he was incorrect in assuming that Hansen did not have a license. In 1905, Hansen sat for a license as master of sail vessels over 700 gross tons, which he had regularly renewed in Seattle, most recently on September 20, 1921.[7] Macarthur's ignorance of Hansen's license status is somewhat excusable, since at that time the Steamboat Inspection Service had no universal system or numerical identification for ship's officers or for seamen in general. What with the relatively primitive state of communications systems and the fact that mates were not required to be licensed, it would have been difficult for Macarthur to try to ascertain Hansen's status through Seattle, where Hansen was known to live, or through the headquarters of the Steamboat Inspection Service in Washington, D.C. This is not to say, though, that such a search could not have been made.[8]

On July 10, 1923, Judge John S. Partridge issued his decree in case 17350 in favor of the libellants, awarding Kohilas $10,000, Kaptein $3,500, Seppinen $500, and Arnesen $500. Following the respondents' unsuccessful appeal, a final decision was rendered in favor of the libellants on May 19, 1924. Six months later in November 1924, Jimmy Rolph's enterprise settled the judgment.

The only key witness to events on board the *Rolph* who did not testify at the seamen's libel was Frederick Hansen. After slipping away in Chile, he was on the loose until March 22, 1922, when he was arrested in Seattle. While Hansen was held in jail in lieu of $2,500 bail, evidence of his misconduct against seaman Arne Arnesen was presented to a grand jury, which indicted him on October 24, 1922. Arnesen's testimony at trial, coupled with Frederick Hansen's reputation, was sufficient for jury foreman Chester E. Roberts to announce to the court on December 20, 1922, that Frederick Hansen was guilty of the four criminal counts on which he had been indicted:

> Count 1: On or about 1 March 1921, on board the vessel *Rolph*, said Frederick Hansen did beat and wound Arne Mikel Arnesen with a knotted rope of large dimension;
> Count 2: On or about 15 April 1921, said Frederick Hansen did kick Arne Mikel Arnesen in the face with great force;
> Count 3: On or about 25 April 1921, said Frederick Hansen did beat

and wound Arne Mikel Arnesen by striking said Arnesen in the face, to wit, on the nose with great force;

Count 4: On or about 27 April 1921, said Frederick Hansen did beat and wound Arne Mikel Arnesen with a knotted rope of large dimensions and weight.

Hansen was sentenced to five years of hard labor for each of the counts, the sentences to be served concurrently. Frederick Hansen, Prisoner 4326 (see plate 15), entered McNeil Island Federal Penitentiary on December 26, 1922.

EPILOGUE

Since the *Rolph* and its tackle were the only assets that the Barkentine Rolph Company had for attachment to satisfy the judgment in the libel suits, what had the court done to safeguard them? After the libel had been accepted in 1921 and with more than $40,000 being asked in damages, Judge Dooling had ordered that the U.S. marshal seize the *Rolph* to assure it would be available for sale.[1] On August 24, 1921, the vessel's Certificate of Registry was surrendered and replaced with a Consolidated Enrollment and License. Essentially under arrest and unable to move except to offload cargo, the *Rolph* laid idle in San Francisco Bay while the libel slowly proceeded. Following Judge Partridge's decree in July 1923, B. H. Tietjen was asked to survey the barkentine to determine whether, after two years, ther ship still had sufficient value to satisfy the judgment. Tietjen's report, which is part of the court record, is interesting in that it examines the process of decay that a wooden ship endures. This process was somewhat faster in places like San Francisco Bay where, according to the surveyor, wooden ships were especially prone to damage by shipworms known as teredos:

> Wooden vessels are almost invariably attacked by teredos if they lay up in San Francisco Bay and in fact [even] if they run unless they are copper painted at least every eight months.... I was told by a ship carpenter that the *Rolph*, now laying on the mud flats in Oakland Creek was already wormed, that it has been attacked by teredos and would need a new bottom in all probability. If that is the case her deterioration will be very speedy from now on. Her bottom will eventually fall out of her, and it will cost a great deal to put a new bottom in her. The

percentage of depreciation of a vessel increases as they lay up. And they finally get so that they mire rapidly and decay. Their decks have to be wet down with water every night, and even then they dry out and have to be re-caulked when they commence to run. I have seen the barkentine *Rolph*. A fair estimate to be placed on her at Marshal's sale is from ten to fifteen thousand dollars. I do not believe she is worth more than fifteen thousand dollars at any kind of sale as there is no demand for vessels of her kind at this time, nor is there likely to be, steamers having taken the place of sailing vessels. And there are a great many vessels of her kind laid up at this time as they cannot run at a profit. There is also one other vessel, a sister vessel of the *Rolph*, laid up in Oakland Creek.

Eventually the *Rolph* was put up for sale. Even though a buyer never came forth, the record states that the company nevertheless satisfied the judgment in favor of the *Rolph* seamen. The *Rolph* was towed up the San Joaquin River to the Sacramento River to Antioch. There the water was nearly fresh, making wooden ships less vulnerable to teredos. The *Rolph* would share the wet storage with three other Rolph barkentines—the *Hesperian*, the *Annie M. Rolph*, and the *George U. Hind*. All would eventually decay and settle into the mud.

In time a similar fate would await the *Puako*, although for a wooden vessel she would carry on into economic old age. The *Puako*'s last voyage began in Vancouver on September 28, 1920. Under the command of Captain Helms, she sailed nonstop to Sydney, arriving there with a load of Canadian lumber on December 20. She sailed in ballast to Newcastle, where she loaded her return cargo, departing on February 17, 1921, and sailing nonstop to Victoria. Her arrival was reported in the May 24 edition of the *Daily Colonist*, which noted:

The length of the voyage [94 days] was due to no misfortune, however, beyond that of frequent calm spells and adverse winds. The ship was never in any trouble but was becalmed near the Equator for some time. Off [Cape] Flattery she met unfavorable breezes, and it was only after two days of waiting for a favorable wind that she put the finishing touch to her voyage. The hull of the *Puako* is in poor condition, coated with barnacles, and she will be hauled out at Esquimalt [Harbor] in the course of a day or so and attended to by Yarrows

[Shipyard]. . . . The *Puako* is one of the fleet owned by Hind, Rolph & Co. whose intention had been to tie the vessel up here pending a brightening up of the charter situation.

The charter market for sailing vessels never did brighten, and in 1925 the *Puako* was sold to Hecate Straits Towing Co. of Vancouver, which removed her rigging, renamed her the *Drumwall*, and used her first as a log barge and then for the carriage of wood chips. Hecate Straits Towing merged in 1926 with others to form Pacific Coyle Navigation Co. Pacific Coyle retained the *Drumwall*, ex *Puako*, until 1933, when the Island Tug and Barge Co. of Victoria acquired her. In her final transfer in 1951, the *Drumwall* was sold to Crown Zellerbach's Comax Logging Division. Archeologists are currently trying to locate her rotted remains which eventually sank into the mud and disappeared from view.[2]

On March 1, 1921, a month before entering prison and despite his conviction as a felon, Adolph Cornelius Pedersen renewed his license as master of sail vessels over 700 gross tons, any ocean, as well as his license as chief mate of steamers, any tons, any ocean. That he was allowed to renew his licenses anywhere, but particularly in San Francisco, is in and of itself amazing, since in a high-profile proceeding he had been found guilty of serious misconduct while serving under his master's license, and in recent months all three San Francisco newspapers—the *Bulletin*, the *Chronicle*, and the *Examiner*—had run sensational stories about what had occurred on the *Puako*. Despite that notoriety, at the time of the license renewal the San Francisco office of the Bureau of Navigation, Steamboat Inspection Service opened a new license file on him, L-14045, apparently never requesting a copy of his extant file L-3648, which was held by Portland, Oregon. That license file had connected him to the *Puako* and certainly would have raised a red flag for even the most uninformed license clerk. His new San Francisco issues made no mention of the *Puako*, rather stating that he was presently the master of the *Annie M. Rolph*, even though he would not take the oath as master until February 21, 1923, at Eureka, California. When Pedersen finally did take command of the *Annie M. Rolph*, his time under sail with her was short. He left Grays Harbor, Washington, on May 10 and sailed nonstop to Sydney, arriving August 19 with a load of West Coast lumber. The vessel proceeded in ballast to Newcastle and loaded 2,222 tons of coal. On December 20 she arrived in San Francisco.[3] Three months later, on March 19, 1924, the vessel's Certificate of Registry was surrendered and replaced by a Consolidated

Epilogue

Enrollment and License naming N. P. Carlsen as master. Even though Pedersen had been replaced by Carlsen, when he again renewed his licenses, this time on March 1, 1926, he stated that he was still master of the *Annie M. Rolph*. Six months later, on September 1, 1926, Pedersen's licenses were revoked, the cause a notation "Telegram from Bureau." This leaves one to conjecture that the government's proverbial right hand had finally caught up to its left and put an end to the probable collusion that had been going on for some time between Pedersen and/or his employer and officials at the West Coast offices of the Bureau of Navigation. The public record of Adolph Cornelius Pedersen ends there. The Office of Vital Statistics, State of California, has no record of Pedersen's death. During an interview in 1989, Leonard Pedersen told West Coast historians Karl Kortum and Harold Huycke that following his last voyage on the *Annie M. Rolph*, his father had worked as a caretaker aboard that laid-up barkentine until his death in the late 1920s from cancer.

Leonard Roy Pedersen attended the Taylor Nautical Academy in San Francisco following his release from prison. This education combined with his experience at sea may have helped him get his own command. On August 31, 1923, Leonard took the oath as master of the twenty-five-year-old four-masted schooner *Eric* which, being less than 700 gross tons, did not require a licensed master. Leonard made one trip on the *Eric*, a voyage he recalled in a story by Denis Cuff that appeared in the December 7, 1975, edition of the *Antioch (California) Daily Ledger*. At the time he took command, Leonard at twenty-four was a year younger than the schooner. During a storm, the seams of the old schooner opened, letting in water. Cuff wrote, "Pedersen realized it was useless for his eight crewmen to continue pumping out the water because the boat had taken on as much water as it would hold." The cargo of timber was actually keeping the *Eric* afloat. Leonard ordered the men to stop pumping and rest. The *Eric* was in an unstable condition, and the men, Leonard said, "were afraid the boat might tip over, but as long as it didn't we could sail toward Honolulu." The crew, Cuff wrote, "was uncertain whether the boat would capsize until the day it limped into Honolulu harbor with its edges no more than a few feet above water." The vessel was so low in the water that for the two weeks it took to reach Honolulu, everyone including Leonard was forced to live in the open atop the cargo of timber. Asked if he was scared, Pedersen in a matter-of-fact tone said, "No, we didn't have time to be scared. There were too many things to do. Like other voyages, you don't have time to be scared when you're in trouble, and there's no reason to be scared when it's over." For his efforts in saving the schooner, her owner presented him with the ship's clock. Leonard relinquished command of the *Eric* to Daniel J. Martin on December 29, 1924. That would be his last deep-sea adventure. In 1939 Leonard was issued a license as operator, motor, which qualified him to operate small commercial motorboats such as launches. He never sat for a large-tonnage license. Leonard died in Antioch, California, on July 2, 1992, at the age of ninety-three. His obituary in the *Antioch Ledger Dispatch* on July 3 stated: "He was caretaker for Gov. James Rolph's schooner fleet for many years, and he enjoyed speedboat racing. He was a past member of the United Pulp and Paperworkers Union." Leonard's cremated remains are at Oakview Memorial Cemetery in Antioch.

Adolph Eric "Dolph" Pedersen also returned to the sea after his release from prison. In 1923 and into 1924, Dolph sailed as chief mate with his father on the *Annie M. Rolph*. That was to be his last deep-sea voyage. By 1925 he had obtained a California state license for pilotage as well as a federal inland masters license for steam and motor vessels, any gross tons, any bays, sounds, rivers, lakes. With these in hand, he bought into the San Francisco Bar Pilots Association, with which he worked from 1925 until he retired in 1967. On December 19, 2003, retired San Francisco bar pilot Captain John Winterling shared with me his remembrances of working with "Little Pete" Pedersen, whom he described as a "loner with a real bad temper." According to Certificate of Death 39156001583 issued by the county of Ventura, California, Dolph died of senile dementia in Ojai on June 6, 1991.[4] His obituary in Ventura County's *Star Free Press* the next day stated that his cremated remains were to be interred at Chapel of the Chimes Cemetery in Oakland, California.

Because of credits for good behavior, Frederick Hansen, Prisoner 4326, was released from McNeil Island Federal Penitentiary by Warden Finch R. Archer on September 1, 1926, several months short of his maximum term. Nothing further is known of his activities.

Consul General George H. Murphy was promoted and transferred to Zurich, Switzerland, on October 20, 1920. Three weeks after his sixty-fourth birthday, he died in Zurich on October 16, 1924, after a lengthy illness. He had been employed in the Consular Service nearly forty years.[5]

James Rolph Jr., born in San Francisco on August 23, 1869, had a many faceted career. In addition to operating his various shipping enterprises, he had also served a record eighteen years as mayor of the fast-growing city of San Francisco. On January 7, 1931, the day he resigned as mayor, he was sworn in as governor of California. Rolph died of heart failure on June 2, 1934, having served three years of his four-year gubernatorial term.

The seamen who had sailed aboard the *Puako* and the *Rolph*, some of them sustaining injuries that would make them unemployable for the remainder of their lives, disappeared into the fabric of society, their fates unknown.

AUTHOR'S REFLECTIONS

Throughout the writing of *Brutality on Trial*, a question kept surfacing: Why did the *Puako* and *Rolph* seamen let themselves be subjected to the abuse and sometimes outright terror foisted upon them by the master and mates? Richard Henry Dana Jr. perhaps explained the reasons best when he himself in the mid-1800s was trying to make sense of the first flogging he witnessed.

> Sam was "*seized up*, as it is called, that is, placed against the shrouds, with his wrists made fast to the shrouds, his jacket off and his back exposed. The captain . . . held in his hand the bight of a thick, strong rope. . . . The crew grouped together. . . . These preparations made me feel sick. . . . A man . . . fastened up and flogged like a beast! . . . The first and almost uncontrollable impulse was resistance. But what was to be done? . . . If they resist, it is mutiny; and if they succeed, and take the vessel, it is piracy. If they ever yield again, their punishment must come; and if they do not yield, they are pirates for life. If a sailor resists his commander, he resists the law, and piracy or submission are his only alternatives. Bad as it was, it must be borne. (112)

Back in Dana's time, circa 1835, a seaman's options were limited—the scales of justice were clearly weighted in favor of the master. Eighty years later, however, thanks to the courageous efforts and dedication of men like Richard Henry Dana Jr., Andrew Furuseth, and Silas Blake Axtell—all advocates for seamen's rights—the scales of justice had become somewhat more balanced.[1]

Frank Fredette, a victim of brutality at sea on the *Rolph* in 1920, articulately echoed sentiments similar to Dana's when in June 1958 in a letter to Karl Kortum, director of the National Maritime Museum in San Francisco, he described the plight of the crew of the *Rolph*, noting that on that hellship at least three of the seamen were Canadians who had only recently returned from the trenches. "What I am trying to impress [on you] is that we, the crew of the *Rolph*, were not cowards as some people might think who have never been to sea; as some have said to me, why didn't we gang up on him? Only a seaman knows that he hasn't a chance against such terrible odds and will usually do his duty under any conditions for the good of his ship."[2]

Prior to passage of the Seamen's Act of 1915, although charges had successfully been filed against a few bucko masters and mates who were subsequently convicted, there was no incentive for owners to keep such men off their ships. Section 9 of the act, which made shipowners culpable, was designed to change that. The seamen from the *Puako* and the *Rolph* who successfully sued over an owner's lack of diligence in its hiring practices proved in a very public way that the law had teeth and that the new system worked. While there were some isolated instances of brutality in the years to come, following the successful settlements of the libels brought by the crewmen of the *Puako* and the *Rolph*, unrestrained brutality against seamen was finally a thing of the past.

APPENDIX 1

The Evolution of Maritime Laws Affecting Seamen, 1790–1915

Laborers in dry-land occupations have generally taken for granted certain work-related freedoms. Specifically, they are free to leave their places of work and return daily to their homes. They are free to give up their employment at whim without prejudice or punishment. They are even free to speak their minds to their employers, though they may soon find they are looking for new jobs. Contrast this to the marine laborer, the seaman who up to the early 1900s was without recourse as if in servitude. In many cases, his vessel was his only home. Some vessel masters—fortunately they were in the minority—thought of themselves almost as kings or deities. These men ran their ships with quasi-military authority and often exacted discipline by creative and brutal means. If things became intolerable under such a master, desertion was the seaman's only hope of escape—but it carried severe penalties if the seaman was found. This was a system that had historic origins dating, some suggest, to Rhodian law. Formulated by the people of the island of Rhodes circa 900 B.C., Rhodian law is the earliest collection of maritime laws. Under them, "Mariners who, without sufficient reason, quit their service during the period of their engagement shall be severely punished . . . to the amount of the loss if as a result of their absence the vessel was lost."[1]

The Code of Visby, promulgated in the early part of the thirteenth century, applied generally to ports in the Baltic region. Under that code, corporal punishment was added as a penalty for desertion, specifically "execution by hanging."

The next important code in maritime law was written around the fourteenth century. The Consolato del Mare (Consulate of the Sea), which is thought to have been compiled on order of the kings of Aragon, comprised the maritime ordinances of the Roman emperors, of France and Spain, and of the Italian commercial powers. European maritime law was considerably influenced by this code. Under the Consolato del Mare, the basic punishment for desertion was loss of wages, although in some situations a seaman could be imprisoned.

The laws of the Hanseatic League of the Baltic and North Sea states seemed to combine the worst of all of these codes by subjecting the deserting seaman to loss of wages, imprisonment for a year on a diet of bread and water, and, "If the vessel is lost and loss of life results, he shall be punished by death."[2]

According to *Black's Law Dictionary*, British maritime laws, first published at the French island of Oléron in the twelfth century and often referred to as the Judgments of Oléron, were adopted successively under the reigns of Richard I (1189–99), Henry III (1216–72), and Edward III (1327–77). Under these laws, "If they deserted the vessel and if by that means she happens to be lost or damnified, they shall be answerable for the damage."[3] The Judgments of Oléron have a direct bearing on American maritime law and are often cited even today in courts of admiralty. In the Judgments, seamen are called "the companions of the vessel," wording that underlines the seaman's unique attachment to his ship.

Under all of these early codes or judgments, only when a voyage ended was a sailor free of his attachment to his ship. Since British seamen did not always agree with or respect that attachment, it was thought necessary in 1729, during the reign of George II, to establish an act "For the Better Regulation and Government of Seamen." Under this act, if a seaman deserted, he automatically forfeited his wages. If apprehended, he could be imprisoned if he refused to return to the vessel.

On April 30, 1790, the young United States enacted its first statute to address maritime affairs. This act focused primarily on means of dealing with murder, manslaughter, revolt and mutiny, "laying violent hands on the commander," and piracy. A new act adopted on July 20, 1790, was more far-reaching, dealing with the seaworthiness of the vessel and with penalties for shipping seamen without signing them on articles, as well as with wages, medicines, provisions, and the treatment of deserters. It provided in Section 7 that a justice's warrant could be issued for apprehension of a deserter. Once caught, he was to be held in a house of correction or common jail until the vessel was ready to proceed or until he was discharged by the master. The cost of this imprisonment was to be deducted from the wages due the seaman. There was little a seaman could do in retaliation. For certain he could not take physical action against the vessel's master. To do so would be mutinous.

In upholding challenges to the two 1790 acts, American courts ruled that seamen presented an exceptional situation in that, once they had signed shipping articles, they surrendered their personal liberty for the life of the contract they had made with the vessel.

Enforcement of these early laws was at the discretion of and under the jurisdiction of the vessel's master—a man who often was part owner of the vessel. In the eyes of some, it made economic sense for such a man to make life on board so uncomfortable and downright miserable that seamen were willing to forfeit their wages after serving for weeks or even months if they could but find a way to escape from the ship without being captured. There clearly was a conflict between an unscrupulous master's fiscal interest and a seaman's physical interest. This sometimes could lead to abuses by ships' officers that are today beyond our ability to comprehend.

For little if any reason, seamen were viciously beaten by masters and mates. Food rations were of the poorest quality and sometimes reduced. Living quarters were, more often than not, below even minimal standards. Is it any wonder, then, that on such "hell ships" it was often only the dregs of society—men who simply could not exist in land-based employment—who signed on to sail the world's seas?

This was the state of affairs in 1834 when Richard Henry Dana Jr. signed as a green hand before the mast. Dana had been attending Harvard College when his eyesight was adversely affected by a case of measles. With the intent of giving his eyes a rest, he left college in his junior year and signed aboard the brig *Pilgrim* as a seaman for a two-year round-trip voyage from Boston to California via Cape Horn. In addition to helping his eyes, he thought such a trip would be a great adventure. During his time away from Boston, Dana kept a diary that became the foundation for the classic *Two Years Before the Mast*, a book that had a decided impact in focusing the public's attention on the deplorable plight of many mariners.

Midway through Dana's adventure, while the young man was on the foreign west coast of North America and out of touch—California was then under the control of Mexico—Congress took what seemed like a significant step to rein in masters and mates who were overstepping the bounds in their treatment of seamen. The meat of the act stated clearly:

> Every master or other officer of any American vessel on the high seas, or on any other waters within the admiralty and maritime juris-

diction of the United States, who, from malice, hatred, or revenge, and without justifiable cause, beats, wounds, or imprisons any of the crew of such vessel, or withholds from them suitable food and nourishment, or inflicts upon them any cruel and unusual punishment, shall be punished by a fine of not more than one thousand dollars, or by imprisonment of not more than five years, or by both.

Those words, enacted into law by the United States in the Act of March 3, 1835, looked good on paper. However, for American seamen they proved to be relatively meaningless, as a master's word carried far greater weight than the average nineteenth century seaman's. It is ironic that only days after enactment of that law, the crew of the *Pilgrim* witnessed a brutal and seemingly senseless flogging. On the orders of the master, two seamen were triced up, then spreadeagled and viciously whipped by the enraged captain. His extreme actions made a profound impression on young Dana, who would describe the flogging in graphic detail in his book. While he deplored the captain's flogging of the two men, at the same time he understood the need to maintain order and discipline. Dana even seemed to feel some compassion for the captain, mentioning the loneliness and heavy responsibilities and frustrations that could drive a seemingly reasonable man such as Captain Thompson to commit such a violent act against another human being. That understanding aside, the cruelty of the actions of Thompson and masters like him was not to be dismissed by Dana. In his book, published five years after the flogging, Dana "vowed that if God should ever give me the means, I would do something to redress the grievances and relieve the sufferings of that poor class of beings, of whom I then was one."[4]

At the conclusion of *Two Years Before the Mast* Dana expressed concern about the status of maritime law. He recognized that the power and absolute authority of the master must be sustained, noting the many lives and considerable property for which a ship's master is responsible. He recognized, too, that seamen are often dangerous and of the lowest classes—men prone to exaggeration and false claims—although Dana knew from firsthand experience that many complaints of seamen were well founded. He felt, probably correctly, that long voyages on ships carrying only cargo tended to be more troublesome than shorter passages or voyages where passengers might provide friendly witness for abused seamen. Should a seaman's complaint result in a trial, the system was heavily weighted in favor of the master, who could generally produce more credible witnesses of the nature of ship's owners, other ship's officers, family members, and individuals from the master's home community who would not hesitate to attest to his character. After all, it was not uncommon for a hard-driving master to wear two personalities. This enabled him to be an upstanding citizen during those short periods at home between voyages when he was neither agitated by complaining seamen nor overburdened by the responsibilities and burdens connected to the operation of his ship. Seamen who lived a more migrant lifestyle had fewer opportunities to be so well represented.

Assessing all sides, Dana seemed to question whether legislation that might hamper a master's authority was the whole answer to the seaman's problems. He urged that ship's masters be better educated and of a higher moral level, stressing highly the role religion might play in this regard. He suggested that religion and religious-based institutions and societies could also play a role in developing a better class of seamen, noting strides being taken by the American Seamen's Friend Society, Windward-Anchor Societies, seamen's bethels, and the like. "The good a single religious captain can do can hardly be calculated [in establishing] a kinder state of feeling" on board the ship.[5]

While Dana was perhaps on the right track in his desire to make ships and shipboard life kinder and more comfortable for seamen, he overlooked a salient fact. If a master made money for the ship's owners, those owners—who often included the master—saw no incentive for changing the status quo or for inquiring what transpired once the ship left port. For most shipping companies, "Out of sight, out of mind" was the motto to follow. Those masters who felt they were king once land faded away in the distance generally had, if not the law, then at least the system on their side.

Ten years after publication of *Two Years Before the Mast*, the United States Congress, by its act of September 28, 1850, took a step to lessen the abuse of seamen when it decreed, "Flogging on board vessels of commerce is hereby abolished." Despite its good intent, still the abuses continued.

In the late 1800s, a period of early labor militancy, the responsibility for American seamen was in the purview of the Treasury Department, Bureau of Navigation. With an eye to establishing laws for the better protection of American seamen, Commissioner of Navigation Eugene Tyler Chamberlain had been studying the subject in Europe. At the same time, a team made up of Special Treasury Agents Baldwin, Irving, and Durham was set up to examine and suggest legislative reforms that could rid the industry of the long-existing abuses that were making it so difficult to obtain good seamen for American ships. In reinforcing the claim that seamen on American ships suffered more from brutality and poor food than those of most other nations, Baldwin was quoted as saying that American seamen were underpaid, underfed, overworked, and "generally driven about like slaves."[6] The bad reputation of American ships was far-reaching. In 1902, British author A. Basil Lubbock, himself a former seaman under the red ensign, wrote, perhaps with a degree of exaggeration:

> On some of the Yankee hellships, the things that go on are almost incredible, and the captains have to be skilled surgeons to cope with the work of destruction wrought by their mates. Legs and arms broken were considered nothing, ribs stamped in by heavy sea boots had to mend as best they could, faces smashed like rotten apples by iron belaying pins had to get well or fear worse treatment, eyes closed up by a brawny mate's fist had to see. There have been many instances of men triced up in the rigging, stripped, and then literally skinned alive with deck scrapers. Thus the reputation of American ships has got so bad that none but a real tough citizen or a stolid long-suffering Dutchman (as sailors call all Germans, Swedes, Norwegians, or Russian-Finns) will ship in them.[7]

Seamen like Andrew Furuseth (see plate 19), who first went to sea in 1873 aboard the bark *Marie* out of Draman, Norway, and who later sailed on American ships, knew from firsthand experiences the abuse and ill-treatment to which seamen were subject. Furuseth was particularly incensed by the hiring system to which many seamen were tied and by which they were victimized. It was an economic system involving masters, operators of boardinghouses, and middlemen or agents known commonly as "crimps." Since many masters would hire only men supplied by crimps, seamen who wanted to go to sea were forced to become victims of the triangle. Once entangled in the web, escape was all but impossible.[8] Exactly when Furuseth first came up against the crimp system is unclear, but for certain he fell into its clutches once he arrived in San Francisco in 1880 and made one of the cooperating boardinghouses his home base. As long as he was part of the system, he had no difficulty finding a ship, but after he and some friends—also seamen—moved from the boardinghouse into an independent rooming house sometime in early 1885, Furuseth found work hard to come by. Once it took him six weeks to locate a master who would sign him on. Fed up with the boardinghouse crimp system, but realizing he could not buck it alone, on June 3, 1885, Andrew Furuseth applied for membership in the fledgling Coast Seamen's Union (CSU).[9] At about the time that

Furuseth joined the CSU, the organization established its headquarters at 6 Eddy Street in San Francisco. In 1887 Furuseth was elected to the powerful position of secretary of the CSU.[10] Thereafter he would devote his life to the improvement of conditions for seafarers.

Early in his tenure with the CSU and in order to make the union a more visible organization, Furuseth urged establishment of a newspaper, something no other seamen's organization had up to that time. He envisioned the newspaper as a tool to further the union's objectives. The weekly publication, the *Coast Seamen's Journal*, made its debut on November 2, 1887, under the direction of its first editor, Xavier H. Leder. The opening message of the first issue announced in somewhat flowery terms,

> With a feeling of natural pride, we venture to present to the public this opening issue of the *Coast Seamen's Journal*—beyond a doubt the first newspaper that has ever been published exclusively in behalf of the myriads who live upon the watery part of this globe of ours, the seafaring class. In taking this step, we do not lend ourselves to any delusion; we fully conceive the immensity of our task. Descendants, as we are, of the House of Want, and the pupils of such grim teachers as extreme hardship and continuous toil, we have even now a woeful apprehension of the scolding, cuffing, and general ill-treatment which this offspring of ours is to receive, especially at the hands of that class of parasites who have grown corpulent and lazy on the hard earnings, the ignorance, and the proverbial generosity of the sailors. How they will hate its voice; how they will endeavor to stifle it; how they will employ each conceivable soothing charm to rock it to sleep again—for its voice, tiny and insignificant as it may seem, is a menace to their objects, a death message to their very existence.

In early 1892 the Coast Seamen's Union and the Steamshipmen's Protective Union combined into the Sailors' Union of the Pacific (SUP). The new union formed a committee to formulate a comprehensive legislative program that would address the many deplorable conditions faced by seamen. The committee drew up a document titled *An Appeal to Congress* which suggested nearly thirty reforms. Most of those were restrictions against shipowners.[11] The points covered by the *Appeal* ran the gamut from crew size through crew's provisions and quarters to the seaworthiness of a vessel.

In the fall of 1892 the union took its first open step into politics by endorsing for election James G. Maguire, a Democrat from the Fourth Congressional District of California. Maguire, who had served in the California Assembly in 1875 and as Superior Court judge from 1882 to 1888, had most recently been in private law practice.[12]

In return for the union's support of his campaign for election, Maguire became an enthusiastic sponsor of several bills that together could go a long way in ameliorating the seafarer's working conditions. At Maguire's request, Furuseth and Per T. J. Eiderkin journeyed in the spring of 1894 to Washington, where they were joined by Charles Hagen of New Orleans and John R. Bell of New York. The four men, all maritime labor activists, testified on the Maguire bills before the House Committee on Merchant Marine and Fisheries. One of the bills Maguire had introduced provided

> that any master or mate, or other officer of a vessel of the United States who directs or superintends the labor of seamen, who shall unnecessarily place or order any seaman into a position of danger to life or limb, or commit an assault or battery upon a seaman, shall, upon conviction be fined not less than one hundred dollars, nor more than five hundred dollars, or be imprisoned for not less than three months nor more than one year; any punishment which may be inflicted upon the master, mate, or other officer of such vessel will not exempt such vessel from liability for damages for injuries sustained by such seamen, and all vessels are liable for damages for an assault or battery committed by any officer upon a seaman.

The latter wording was unique as it would hold shipowners equally liable for the actions of their shipmasters. Maguire's apparent goal was to provide an economic incentive for shipowners to exercise greater care in hiring their ships' masters. This was a far more muscular approach than anything previously suggested and thus met with considerable opposition from shipowners. To counter some of that opposition, Furuseth enlisted the aid of groups such as the American Seamen's Friend Society, which had a network in place for effectively lobbying members of Congress.[13]

One important factor in the process of pushing Maguire's bill was the dissemination to Congress and the press (and thus the public) of the aforementioned *Appeal* which alleged that public apathy was partly to blame for the poor working conditions of seamen, stating that an uninformed public commonly believed that abuses to seafarers no longer existed after flogging was abolished by the Act of September 28, 1850. The actual truth was that, while the act of flogging had been abolished on commercial vessels, it had been "superseded by the more brutal method of the belaying pin and the handspike."[14] Attached to the *Appeal* was a summary prepared by Walter Macarthur, who had joined the CSU in 1889 and by 1894 had become editor of the *Coast Seamen's Journal*.[15] The summary Macarthur compiled, which is commonly referred to as *The Red Record*, contains details of sixty-four of the worst cases of brutality committed against seamen on U.S.-flag merchant vessels between 1888 and 1895. It is not pleasant reading. The summary was derived from "The Red Record" column, which first began appearing on February 14, 1894, as a feature in the *Coast Seamen's Journal* after Macarthur took over as editor. The column was headed by an engraving, printed in bright red ink, of a hand gripping a blood-covered belaying pin (see plate 18) and was clearly intended to inflame the membership of the seamen's union. The cases selected by Macarthur for the *Red Record* summary within Eiderkin's *Appeal* dealt only with incidences of actual physical violence, making no mention of such other abuses and violations of maritime law as inadequate wages, inadequate rations, and inferior or substandard living spaces for crews. Although perhaps isolated instances, these were obviously selected to illustrate the brutality that was occurring within the industry. In his accounts, it seems that Macarthur at times gave rather one-sided presentations, with no space for a defensive reaction that may have been possible in some of the cases cited. That said, there is no reason to believe that there were any outright fabrications on his part.

Forty-six of the sixty-four selected cases were reported at West Coast ports, forty of those at the port of San Francisco. Of the cases summarized by Macarthur, only three convictions resulted—those in trials for murders committed by the most brutish officers. The rest of the cases, including eleven others involving murder, were dismissed for lack of evidence or lack of witnesses, or because the alleged brutality was deemed to have been justifiable discipline (*RR*, 6). Often accused officers disappeared even before they could be arrested. This seems to have been a favorite habit of Captain Edward Robinson Sewall of the ship *Solitaire*, built in 1879 in Bath, Maine. The *Solitaire* arrived in Dunkirk, France, around January 1888. While she was in the English Channel, "the second mate called a seaman from aloft, knocked him down, jumped on his breast and inflicted wounds from which he died the next day." The body was placed in an after hatch. Four days later "the corpse was so black that the bruise could not be distinguished," the claim could be made that the seaman had died of consumption. The second mate of the *Solitaire* fled to England, where he stayed until the ship was ready to go to sea, thus avoiding a trial for murder (*RR*, 13). During the same voyage, Captain Sewall beat up two men for talking while at work.[16] The first mate joined in, breaking the nose of one of the men. On the arrival of the *Solitaire* in Philadelphia more than a year later on April 8, 1889, warrants were issued for the arrest of Captain Sewall and both of his mates on new charges of murder and attempted murder based on statements made by the seamen. In one case, a man hit while aloft fell eighty feet into the buntlines, which saved him. Another wasn't so lucky. When he was struck while aloft, he fell to the deck and died. While the ship was being towed up Delaware Bay, the mates somehow managed to desert and escape. Sewall also disappeared for a time, but not before he had "healed the wounds of all complainants with $440 in cash and proceeded on his way" (*RR*, 15).

Edward R. Sewall's cousin Joseph Ellis Sewall also shows up in *The Red Record*, having arrived in April 1893 at San Francisco aboard the four-masted Bath-built bark *Susquehanna*, which he commanded between 1891 and 1899.[17] Before sailing from New York, he is reported to have made the remark that he would "knock down and kick sailors whenever he felt like it, and moreover that he would use a belaying pin upon their heads and bodies to save hurting his knuckles when he felt disposed to punish one of the crew" (*RR*, 29). When a crewman, a "lime-juicer," charged he had been viciously assaulted on the voyage by the first mate, Sewall feigned ignorance. Without witnesses and evidence, no case could be made. The last entry of *The Red Record* also involves the *Susquehanna* and Joseph E. Sewall. On November 12, 1895, having again arrived in San Francisco from New York, the master and mates were charged with ill-treatment. An arrest warrant was put out for first mate Ross. Sewall threatened that if Ross was arrested, he would lay charges of mutiny against the crew. The case was brought before U.S. Shipping Commissioner Thomas E. Heacock, who Macarthur claimed was a particularly lenient examiner with a tendency to reject charges laid against ship's officers by seamen (*RR*, 40). Heacock dismissed the charges against the *Susquehanna*'s officers.

When the square-rigged ship *Hecla* arrived on April 25, 1894, from Baltimore, the crew brought charges that they had been variously struck with belaying pins, hammers, and marline spikes. The mates were arrested, but the case was dismissed by Heacock for lack of evidence (*RR*, 33). According to charges filed against Captain E. D. P. Nickels, a native of Searsport, Maine, when his ship *May Flint* arrived in San Francisco on August 26, 1895, Nickels had kicked one man in the testicles, causing a permanent rupture, and had "laid bare with a holystone" the face of another. Another man was "beaten for unavoidably spitting on the deck while aloft and another [was] triced up to the spanker-boom for some trifling fault." Here, as in earlier instances, Macarthur's impartiality is rendered somewhat suspect by his own use of such terms as "unavoidably spitting" and "trifling fault." Heacock allegedly examined Nickels and the second mate, exonerating both (*RR*, 38–39).

When the ship *Benjamin F. Packard* arrived on October 24, 1895, from Swansea, Wales, the crew charged that Captain Allen had terrorized them even before the vessel left Swansea and that during the voyage Allen, his mates, and the carpenter assaulted them on numerous occasions. Two crew members swore out warrants for the arrest of the second mate and the carpenter. Before he could be charged, the second mate disappeared. Although the carpenter was detained initially, Heacock dismissed all charges against him for "lack of evidence" (*RR*, 39).

While most of the cases of brutality reported in *The Red Record* centered on the use of belaying pins, knuckle dusters, or bare fists, the second mate on the ship *Tam O'Shanter*, built in Freeport, Maine, was more imaginative. R. Crocker, who stood 6'3" tall and weighed 260 pounds, was charged on arrival in San Francisco with assaulting several seamen. "One in particular, Harry Hill, bore nine wounds, five of them still unhealed," when the *Tam O'Shanter* came into port in July 1893. "A piece was bitten out of his left palm, a mouthful of flesh was bitten out of his left arm, and his left nostril torn away as far as the bridge of his nose" (*RR*, 31). Crocker had also kicked the seaman out of "pure devilment." This case at least went to court, and Crocker was held pending trial on $500 bail. But even though the seaman still had visible wounds, Crocker was acquitted. In October 1893 Crocker was again arrested, this time on charges stemming from a voyage on the full-rigged ship *Francis*, built in Bath. The case was dismissed for lack of evidence, because the injured party failed to show up for the trial.

Despite the best efforts of the seamen's unions, the Maguire bill never passed, but its goals continued to be pressed by Furuseth to members of Congress. On December 21, 1898, Congress passed a new piece of legislation, the White Act. This act addressed some, but far from all, of the concerns about which Furuseth had lobbied. In fact, an examination of the White Act shows that most of its twenty-four sections did not cover new territory but rather only clarified, tightened, or strengthened existing regulations. Section 22 of the bill is a case in point. Where the 1850 law had simply stated, "Flogging on board vessels of commerce is hereby abolished," Section 22 of the White Act broadened the earlier statute by prohibiting flogging as well as "all other forms of corporal punishment," and it established a penalty. Violators would be guilty of a misdemeanor and subject to imprisonment of up to two years. A flaw of Section 22 of the White Act was that it fell to the master to surrender to the authorities the ship's officer who was guilty of the application of corporal punishment. This ignored the clear reality that the master often was the perpetrator of the crime. Unlike the earlier Maguire bill that had been proposed but did not pass, the White Act lacked teeth, since it had no provision to make either the vessel or the vessel's owner liable for actions by the master or his officers.

Seamen's leaders, led by Furuseth, were rankled that the White Act had left open this large loophole. Furuseth knew well that discipline on board ship was of uppermost concern, and he not only endorsed but staunchly defended the right of masters to punish seamen who disobeyed a lawful command at sea. But discipline needed to have law as its basis. Its exercise could not be at the arbitrary whim of masters and mates. Furuseth and other labor leaders were also upset that it continued to be a criminal rather than a civil offense for a seaman to leave a vessel—even an unseaworthy one—before the end of the term contracted in the shipping articles. To correct these deficiencies, Furuseth again lobbied members of Congress. His efforts were strongly opposed by shipowners, who put up a united front to defeat any new legislation. One of the two exceptions to this opposition was James Rolph Jr., president of Hind, Rolph & Co., whom Furuseth had openly supported in Rolph's recent mayoral campaign in San Francisco. This was an interesting alliance, considering later violations of the law by ships' officers of the *Puako* and the *Rolph* for which Jimmy Rolph's enterprises would be held liable.

Little notice was taken of the union's message until after April 15, 1912, when the *Titanic*, advertised as the safest ship ever built, sank in the North Atlantic with a high loss of life. Although the concern specific to the *Titanic* was safety—the lack of sufficient lifeboats—at last the public's attention was aroused.

The program for seamen's relief which the unions under Furuseth had begun formulating in the late 1800s and for which they had been lobbying continually to Congress over the years was freshly honed and made ready to be turned into legislation. This time, Senator Robert M. LaFollette became the congressional messenger for the cause of American seamen. The majority of the Committee on Merchant Marine and Fisheries reported favorably on the LaFollette bill. The minority, however wrote a blistering report calling the bill extreme and revolutionary, objecting that it was an attempt to dictate to foreign nations, because if it passed, all ships within U.S. waters would eventually become subject to its provisions. "It would also," they said, "encourage the scum of all the foreign sailors" to desert in this country.[18]

Although the minority openly accused the majority of playing politics to win votes in the November presidential election, both sides used the seamen's cause for their own interests. At their convention, the Republicans remembered the seamen in their platform: "We favor the speedy enactment of laws to provide that seamen shall not be compelled to endure involuntary servitude, and that life and property at sea shall be safeguarded by the ample equipment of vessels with life-saving appliances and with full complements of skilled able-bodied seamen to operate them."[19]

Not to be outdone, in their platform adopted July 2, 1912, the Democrats urged "the speedy enactment of laws for the greater security of life and property at sea, and . . . the repeal of all laws and the abrogation of so much of our treaties with other nations as provided for the arrest and imprisonment of seamen charged with desertion or with violation of their contract of service. Such laws and treaties are un-American and violate the spirit, if not the letter, of the Constitution of the United States."[20]

LaFollette's bill introduced in 1912 passed the House and Senate, but at the last moment President William Howard Taft refused to sign it into law. Soon after, Taft was soundly defeated in his bid for reelection, receiving only 8 electoral votes against Woodrow Wilson's 435 and Theodore Roosevelt's 88.

LaFollette reintroduced the bill following Wilson's election. After again passing both houses of Congress, the legislation, which has come to be known simply as the Seamen's Act, was signed into law by President Woodrow Wilson one hour before Congress was scheduled to adjourn on March 4, 1915.[21]

For U.S.-flag vessels, the provisions of the Seamen's Act went into effect eight months following its passage. Foreign-flag vessels operating in U.S. waters became subject to its provisions one year after its signing, with the proviso that it would not take precedence over any standing treaties between the United States and a foreign power. Section 16 directed the president, within ninety days of the act's signing, to serve notice on all foreign governments with which we had treaties and which might be affected.

LaFollette's bill, which recodified many provisions of earlier legislation and added new strictures against abuse, was one of the most far-reaching actions taken to that time by the United States to protect the seamen of its merchant marine. It addressed desertion, advances, allotments, provisions, wages, qualifications, crew space, hospital compartments, washing areas, and numerous other matters concerning the living conditions and safety of seamen at sea. Furuseth wrote to Wilson: "In signing the Seamen's Bill, you gave back to the seamen, so far as the United States can do it, the ownership of their bodies, and thus wiped out the last bondage existing under the American flag. The soil of the United States will be holy ground henceforth to the world's seamen. If you should need them, you would only have to call on them."[22]

APPENDIX 2

The Seaman's Diet

The table presented here, drawn from Section 10 of the Seamen's Act, lists the minimum provisions that were to be provided daily to seamen following passage of the act in 1915.

Item	Unit	Sun	Mon	Tues	Wed	Thurs	Fri	Sat
Water	quarts	5	5	5	5	5	5	5
Biscuit	pounds	½	½	½	½	½	½	½
Beef, salt	pound			1¼		1¼		1¼
Pork, salt	pound		1		1		1	
Flour	pound	½		½		½		
Canned meat	pound	1			1			
Fresh bread	pound	1½	1½	1½	1½	1½	1½	1½
Fish, dry, preserved, or fresh	pound						1	
Potatoes or yams	pound	1	1	1	1	1	1	1
Canned potatoes	pound	½					½	
Peas	pint			⅓			⅓	
Beans	pint		⅓		⅓			
Rice	pint		⅓					⅓
Coffee (green berry)	ounce	¾	¾	¾	¾	¾	¾	¾
Tea	ounce	⅛	⅛	⅛	⅛	⅛	⅛	⅛
Sugar	ounces	3	3	3	3	3	3	3
Molasses	pint	½		½		½		
Dried fruit	ounces	3		3		3		
Pickles	pint		¼		¼		¼	
Vinegar	pint			½				½
Corn meal	ounces	4				4		
Onions	ounces	4				4		4
Lard	ounce	1	1	1	1	1	1	1
Butter	ounce	2	2	2	2	2	2	2

Mustard, pepper, and salt sufficient for seasoning.

APPENDIX 3

An Attempt to Weaken the Seamen's Act of 1915

This undated rebuttal was written by Silas Blake Axtell. It first appeared in the May 1919 issue of the monthly magazine *Democracy*. It was reprinted in *A Symposium on Andrew Furuseth*, 145–47.

Senator Calder of New York has recently introduced a bill in the United States Senate to amend the Seamen's Act. Representative Gould of New York has introduced a similar bill in the House of Representatives. The bills propose to do two things.

First: Restore the right of the shipowner to cause the arrest and imprisonment of seamen who desert their ships or break their contracts of hiring.

Second: Repeal the provisions of the Act [Section 4] that give seamen the right to demand half wages earned in any loading or discharging port after the voyage is commenced.

These are the provisions of the Act that caused the opposition of owners of foreign vessels, for the most part, foreigners.

The people of the United States are deeply concerned in these provisions, for a large part of our national prosperity depends on our ability to get out goods to foreign markets cheaply and quickly. Our capacity to manufacture is four times our capacity to consume, and unless we have proper outlet for our manufactured goods, our factories must be closed from time to time and men laid off. This means idleness and hardship, discontent and unrest.

We don't intend to depend upon our competitors to deliver our goods any longer. To do it ourselves, we must have ships. In 1922 we will have twenty million tons, or nearly one-half of the world's prewar tonnage. We desire seamen; we want American seamen. Yet we cannot get them if the old way of things is restored.

We may get the East Indians and Chinamen, the Coolies and Malays, and perhaps some few Japanese, to work as slaves in antiquated hot fire-rooms or scrub decks under the domination of a brutal boatswain or first officer. But free American boys will never enter such a calling. We don't want them to. Centuries ago shore servants and sea servants were both slaves; one class bound to the soil and sold with it, and the other to the ship. The former class were gradually liberated, but the seamen remained a slave to his ship under the laws of all nations, until America set him free by the Seamen's Act of March 4th, 1915.

Shall we again enslave him? The American people would sooner do without a merchant marine than enslave any class of workmen.

However, these very provisions are the principles of the Seamen's Act and are its chief business assets. By giving the seamen freedom to leave their ships, wages heretofore vastly unequal have been equalized on American and foreign vessels in the same trade. Hence the opposition of Mr. Foreigner, and also, I am sorry to state, Mr. American, who had his money in foreign ships.

Broadly speaking, these bills declare for the forces of conservation, reaction, property.

The Seamen's Act declares for the rights of human beings to be free, or reasonably so, on shipboard. These bills urge antiquated methods of doing business, and operating ships.

The Seamen's Act stimulates the forces of America's inventive genius and efficiency to fullest functioning.

Which will win?

Already thousands of the ablest and most intelligent of foreign races have declared their intention of becoming American seamen. Unless foreign nations quickly grant to their seamen similar or greater rights, privileges and liberties, and afford them better treatment, living conditions and food than is afforded by American shipowners, they will have no able or intelligent seamen left.

In the meantime we are building oil burners, thereby reducing the fire-room crew by 90%, and the total crew cost by about 35%. We are doing away with the dirtiest, heaviest and hottest job on shipboard. We are manufacturing labor and time-saving devices for loading and unloading that far excel foreign inventions. Modern coal burning vessels will soon be antiquated and unprofitable.

Meanwhile the Seamen's Act has equalized the wage operating cost and given us seamen. Only by the maintenance and enforcement of its principles, can we ever hope to induce a steady and growing stream of loyal and intelligent American boys to go to sea.

Thousands of alien seamen are becoming citizens of the United States under the stimulus of the Seamen's Act. It is our task to Americanize them, and take immediate steps to give all merchant seamen absentee voting privileges.

The Act is worthy of the great man who conceived it—Andrew Furuseth. He is less an organizer of labor than a humanitarian and statesman. Some day his great contribution to America at a timely moment will get deserved recognition.

Author's Note: Following Furuseth's death on January 22, 1938, Secretary of Labor Frances Perkins allowed his body to lie in state in the Department of Labor, an honor never before accorded to any American labor leader. Paul Scharrenberg, Furuseth's colleague, later carried the old seaman's ashes to Savannah, Georgia, where he transferred them to the custody of Captain Thomas F. Webb of the American steamship *Schoharie*. In mid-Atlantic, Captain Webb stopped his ship. The ceremony Webb conducted may have included a reading of the tribute Scharrenberg had written to honor his friend:

> When I am dead—
> Then take my ashes far from shore
> And scatter them upon the waves,
> For I have loved the restless sea
> And all the years of life I've known
> Were ever lashed by storm and swept
> By lightning flame and driving hail;
> And I at close of day would sleep
> Where all God's wildest storms of Earth
> Shall thunder requiems for me—
> When I am dead.

APPENDIX 4

Lyrics from *Songs of the Workers: To Fan the Flames of Discontent*

Leaders of the radical Industrial Workers of the World movement wrote songs designed to recruit and rally members. Many of these were published in the IWW songbook that the mates of the *Puako* found when they made a search of the fo'c'sle. The lyrics from some of the songs are reproduced below. They were not read aloud in the courtroom; however, by agreement with the court, they were introduced into the trial record and were made available to the jury as part of the testimony (folios 2795-811) given by second mate Adolph Eric Pedersen in the trial *United States vs Adolph Cornelius Pedersen, Leonard Roy Pedersen, and Adolph Eric Pedersen*. The lyrics give a clear indication of the revolutionary nature of the labor organization.

Workingmen, Unite

by E. S. Nelson (Tune: "Red Wing")

Conditions they are bad, and some of you are sad.
You cannot see your enemy, the class that lives in luxury.
You workingmen are poor, will be forevermore
As long as you permit the few to guide your destiny.
    Shall we still be slaves and work for wages?
    It is outrageous—has been for ages;
    This earth by right belongs to toilers,
    And not to spoilers of liberty.
The master class is small, but they have lots of "gall."
When we unite to gain our right, if they resist we'll use our might.
There is no middle ground; this fight must be one round.

To victory, for liberty, our class is marching on.
Workingmen, unite! We must put up a fight
To make us free from slavery and capitalistic tyranny.
This fight is not in vain; we've got a world to gain.
Will you be a fool, a capitalist tool, and serve our enemy?

Scissor Bill

by Joe Hill (Tune: "Steamboat Bill")

You may ramble around the country anywhere you will,
You'll always run across the same old Scissor Bill.
He's found upon the desert; he is on the hill.
He's found in every mining camp and lumber mill.
He looks just like a human; he can eat and walk.
But you will find he isn't when he starts to talk.
He'll say, "This is my country," with an honest face,
While all the cops they chase him out of every place.
   Chorus:
   Scissor Bill, he is a little dippy,
   Scissor Bill, he has a funny face,
   Scissor Bill should drown in Mississippi,
    He is the missing link that Darwin tried to trace.
And Scissor Bill, he couldn't live without the booze,
He sits around all day and spits tobacco juice.
He takes a deck of cards and tries to beat the Chink,
Yes, Bill would be a smart guy if he only could think.
And Scissor Bill he says: "This country must be freed
From Niggers, Japs, and Dutchmen, and the gol durn Swede."
He says that every cop would be a native son
If it wasn't for the Irishman, the sonnafur gun.
   Chorus:
   Scissor Bill, the "foreigners" is cussin;
   Scissor Bill, he says, "I hate a coon";
   Scissor Bill is down on everybody
    The Hottentots, the bushmen and the man in the moon.
Don't try to talk your union dope to Scissor Bill,
He says he never organized and never will,
He always will be satisfied until he's dead.
With coffee and a doughnut and a lousy old bed.

And Bill, he says he gets rewarded thousand fold,
When he gets up to Heaven on the streets of gold,
But I don't care who knows it, and right here I'll tell,
If Scissor Bill is goin' to Heaven, I'll go to Hell.
  Chorus:
  Scissor Bill, he wouldn't join the union,
  Scissor Bill, he says, "Not me, by Heck!"
  Scissor Bill gets his reward in Heaven,
  Oh, sure. He'll get it but he'll get it in the neck.

The White Slave

by Joe Hill (Tune: "Meet Me Tonight in Dreamland")

  One little girl fair as a pearl
  Worked every day in a laundry.
  All that she made for food she paid,
  So she slept on a park bench so soundly.
  An old procuress spied her there.
  She came and whispered in her ear.
Chorus:
Come with me now, my girly, don't sleep out in the cold.
Your face and tresses curly will bring you fame and gold.
Automobiles to ride in, diamonds and silk to wear,
You'll be a star bright, down in the red-light,
You'll make your fortune there.
  Same little girl, no more a pearl,
  Walks all alone 'long the river,
  Five years have flown; her health is gone.
  She would look at the water and shiver,
  Whene'er she'd stop to rest and sleep
  She'd hear a voice call from the deep:
[*Chorus*]
  Girls in this way fall every day
  And have been falling for ages.
  Who is to blame? You know his name.
  It's the boss that pays starvation wages.
  A homeless girl can always hear
  Temptations calling everywhere.

GLOSSARY OF TECHNICAL AND/OR OBSCURE TERMS

Bark: A sailing vessel that is square-rigged on the fore, main, and mizzen masts and is fore-and-aft-rigged on the after mast (Bradford). Referenced by some authorities as a ship.

Barkentine: A sailing vessel that is square-rigged only on the foremast, her remaining rigging being fore-and-aft (Bradford).

Belaying pin: "A device of brass, iron or wood which is set in the pin or fife rails for securing the running rigging" (Bradford). Given the amount of secured lines aboard a large vessel such as a barkentine, large numbers of these pins were readily available for use as a "disciplinary tool" by a so-inclined ship's officer.

Billet-head: "A small scroll used in place of a more pretentious figurehead" (Bradford).

Brass knuckles or **knuckle dusters**: A set of rings permanently attached to a bar that can be fitted over the fingers to increase the impact of a blow with the fist. Easily concealable, it was a favorite weapon aboard ship.

Bucko: A bully, particularly one who uses physical means to dominate employees (*Webster's*). During the days of sail, "bucko" was a term most often used in connection with overzealous mates.

Bull Durham: A brand of loose tobacco packaged in a pouch and used to make hand-rolled cigarettes.

Certificate of Registry: A document carried by U.S.-flag ships engaged in foreign trade. Until 1907, U.S.-flag vessels over 20 tons engaged in the domestic coasting trade were required to possess a Certificate of Enrollment. After 1907, that document was changed to a Consolidated Enrollment and License. Every U.S.-flag vessel engaged in commercial trade must possess either a Registry or an Enrollment, depending on its type of service (*Badger vs Gutierrez*, LA. 1884, 4 S Ct, 563, 111 US 734, 28 L.Ed.581). All of these documents are issued by collectors of customs.

Consulate General: A large consulate headed by a consul general. The United States maintained a consulate general in Cape Town. In other ports discussed in this work, such as those in Australia and Chile, the United States had smaller consulates, headed by a consul.

De bene esse: In anticipation of future need. To depose "de bene esse" is to examine an important witness in advance of a trial with the understanding that the testimony so taken may be used during trial in the event the witness cannot be present in person (Black).

Elliptical stern: "A form of stern with short counter in which the upper part above the knuckle is approximately an elliptical cone enlarging upward from the knuckle, the surfaces below being a continuation of the forms of the ship's bottom. Also called a round stern" (Kerchove).

Fathom: A measure of water depth equaling six feet.

Handspike: A bar used as a lever for various purposes, as in moving weights or heaving about a cargo; also, a short spike used for splicing wire cable (Kerchove).

Hold: Generically, a storage space on a ship below deck, usually for stowage of cargo. More particularly, a space located between the weather deck and the bottom of the ship (Kerchove). The *Puako* seamen used the term "hold" to refer both to the lazarette and to a small storage locker adjacent to the after cabin. The "pump hold" on the *Puako* was a confined area created by stacked lumber where the ship's bilge pump was housed.

Intervenor: A person or party that with permission of the court voluntarily joins or interposes in an action (Black's).

Lime juicer: A British vessel and/or seaman. The name stems from British law which required that a ration of lime juice be distributed on a regular basis to prevent scurvy (Bradford).

Marline spike: "A pointed steel tool about 16 inches long, used by riggers and seamen to separate strands of rope when splicing and also as a lever when putting on seizing, marling, etc." (Kerchove). Another handy object used against seamen by "bucko mates."

Proctor in admiralty: An attorney specializing in admiralty (maritime) law. Prior to the unification of the civil rules and the admiralty rules in 1966, a proctor in admiralty was an individual qualified to practice on "the admiralty side" of the court, where a special terminology and procedure were used: the complaint was called the "libel," the plaintiff was the "libellant," the defendant the "respondent," and admiralty lawyers themselves referred to as "proctors," a term that dates to the thirteenth century in England.

Rations: Minimal food allowances required by law to be issued to every seaman aboard an American ship. Appendix 2 contains the complete scale of provisions stipulated by the Seamen's Act of 1915.

NOTES

Chapter 1. Cape Town, 1917

1. Matthews, *American Merchant Ships*, 1:62. Matthews misspelled Pedersen's name.

2. Although the legal term for the person in command of a merchant ship is "master," the familiar term that has come to be used when referring to a ship's master is "captain." Ship masters possess master's licenses; they do not possess a "captain's license," which is a recent misuse referring to a license to operate a commercial vessel of less than 100 gross tons. While I have usually used the term "master" in generically discussing a person's command position aboard a vessel, often when discussing Adolph Cornelius Pedersen and other specific ship's masters, I have used the familiar term "captain." This follows the pattern within the trial transcripts I examined.

3. *Record of the American Bureau of Shipping* (1905), 888.

4. An examination of the *Puako*'s documents at NARA in Washington, D.C., indicates that when Pedersen first took command she was operating in foreign trade under a Certificate of Registry issued September 17, 1907, in San Francisco. This was surrendered March 18, 1908, and replaced by a Certificate of Enrollment when her home port was changed to Honolulu and her trade was changed to domestic. This in turn was surrendered April 27, 1908, and replaced with a new Certificate of Enrollment when the ship's home port was changed to San Francisco and her owner changed from George U. Hind to James Rolph Jr. On June 10, 1908, at Port Townsend, Washington, the *Puako* was issued a Certificate of Registry allowing her to again participate in foreign trade, with A. C. Pedersen named as agent and master. More changes came on October 16, 1909. The Certificate of Enrollment issued that day names the owner as the Barkentine Puako Company, George Hind secretary, A. C. Pedersen master. It was then and remains today a common practice for a corporation—often a subsidiary of a parent corporation—to be established for the sole purpose of ownership of a particular ship. This is done for two major reasons. It limits the liability to the value of the ship and thus safeguards the parent corporation. It also provides a structure whereby individuals may purchase or be

given a share in the ownership of that ship. In the case of the *Puako*, for instance, Adolph Cornelius Pedersen owned two shares, which was equivalent to one-thirty-second ownership in the vessel (see letter, Hind, Rolph & Co. to Secretary Lansing, October 24, 1918, Bureau of Navigation file 101975). A Certificate of Registry issued November 22, 1909, showed no change of master or owner. The next trade change occurred on March 7, 1911; that Certificate of Enrollment shows James Rolph Jr. as president of the Barkentine Puako Company. There followed: April 25, 1911, Certificate of Registry; November 16, 1911, Consolidated Certificate of Enrollment and License (note the new document title for vessels participating in domestic trade); December 23, 1911, Certificate of Registry; December 7, 1914, Consolidated Certificate of Enrollment and License; January 30, 1915, Certificate of Registry; August 4, 1915, Consolidated Certificate of Enrollment and License; September 17, 1915, Certificate of Registry. These frequent document changes indicate that during this period she operated back and forth between foreign and domestic trade. Her last document, a Certificate of Registry, was issued February 8, 1918. This was surrendered August 4, 1925, at which point she was "sold foreign" to a Canadian buyer. A. C. Pedersen was named as master on all of these latter documents. Although Eric Pearson and Charles E. Helms served as master after Pedersen was detained in 1918 in Cape Town and later arrested in New York in 1919, their names do not appear as endorsements on the documents held at the NARA archives.

5. DOS 196.3/35. Unless otherwise noted, quotations in this chapter are from this Department of State file.

6. Under the provisions of Section 4 of the Seamen's Act, the discharged seamen were due in full all earned wages.

7. By June 1917, war-related demands on shipping were already tightening the labor market, and Pedersen probably would have had a hard time replacing these two men.

8. When the gasoline engine was inoperative, the crew manually operated the pump using cranks, although this was far less efficient. The *Puako* also carried a small amount of coal to fire her steam-driven donkey engine, which was used to load and unload cargo, hoist sails at the beginning of a voyage, and weigh the ship's anchor. The donkey engine was rarely used to adjust sails at sea because it took too long to bring up steam and consumed too much fresh water. See trial transcript, folio 2616. (Unless otherwise specified, "trial transcript" hereafter refers to the appeal *Adolph Cornelius Pedersen, Leonard Roy Pedersen, and Adolph Eric Pedersen vs United States of America*, heard in New York City during the October 1920 term of the United States Circuit Court of Appeals, Second Circuit.)

9. Quotes in this paragraph and the next are from DOS 196.3/42.

10. It is not known whether Pedersen and/or his employer, Hind, Rolph & Co., ever knew such a hearing had taken place.

Chapter 2. Vancouver-Victoria, B.C., April 1918

1. Quotes in this paragraph and the next are from Weisberger, "Here Come the Wobblies!" 87–90.
2. See Weintraub, *Andrew Furuseth*, 159, 163.
3. See Lyman, "Pacific Coast–Built Sailors," 2.
4. Blume, "The Hairy Ape Reconsidered." Blume's tables are specific only to the late 1800s; however, they show a trend that continued into the 1900s as the gap widened in wages paid within various segments of the American merchant marine. In 1905, the year Pedersen assumed his first command, there were 490 U.S.-flag sailing ships in excess of 1,000 gross tons. By 1917 that number had dropped to 371, and it would continue to decline as the numbers of large-tonnage steamships increased. See *Merchant Vessels of the United States* for the years 1905 and 1917.
5. Consular form no. 79 contains an error concerning the vessel's routing. The form states the ship was "bound to South Africa via Australia and Philippine Islands." The actual planned routing was directly to South Africa via Cape Horn, thence to Australia, thence to the Philippine Islands, from where the ship was to return to California with a possible stop at Honolulu. Although the ship's papers were all dated April 24, 1918, the *Puako* did not actually depart from Victoria until April 27.
6. The consular forms and cable are found in DOS 196.3/106, enclosure 10.
7. Trial transcript, folios 2324–25.
8. Logbook entries indicate that Captain Pedersen expressed time based on 12-hour cycles rather than the 24-hour cycle that is standard today aboard ship. Under the 24-hour cycle, 7 a.m. would have been expressed as 0700, and 7 p.m. as 1900 hours.
9. Department of State records and trial records both refer to this vessel incorrectly as *Soldack*. The ferry *Sol Duc*, home port Seattle, O.N. 210133, was a 189-foot passenger vessel built in Seattle in 1912.

Chapter 3. Off Cape Town, August 27, 1918

1. Around 1901 the International Code for Signal Flags was changed to Y-F. Prior to that change, the two-flag signal for "want assistance; mutiny" was P-C. For signal flag codes, see *The International Code of Signals for the Use of All Nations*, 44.
2. DOS 196.3/106. All quotes in this chapter, unless otherwise noted, are from this Department of State file.
3. Although William Clark Russell (1844–1911) was born in New York, he is remembered as an "English novelist." After leaving the British merchant service in 1866, he took up a literary career. His fifty-seven novels of the sea include such titles as *An Ocean Tragedy*, *The Emigrant Ship*, and *The Convict Ship*. He is perhaps best known for *The Wreck of the Grosvenor*. His books stimulated public interest in

the deplorable conditions under which seafarers existed and helped pave the way for reforms.

4. Bureau of Navigation file 101975.

5. Excerpts copied by Captain Howe from *Puako*'s official logbook and the full text of all statements turned over by Pedersen are in DOS 196.3/106, as is Howe's complete report.

6. A daily logbook kept by one or both of the mates was found days later during a police search of the ship. Unbeknownst to Police Sub-inspector Captain Howe, Captain Pedersen had also kept a personal diary or daybook, which he kept hidden and spirited ashore before he was removed from command of the ship. The existence of the master's daybook would come to light months later during a trial to be held in New York.

7. Reilly's remarkable statement is item 2-h of DOS 196.3/106.

8. Reilly incorrectly referred to this man as Levi Maxwell. He was Maxwell Levy.

9. Which seamen's union Hansen belonged to is not made clear in any statements or trial record available to me.

10. Englebach's report is item 2-m of DOS 196.3/106.

11. Bureau of Navigation file 101975.

12. DOS 196.3/52.

13. DOS 196.3/79.

14. Bureau of Navigation file 101975.

15. DOS 196.3/79.

Chapter 4. Digesting the Official Logbook

1. Bureau of Navigation file 101975.

2. DOS 196.3/106. Unless otherwise noted, quotations in this chapter are from this Department of State file.

3. The stiff monetary penalties that Pedersen might have faced for noncompliance were contained in Section 60 of the act; however, from a strict reading of the regulation, these would normally be assessed only following the arrival of a vessel at her final port of discharge—in other words, at the completion of the entire voyage. Pedersen was removed from the *Puako* months before she reached her final destination.

4. See chart *The World Sailing Ship Routes*.

5. Trial transcript, folios 2936–37. When this statement was read into the trial record by the government's attorney, S. Lawrence Miller, Dolph (as the second mate was by then known) claimed that he had not personally written the last few words, "stick his sunken mush up to Jesus any more." Without extending the trial by calling on handwriting experts, there was no way to either prove or dispute Dolph's claim, leaving the question: If Dolph did not write it, who did?

6. Croton oil, which has a cathartic action too violent for human use, is obtained from the seeds of a tropical Asian shrub or small tree, *Croton tiglium*.

7. It is not clear whether Pedersen wrote "9 miles per hour" or whether Howe's typist misunderstood nautical terminology and used that wording. The correct term for a ship's speed is "knots." The term "9 knots" means 9 nautical miles per hour; it is incorrect to state a vessel's speed as "knots per hour."

8. Since this entry is out of chronological order, one might initially suspect that an error by a typist in Howe's office may have changed this entry from August 13 to August 3, but that is unlikely. Jensen's signature appears on a number of unbound statements, each one dated August 3 and all aligning themselves with Pedersen's log entry. It is impossible to ascertain when the entries were actually written.

9. Schevek, who was determined to be fictitious, was in other confessions variously identified as Schlanger or Schlager with the first initial J or L.

Chapter 5. The "Plot" Enlarges

1. These statements are all contained in DOS 196.3/106.

2. Joe Hill, an IWW leader, had composed many of the society's radical songs, such as "The White Slave" and "Scissor Bill." The lyrics of both songs are reproduced in appendix 4. Following his execution in 1915 for the murder of a Utah grocer, Hill became a martyr in the eyes of IWW members.

3. Anyone who has spent time at sea as a crew member is not surprised at the repetitious emphasis on the quantity and quality of food. A warm meal, even if it was not a tasty one, was one of the few pleasures a seaman could look forward to. This was especially true on sail vessels when men were exposed to the elements for hours, even days, on end.

Chapter 6. The Search for the Truth

1. DOS file 196.3/106 contains all of these statements.

2. Pedersen overlooked Bjarne Olsen when he made this assertion. According to crew statements, Olsen, who had shipped as boatswain, had considerable experience which possibly included some knowledge of the art of navigation.

3. There are conflicting stories about how Pedersen came to acquire the songbook. Most likely the book was found by the mates when they made a search of the forecastle. At that time they took a number of personal items including diaries and jewelry. Most of those items were never returned to their owners.

4. The "Society," the Industrial Workers of the World, distributed many pamphlets to attract potential members, but the only piece of IWW literature known to have been on board *Puako* was the small songbook Pedersen initially handed over to Howe.

5. This letter and the reply are items 7-a and 7-b of DOS 196.3/106.

6. The death certificate is reproduced in plate 8. As far as can be determined, no autopsy was performed on Olsen's body.

7. Trial transcript, folios 2271–76.

8. The information for this daily report, which could not be located, came from Captain Pedersen's daybook.

9. Bureau of Navigation file 101975.

10. Lester Jensen deposition, *Lester Jensen vs Barkentine Puako Company*.

11. Letter, Hind, Rolph & Co. to Secretary Lansing, October 3, 1918, Bureau of Navigation file 101975.

12. During one of the trials of the Pedersens in 1919, their attorney, Dudley Field Malone, took issue with the way the three *Puako* officers had been handled. He insinuated that George Murphy had acted outside the law when he enlisted the assistance of South African Immigration officials. In various communications Murphy seemed to vacillate as to whether John Walter Campbell would be a defense or prosecution witness. Mattson was always viewed by Murphy as a defense witness, although he ended up as a government witness.

13. As earlier noted, when the *Puako* left Cape Town under her new master, Smithson and Jorgensen decided to resail on her rather than return to the United States as material witnesses. And Olsen did not live to testify.

14. DOS 196.3/73.

Chapter 7. Transportation Secured

1. Navy Department file 20958-823, A4, enclosure 21123.

2. DOS 196.3/82 is quoted here and in the next two paragraphs.

3. Bureau of Navigation file 101975.

4. This dispatch is in DOS 196.3/110.

5. In October 1918 when the outbreak of influenza was at its peak in Cape Town, 250 to 300 persons—60 percent of them of working age—died each day in the city. See trial transcript, folio 3063; Barry, *The Great Influenza*, 239.

6. This dispatch is item 4-a of DOS 196.3/106.

7. DOS 196.3/122.

8. DOS 196.3/125.

9. DOS 196.3/127.

10. DOS 196.3/112. On March 29, 1919, U.S. Marshal Thomas D. McCarthy submitted a statement of expenses totaling $4,689.62 for the incarceration and transportation of the Pedersens, the witnesses, and their guards for the period January 1 through March 31, 1919. The bulk of those expenses were incurred in Cape Town by the consul general. The guards, Edmund Joseph Tuohy and James Keely (or possibly Kealy), were relieved in England once the men came under the custody of the U.S. Navy Department.

11. DOS 196.3/118.

12. Department of State records misidentify the USS *Woolsey* as a torpedo boat. She was in fact a destroyer. During 1918 and 1919 the *Woolsey* was engaged in regular

cross-channel runs between southern England and Brest. See *Dictionary of American Naval Fighting Ships*, 8:461.

Chapter 8. Captain and Son Indicted for Murder

1. When the seamen witnesses were finally released months later, the government gave each a check which represented the maximum allowable of $1.00 per day for "witnesses or seamen who are sent to the United States from a foreign port to give testimony in any criminal case tried in any court of the United States" (Act of February 26, 1853, Section 3).

2. DOS 196.3/138.

3. Sometime around 1859 the New York Quarantine Station, which had been located on Staten Island near Fort Wadsworth, was relocated to two small artificial islands below the Narrows; see Albion, *New York Port*, 219. Although the quarantine station no longer exists there, ruins of its buildings are still evident on one of the islands, now called Swinburne Island.

4. In the murder trial, Judge Charles Merrill Hough took the matter under advisement but let the trial proceed. When the defendants were later found not guilty, the question of jurisdiction became moot. In the second trial, Judge George Whitfield Jack followed Judge Hough's lead and did essentially the same thing, "reserving to counsel the right to renew his motion later in the trial of the case or when the evidence is all in"; see trial transcript, folio 75.

5. *New York Times*, April 2, 1919. The *New York Times* stories, which reported daily on the trial's progress, are the only extant record of the murder trial.

6. Charles Merrill Hough, Dartmouth College, class of 1879, was admitted to practice in the state of New York in 1884. He was appointed to the Court of the Southern District of New York (SDNY) in 1906 by President Theodore Roosevelt. After President Wilson appointed him to the Court of the Second Circuit in 1916, Judge Hough continued to serve on an as-needed basis in the SDNY. See *Judges of the United States*.

7. *New York Times*, June 1, 1919. This sensational news hit the wire services and traveled from coast to coast. In Victoria, Cecil Clark, a policeman stationed at the Bastian Street headquarters of the British Columbia Provincial Police, paid particular attention to the news stories. Clark later claimed that he had tried without success to help Pedersen locate three crewmen who in early April 1918 had come on board the *Puako* but had jumped ship prior to signing ship's articles and had rowed ashore in the *Puako*'s boat. In 1967 Clark, who was still fascinated with Captain Pedersen and the *Puako*, wrote a story titled "Hellship Sailed from Victoria," which appeared in the March 12 issue of Victoria's paper the *Daily Colonist*. In that article Clark mentioned not only the *Puako* but also the *Rolph*, a Hind, Rolph & Co. ship on which mayhem had occurred at the hands of mate Frederick "Fighting" Hansen. That mayhem is discussed later in this volume. On August 13, 1972, T. W. Paterson's

article "Hell Ship *Puako* Visited Island" was published in the *Daily Colonist*. In 1974 Paterson incorporated that article with others in a self-published booklet titled *Hellship: A Collection of True Stories of Jinxed Ships, Bucko Mates, and Terror on the High Seas*. Paterson's writings borrowed from Clark's 1967 story. Clark's continuing fascination with the *Puako* story led him to write another feature article published in 1980 in the *Islander*. Clark's embellishments went too far when he stated that "the United States formula for dealing with murder on the high seas had been copied from a very early English statute which prescribed that the prisoners should be arraigned in court in a cage. Though it smacked a little of the days of Captain Kidd, anyway a cage was built and the two prisoners ensconced in it. Their defense counsel, Dudley Field Malone, objected saying the prisoners could not see the witnesses properly nor hear what they said. The cage was abandoned."

Was there in fact a cage, or was that aspect of the story—written some sixty years after the trial—the creation of an elderly author whose memory had begun to play tricks upon him? The record of the murder trial could not be located despite repeated archival searches, so it is not possible to confirm or refute Clark's claim. It is worth noting, though, that none of the East Coast newspaper accounts I have read mentions use of a cage.

8. *New York Times*, June 4, 1919.
9. *New York Times*, June 6, 1919.
10. *New York Times*, June 7, 1919.
11. *New York Times*, June 8, 1919.
12. *New York Times*, June 10, 1919.

Chapter 9. The Government's Second Round

1. The original transcript of this trial involving all three of the Pedersens appears no longer to exist. Repeated searches have failed to turn up any part of it. Fortunately, soon after the defendants were found guilty on several counts, that original transcript was printed for distribution to attorneys and other need-to-know parties during an appeal action, Appeal Case No. 87, U.S. Court of Appeals for the Second Circuit, October 1920 term. It is from a copy of that published transcript that I have worked. All folio numbers in the text and all citations of the "trial transcript" refer to this published transcript.

2. DOS 196.3/179.

3. DOS 196.3/170.

4. *United States vs Pedersen, et al.* was the first case Judge George Whitfield Jack presided at during his term with the United States District Court, Southern District of New York. Jack, born in 1875 in Natchitoches, Louisiana, entered federal judicial service in March 1917 and served until his death on March 15, 1924. See *Judges of the United States*.

5. Because of desperate conditions in Cape Town in the aftermath of the influ-

enza epidemic, Doctor Engelbach, who examined the seamen when they arrived in Cape Town, could not be spared for such a long period to attend the trial.

6. On November 21, 1919, S. Lawrence Miller, age thirty-five, offered his resignation by penned note to Francis G. Caffey, the explanation being his desire to return to private practice. The 1920 New York City directory lists his office at 52 William Street. Between 1925 and at least to 1933, he was an associate at Frueauff, Robinson and Sloan with offices at 67 Wall Street. In 1929 he represented the owner of a painting by Leonardo da Vinci in a suit against an art critic who claimed the painting was not a Leonardo. The well-publicized case seems to have ended in a hung jury. By 1940 Miller was practicing at 25 Broad Street.

7. Dudley Field Malone became well known in legal circles when in June 1925, at the age of forty-five, he joined Clarence Darrow in defending John Scopes, arguing against William Jennings Bryan in what has come to be known as the Scopes Monkey Trial. Following a brilliant twenty-minute oration that Malone delivered to a spellbound courtroom, Bryan told Malone, "Dudley, that was the greatest speech I ever heard" (Ragsdale, "Three Weeks in Dayton," 101.) A search of the Field family's genealogical records held by the Stockbridge (Massachusetts) Public Library failed to establish a familial connection between Dudley Field Malone and American jurist David Dudley Field. The similarity in names was apparently coincidental.

8. Grielen was held primarily in this small boxlike space, which the ship's officers called the paint locker. Occasionally another seaman would be thrown into the storeroom with Grielen, but usually the others were cuffed and put into the lazarette, which the seamen called the hold. Although several were at times also kept in the pump hold, Grielen was never placed there.

9. These were the types of activities for which the Wobblies were known, but Pedersen did not directly charge Grielen with being an IWW member.

10. Worldwide, one of the worst hit cities during the influenza epidemic was Philadelphia. Like Cape Town, it came to a complete standstill. For a vivid description of conditions in Philadelphia in 1918, and hence a better perspective of the situation as it must have existed in Cape Town, see Barry, *The Great Influenza*, 220–27, 321–32.

Chapter 10. The Defense

1. Smithson had opted to return to the *Puako* at Cape Town when the new master, Eric Pearson, was hired. Hind, Rolph & Co. reported to the Department of Justice that after the *Puako* arrived in Australia, Smithson deserted the ship.

2. Although the HMS *Bounty* mutiny was never mentioned in any of the material taken from the *Puako* by Captain Howe or in any of the forced confessions the seamen signed under Pedersen's direction or in depositions of the ship's officers, it should be noted that after Fletcher Christian and his band of mutineers took over HMS *Bounty* from Captain William Bligh in 1790, they eventually settled on

Pitcairn Island, which is still home to a few of their descendents. Captain Bligh, whose reputation over the years has been unjustifiably sullied by a number of writers, successfully brought his loyal crewmen to safety in an open boat after what was arguably the most challenging small-boat voyage in the annals of maritime history.

3. The songs, some reproduced in appendix 4, carried such titles as "Dump the Bosses off Your Back" and "Casey Jones, the Union Scab." The lyrics to the last concluded

Casey Jones went to Hell a-flying,
"Casey Jones," the Devil said, "Oh, fine;
Casey Jones, get busy shoveling sulphur;
That's what you get for scabbing on the S.P. Line."

4. It was common to carry clean sand aboard ships especially for use in scouring and cleaning wooden decks with a holystone. Writer Richard Henry Dana Jr. frequently mentioned clean ships with white decks and described clearly how sailors operated holystones.

Chapter 11. Summations

1. Malone's figures were way off, According to Captain Pedersen, the cargo itself, Oregon pine, was worth $30,000. Added shipping charges brought its total value to about $156,000 on delivery at Cape Town.

2. Bowditch, *American Practical Navigator*, chap. 32, "Ocean Currents."

3. Malone's assertion that he had been "Chief of the Consular Service" was an overstatement. During the seven-month period April 22 to November 22, 1913, when he was an employee of the Department of State, he was a third assistant secretary of state. At that time Wilbur J. Carr was director of the Consular Service. Carr had been appointed to that post on November 30, 1909. As third assistant secretary, Malone had the added duty of chief, Division of Western European Affairs. On May 20, 1913, he was President Wilson's special representative with the rank of envoy extraordinary and minister plenipotentiary at the inauguration of Cuban president General Mario G. Manocal. In bringing his own background into his summation, Malone may have overstretched the rules of protocol in the trial game. William H. Welte, proctor in admiralty, hesitated to speak with certainty about the protocol of the early years of the twentieth century; however, in a December 2003 letter to the author, he said, "It is absolutely improper to argue personal history, at least under today's rules of procedure and case law."

4. In *Regulations Governing the Consular Service of the United States*, 1923, and *Regulations Prescribed for the Use of the Consular Service of the United States*, 1896, Section 355 is identical and thus was definitely in effect in 1913 when Malone was employed by the Department of State.

5. Seamen's Act, Section 7(4).

6. In his sworn statement given at Cape Town, Pedersen had said: "About this

time, the whole crew spoke amongst themselves about committing suicide" (trial transcript, folio 2298).

Chapter 13. Appeal Denied

1. DOS 196.3/233.
2. DOS 196.3/229.
3. DOS 196.3/288.
4. DOS 196.3/297.
5. LaFollette did accept the nomination of the Progressive Party in 1924 and received thirteen electoral votes following a campaign centered on farmer and labor rights.
6. Caldwell, "Utah's First Presidential Candidate."
7. Axtell served Andrew Furuseth as a friend, counselor, and advisor from 1908 to 1938. His discussion of congressional challenges made against the Seamen's Act is reproduced in appendix 3.
8. DOS 196.3/113, 114, 116.
9. According to information provided to this author by proctor in admiralty Graydon S. Staring, Esq., of San Francisco, in 1924 Ira S. Lillick maintained a law office in San Francisco "in which he had a number of colleagues whom he took as partners when he started the firm of Lillick, Geary and Olson in 1928." That firm has undergone various transitions and today operates as Nixon Peabody, LLP.
10. Pedersen's prison file contains a summary of incoming and outgoing correspondence. He and his wife Gertrude wrote each other almost weekly. Son Leonard wrote his father twice while he was himself in jail and three times in the fall of 1922; Dolph (who had begun calling himself Duffie) wrote regularly after September 1921. Pedersen received four letters from the Department of Commerce, two letters from Hind, Rolph & Co., and one letter each from Dudley Field Malone, Charles P. Sweeney, J. A. Fletcher, and George U. Hind. While incarcerated, Pedersen wrote three times to Leonard, a dozen or so times to Dolph, three times to Malone, once to C. O. Andersen of San Francisco, and once to New York attorney E. McDonald.
11. File of Inmate 12262-131, NARA, East Point, Georgia.

Chapter 14. "Fighting" Hansen

1. Frederick Hansen, who would become known as "Fighting" Hansen, is not the "Bully" Hansen mentioned by Newell in *Sea Rogues' Gallery*. "Bully" Hansen is much older and from an examination of photographs bears no resemblance to Frederick "Fighting" Hansen. Descriptions of Hansen were obtained from a Seaman's Identification Certificate that had been issued to him on November 6, 1918.
2. Bureau of Navigation file 122808N.
3. Bureau of Navigation file 101975.
4. As quickly as employment at the Rolph Shipyard expanded, it contracted fol-

lowing the cessation of hostilities. The Rolph Post Office which had opened in 1918 was closed by the postal service in 1921, and the citizens of the community voted to reinstate the original name Fairhaven. On December 22, 1959, the Rolph School District joined with the Samoa School District to form the Peninsula District. A photo of the three-room Rolph School, which today houses the Fairhaven Fire Department, may be found in the photo gallery section of the website www.Humboldt.k12.ca.us.

5. *Victoria (B.C.) Daily Colonist*, March 12, 1967.

6. Quotes concerning this voyage, unless otherwise noted, are from case 17350, *Kohilas vs Barkentine Rolph Company*.

7. Consul's memo, May 20, 1921, in Bureau of Navigation file 122808N.

Chapter 15. Four Davids Take On Goliath

1. According to memos prepared by Consul Voetter following the departure of the *Rolph* from Chile, the Chilean maritime governor (captain of the port) at Mejillones had refused to permit Sorensen to pay off and discharge Kohilas, "considering it undesirable to increase the number of unemployed persons in this section."

2. Although such agreements seem unlikely in the case of the *Rolph* seamen, they did exist in that era. For instance, Captain Pedersen of the *Puako* may have had at least one, with the Welshman William Jones, who was desirous of getting paid passage from Canada to South Africa, where he hoped to work in the mines.

3. Kohilas had not been hired "at the last moment" but rather a few days before the ship sailed. At least two other men were hired after him.

4. The depositions of witnesses such as Healy who resided outside the United States were monitored by American consuls.

5. Walter Macarthur's considerable contributions to the seamen's cause are described in appendix 1.

6. Section 1 of the White Act of December 21, 1898, mandated that masters and chief mates of sail vessels over 700 tons be licensed. When that provision was recodified by the Act of Congress of January 25, 1907, the new wording mandated licensing only of masters. This change probably resulted from pressure by ship owners who, as sail was phasing out to steam power, were finding it increasingly difficult to find licensed mates of sailing ships. Starting in 1898 with the White Act, all mates—chief, second, and third—who served on steam vessels were required to possess a license, but this did not apply to sail vessels.

7. Although Hansen had a license to sail as master on sail vessels over 700 gross tons, it does not appear that he ever held command of anything larger than the four-masted schooner *William H. Smith* of 566 gross tons in which he owned a one-sixteenth share. Hansen was entered on the ship's papers as master of the *William H. Smith* from 1903 to 1916. The schooner carried a crew of nine.

8. Hansen's license as master of sail vessels would come up for the five-year renewal cycle in 1925, but by that time he was behind bars. Since he was unable to ap-

pear for the renewal in person as required, the license automatically lapsed. Hansen was released from prison in 1926. Several years later, on January 18, 1935, J. J. O'Hara, Office of the Solicitor, Department of Commerce sent a memo to Director, Bureau of Navigation and Steamboat Inspection which in part read, "Hansen says that he is a master mariner and now asks that he be granted a full and unconditional pardon which will assist him in obtaining a position as a ship's officer." After reviewing Hansen's file, J. B. Weaver, director of the Bureau, responded on February 28, "It is the opinion of this Bureau that he is not a fit person to be placed in any position where he would have authority over seamen" (NARA, Bureau of Navigation file 122808N).

Epilogue

1. About this time and for a variety of reasons, many of which were no fault of his own, James Rolph Jr. and his shipping enterprises were rumored to be falling on hard times. Because of these circumstances, and just in case there was not enough value in the Barkentine Rolph Company to satisfy a favorable judgment, Hutton had taken out an insurance policy on behalf of his clients. This would assure that one way or another they would obtain any moneys that might be awarded them. In the later case of the *Puako* seamen's libel, there is no definitive indication that papers were ever drawn to arrest that ship. Even if such papers had been drawn and a subsequent order issued, a U.S. marshal could not have acted on the order: after August 5, 1920, when the libel causes for the six *Puako* seamen were collectively filed in federal court in California, the *Puako* never again touched at a U.S. port.

2. Letter, Susan Buss to author, December 1, 2003, outlining the last years of the *Drumwall*, ex *Puako*. Buss is librarian at the Vancouver Maritime Museum. Letter, Rick James to author, December 1, 2005. James has been working with archeologists.

3. Files of John Lyman held by Harold Huycke.

4. Social Security records incorrectly give the date of death for Adolph Eric Pedersen as June 6, 1994. Leonard's obituary, which mentions his brother's death, states incorrectly that Adolph died in January of 1992.

5. NARA, College Park, RG 59, file for George H. Murphy, 250/47/32/01.

Author's Reflections

1. When Congress enacted the White Act in 1898, its goal was to protect seamen from unjustified abuse. However, enforcement of the act's provisions rested with the ship's master, the very person who was often the violator. Lobbyist Andrew Furuseth's attempts to strengthen the enforcement mechanism by making the ship's owners culpable for offenses by ship's officers resulted in the inclusion of Section 9 in the Seamen's Act passed in 1915.

2. Letter collection of Harold Huycke.

Appendix 1. The Evolution of Maritime Laws Affecting Seamen, 1790–1915

1. Clee, "Desertion and the Freedom of the Seaman," 650.
2. Ibid., 261.
3. Judgments of Oléron, Article 5(m), quoted in Clee, 65D.
4. Dana, *Two Years Before the Mast*, 110–15 (quote, 115).
5. Ibid., 407.
6. *The Red Record*, 3.
7. Lubbock, *Round the Horn Before the Mast*, 33–34.
8. Weintraub, *Andrew Furuseth*, 4–7; Schwartz, *Brotherhood of the Sea*, 4–6.
9. Weintraub, *Andrew Furuseth*, 11.

10. For more on the maritime labor movement and on Andrew Furuseth, see Wissmann, *The Maritime Industry*; Hohman, *History of American Merchant Seamen*; Goldberg, *The Maritime Story*; and *A Symposium on Andrew Furuseth*. While these four publications generally agree regarding the history of the early maritime unions, they differ somewhat on dates. The authors at times seem confused about the names of the various labor organizations.

11. Weintraub, *Andrew Furuseth*, 31.
12. Ibid., 32.
13. Ibid., 40.
14. *The Red Record*, 2. Parenthetical references in the text will refer to *The Red Record* as *RR*.

15. Macarthur held the position of editor of the *Coast Seamen's Journal* until early 1900. When he resigned, he was replaced for a short time by John Vance Thompson, who in turn resigned in September 1900. Thompson regained the post of editor in 1921. He was probably not a Wobbly—a member of the Industrial Workers of the World—but he was at times in sympathy with their views, and during his second tenure as editor he allowed their ideas to be expressed in the *Coast Seamen's Journal* (see Weintraub, *Andrew Furuseth*, 160). That editorial policy under Thompson increased the threat the union posed for shipowners.

16. It was a common practice on sailing ships to prohibit talking between seamen when they were on deck watch. While Dana in *Two Years Before the Mast* frequently mentions this and the *Puako* seamen claim this was Captain Pedersen's policy, British seaman Lubbock (*Round the Horn Before the Mast*) and his shipmates were seemingly not under any such restraint. It would take considerable research to determine if the practice was unique to American-flag ships in the days of sail.

17. Macarthur used only the last names of the two captains named Sewall, making it appear that the same man was guilty on all accounts. Nathan Lipfert, librarian and curator at the Maine Maritime Museum, who is intimately familiar with the Sewall family history, was able to separate the offenders and correctly connect each master to his particular ship.

18. Weintraub, *Andrew Furuseth*, 120.

19. Wissmann, *The Maritime Industry*, 317.
20. Ibid.
21. Weintraub, *Andrew Furuseth*, 108–32.
22. Goldberg, *The Maritime Story*, 61. When Furuseth told Wilson that America's seamen would be ready if he needed them, he was alluding to the strong possibility that America, still neutral in March of 1915, might eventually be at war against Germany and that many U.S.-flag merchant ships would be pressed into service carrying troops and military cargoes to the war zones. That call did come in 1917, and America's seamen—those employed on merchant ships as well as those who volunteered to serve on naval and military auxiliaries—played an important role in bringing about the Allied victory. For a synopsis of events leading up to United States involvement in World War I, including Germany's establishment of maritime war-zones, see *The Literary Digest History of the World War*, 9:235–47, and Gibson, *Merchantman? Or Ship of War*, 28–49.

BIBLIOGRAPHY

Documents

An Act to Promote the welfare of American seamen in the merchant marine of the United States; to abolish arrest and imprisonment as a penalty for desertion and to secure the abrogation of treaty provisions in relation thereto; and to promote safety at sea. Public Law 302, 63rd Congress, 3rd Session, 1164. Enacted March 4, 1915. Also known as the *Seamen's Act of 1915.*

Huycke files. Research files of Captain Harold Huycke.

Huycke-Gibson correspondence, 2002–5. Letters relating Captain Harold Huycke's personal knowledge of the West Coast shipping industry and its personalities in the early twentieth century.

U.S. Coast Guard. National Maritime Center, Marine Personnel Division, Mariner Records Branch, Arlington, Va. Service record of Adolph Eric Pedersen.

U.S. Congress. *Seamen's Act of 1915.* See *An Act to Promote the welfare . . .*

U.S. Department of State. Library of the Department of State. Registers for 1914 and 1918. Records of DOS service of Dudley Field Malone and George H. Murphy.

U.S. National Archives and Records Administration (NARA), College Park, Maryland. Record Group 59: Applications and Recommendations for Appointment to the Foreign Service, 1901–1924, box 178, file for George H. Murphy, 250/47/32/01/. Decimal file 196.3: complete Department of State file on *Puako* matter.

U.S. NARA, East Point, Georgia. Records of Department of Justice, Federal Bureau of Prisons. File of Adolph Cornelius Pedersen, Prisoner 12262-131, Atlanta, in 1922 collection.

U.S. NARA, Northeast Region, New York. Record Group 276: United States Court of Appeals for the Second Circuit. Appeal Case 87, October 1920 term: *Adolph Cornelius Pedersen, Leonard Roy Pedersen, and Adolph Eric Pedersen against United States of America.* This published Appeal Transcript of Record contains the only extant transcript of the trial *United States vs Adolph Cornelius Pedersen, Leonard Roy Pedersen, and Adolph Eric Pedersen.*

U.S. NARA, Pacific-Alaska Region, Seattle, Wash. Record Group 21: Civil, Criminal and Admiralty Case Files, 1912–1928. U.S. District Court, Western District of Washington, Northern Division (Seattle), case 7112, *U.S. vs Frederick Hansen.*

———. Record Group 129: Records of the Bureau of Prisons, McNeil Island Penitentiary. Registers of Prisoners Received 1875–1951, and Inmate Photographs, 1899–1923, for Prisoner No. 4326, Frederick Hansen.

U.S. NARA, Pacific Region, San Bruno, Cal. Record Group 21: U.S. District Court, Southern Division for the Northern District of California, First Division, in Admiralty, case 17068, *James Campbell, Libellant vs The Barkentine Puako Co.*; case 17069, *Frank Grielen, Libellant vs The Barkentine Puako Co.*; case 17070, *Lester A. Jensen, Libellant vs The Barkentine Puako Co.*, case 17071, *William Jones, Libellant vs The Barkentine Puako Co.*; case 17072, *Jack Joe, Libellant vs The Barkentine Puako Co.*; case 17073, *Edward Reilly, Libellant vs The Barkentine Puako Co.*; case 17349, *Kohilas vs Barkentine Rolph Company.*; case 17350, *Kohilas vs Barkentine Rolph Company.*

U.S. NARA, Washington, D.C., Old Military and Civilian Records, Record Group 41, Bureau of Marine Inspection and Navigation. Correspondence 1884–1934: file 101975 re A. C. Pedersen; file 102498 re charges against Frederick Hansen of murder on board *Edward R. West*; file 122808 re inhuman treatment by Frederick Hansen of seamen on board *Rolph*.

———. Vessel documentation: Certificates of Enrollment and Certificates of Registry for Vessel 136681, *Eric*; Certificates of Enrollment, Certificates of Enrollment and License, and Certificates of Registry for Vessel 150973, Barkentine *Puako*; Certificates of Enrollment and License and Certificates of Registry for Vessel 217610, *Annie M. Rolph*, and for Vessel 218534, *Rolph*.

U.S. NARA, Washington, D.C., Record Group 26: Card Records of Licenses Issued to Merchant Marine Officers 1910–1946. Records of Adolph C. Pedersen, Leonard Roy Pedersen, Charles Emil Helms, Albert Henry Sorensen, and Frederick Hansen.

Printed Sources

Albion, Robert Greenhalgh, with Jennie Barnes Pope. *The Rise of New York Port*. New York: Charles Scribner's Sons, 1939. Covers the period 1815–60.

An Appeal to Congress and the Public for Passage of the Seamen's Act. Appended within the *Appeal* are recountings of sixty-eight cases of severe abuse against seamen which were first brought to light by Walter Macarthur, editor, in a feature of the *Coast Seamen's Journal* titled "The Red Record." These cited cases along with many more discussed in the *Coast Seamen's Journal* were brought to the attention of shipping commissioners over the fifteen-year period 1880–95. Only three of the sixty-eight cases contained in the *Appeal* ended with verdicts of any consequence. Over time, the *Appeal* itself has come to be known as *The Red Record*.

[Arnesen, Arne M.] "A Tale of Terrorism: Victim Relates Facts of Frightful Experience on Board Hell Ship." *Coast Seamen's Journal*, June 15, 1921.

Arzt, Frederick K. *Marine Laws: Navigation and Safety*. 3rd ed. 3 vols. Orford, N.H.: Equity, 1985. By comparing Macarthur's *The Seaman's Contract* (1918) against the

"Merchant Seamen" section of Arzt, one can readily see additions and revisions made following 1918 to laws that continue to affect the safety and welfare of American merchant seamen.

Barry, John M. *The Great Influenza*. New York: Viking, 2004.

Black, Henry Campbell. *Black's Law Dictionary*. 6th ed. St. Paul, Minn.: West, 1990.

Blume, Kenneth John. "The Hairy Ape Reconsidered: The American Merchant Seaman and the Transition from Sail to Steam in the Late Nineteenth Century." *American Neptune* 44, no. 1 (1984): 33–47.

Bowditch, Nathaniel. *The American Practical Navigator*. Bethesda, Md.: Defense Mapping Agency Hydrographic/Topographic Center, 1995. My specific interest was chapter 32, "Ocean Currents."

Bradford, Gershom. *The Mariner's Dictionary*. Barre, Mass.: Barre Publishers, 1972.

Caldwell, Gaylon L. "Utah's First Presidential Candidate." *Utah Historical Quarterly* 28 (1960): 328–41.

Clark, Cecil. "Hellship Sailed from Victoria." *Victoria (B.C.) Daily Colonist*, March 12, 1967.

Clee, Charles R. "Desertion and the Freedom of the Seaman." *International Labour Review* 13 (1926): 649–72.

Dana, Richard Henry, Jr. *Two Years Before the Mast*. 1840. New York: Modern Library, 2001.

Dictionary of American Naval Fighting Ships. Edited by James L. Mooney. 8 vols. Washington, D.C.: Naval Historical Center, Department of the Navy, 1991–.

Forsyth, Craig J. *The American Merchant Seaman and His Industry: Struggle and Stigma*. New York: Taylor and Francis, 1989.

Gibson, Charles Dana. *Merchantman? Or Ship of War*. Camden, Maine: Ensign Press, 1986.

Gilbert, Martin. *First World War Atlas*. New York: Macmillan, 1971.

Gill, Peter B., and Ottilie Markholt. *The Sailors' Union of the Pacific, 1885–1929*. Unpublished manuscript. Bancroft Library, University of California, Berkeley, California.

Goldberg, Joseph P. *The Maritime Story*. Cambridge, Mass.: Harvard University Press, 1958.

Harper's School Geography. New York: Harper and Brothers, 1887.

Hohman, Elmo Paul. *History of American Merchant Seamen*. Hamden, Conn.: Shoe String Press, 1956.

International Code of Signals for the Use of All Nations. Washington, D.C.: Government Printing Office, 1903.

Judges of the United States. 2nd ed. Washington, D.C.: Government Printing Office, 1983.

Kerchove, René de. *International Maritime Dictionary*. 2nd ed. Princeton, N.J.: Van Nostrand, 1961.

Literary Digest. *The Literary Digest History of the World War*. 10 vols. New York: Funk and Wagnalls, 1919–20.

Lubbock, A. Basil. *Round the Horn Before the Mast*. London: John Murray, 1903.

Lyman, John. "Pacific Coast–Built Sailors, 1850–1905, Installment No. 26." *Marine Digest* 19, no. 51 (1941): 2.

Macarthur, Walter, comp. *The Seaman's Contract, 1790–1918: A Complete Reprint of the Laws Relating to American Seamen, Enacted, Amended, and Repealed by the Congress of the United States, as Originally Published in the U.S. Statutes at Large, Compiled and Arranged for Purposes of Comparison, Including the Present Law*. San Francisco: [James H. Barry], 1919.

Matthews, Frederick C. *American Merchant Ships, 1850–1900*. 2 vols. Salem, Mass.: Marine Research Society, 1930–31.

McCormick, Evelyn. "School Days at Fairhaven." *Humbolt (California) Historian*, September–October 1993, 10–13.

Merchant Vessels of the United States. Washington, D.C.: Department of Commerce, Bureau of Navigation, 1905, 1917, 1920.

Merriam Webster's Geographical Dictionary. 3rd ed. Springfield, Mass: Merriam-Webster, 1997.

National Maritime Union. *On a True Course: The Story of the National Maritime Union of America, AFL-CIO*. Washington, D.C.: Merkle Press, 1967.

Newell, Gordon. *Sea Rogues' Gallery*. Seattle: Superior Publishing Company, 1971.

"Pacific Coast Marine." *Coast Seamen's Journal*, February 3, 1915. Contains a short notice of charges filed against Adolph Cornelius Pedersen by German seamen.

Paterson, T. W. *Hellship: A Collection of True Stories of Jinxed Ships, Bucko Mates, and Terror on the High Seas*. Langley, BC: Stagecoach, 1974.

Ragsdale, W. B. "Three Weeks in Dayton." *American Heritage* 26, no. 4 (1975): 38–41, 99–103.

Record of the American Bureau of Shipping. New York: American Bureau of Shipping, 1905.

The Red Record. See *An Appeal to Congress* . . .

Regulations Governing the Consular Service of the United States. Washington, D.C.: Government Printing Office, 1923. The pertinent area, Section 355, was the same as in the previous regulations, below.

Regulations Prescribed for the Use of the Consular Service of the United States. Washington, D.C.: Government Printing Office, 1896.

Schultz, Charles. *Forty-niners 'Round the Horn*. Columbia: University of South Carolina Press, 1999.

Schwartz, Stephen. *Brotherhood of the Sea: A History of the Sailors' Union of the Pacific, 1885–1985*. San Francisco: Sailors' Union of the Pacific, AFL-CIO, 1986.

A Symposium on Andrew Furuseth. New Bedford, Mass.: Darwin Press, [1948].

Taylor, David Wooster. *The Life of James Rolph, Jr.* San Francisco: privately printed, 1934.

Webster's New International Dictionary of the English Language. Springfield, Mass.: G. and C. Merriam, 1931.

Weintraub, Hyman. *Andrew Furuseth: Emancipator of the Seamen.* Berkeley and Los Angeles: University of California Press, 1959.

Weisberger, Bernard A. "Here Come the Wobbies!" *American Heritage* 18, no. 4 (1967): 30–35, 87–93.

Wissmann, Rudolf Walter. *The Maritime Industry: Federal Regulation in Establishing Labor and Safety Standards.* New York: Cornell Maritime Press, 1942.

The World Sailing Ship Routes. Taunton, England: Hydrographer of the Royal Navy, 1974. Reference chart prepared by Rear Admiral Boyle T. Somerville, C.M.G., bearing note: "This Chart illustrates the more important routes described in *Ocean Passages for the World* (NP 136) published by the Hydrographic Department. The Routes shown on this chart were those generally used by sailing ships on ocean voyages during the sailing ship era. Short or coasting voyages are not shown. . . . The routes shown are based on general experience, but owing to the variability of winds and currents in all latitudes, it may be necessary to depart from the tracks recommended here."

INDEX

Page numbers in italics refer to plates.

Act of April 30, 1790: Section 8, 126
Act of February 28, 1803: destitute seamen, 149
Act of March 3, 1835, 170
Act of September 28, 1850: abolished flogging, 2, 171, 174
Act of February 26, 1853, 199n1
Act of June 7, 1872 (Shipping Commissioner's Act), 39, 40, 64
Act of December 21, 1898 (White Act), 2, 177, 178, 204n6 (chap. 15), 205n1 (Author's Reflections)
Act of January 25, 1907, 204n6 (chap. 15)
Act of March 3, 1911, 133
Act of March 4, 1915 (Seamen's Act): abuses following passage of, 149, 150; attempts to weaken, 182–84; Axtell's defense of, 133, 182, 203n7; enforcement on U.S. vessels, 179; LaFollette's connection to, 132, 179; passage of, 3; Section 2, 1, 136; Section 4, 1, 194n6; Section 7, 1, 126; Section 8, 1, 27, 63, 122, 149; Section 9, 1, 64, 129, 137, 166, 205n1 (Author's Reflections); Section 10 (scale of provisions), 181; Section 11, 64; Section 16, 179; ship owner responsibility under, 61; ship owner support for, 3
Act of July 1, 1916, 133
Act of May 18, 1917 (Selective Service Act), 16
Adriatic, White Star Line, 27
Agar, Charles, 93
Alcohol, use of: by A. C. Pedersen, 9, 11, 34; by Canadian military officer, 28; by F. Hansen, 146, 148; by Sorensen, 146, 148
Alexander, W., 155
Alfred Docks Police Station, 26
Allen (master, *Benjamin F. Packard*), 177
American merchant marine (mercantile marine), 11, 68, 69; wages, 195n4
American Seamen's Friend Society, 171
Ames, Alden, 136, 137, 150
Andersen, C. O., 139, 203
Anderson, Edward, 139
Annie M. Rolph, 160–63
Archer, Finch R., 163
Arnesen, Arne Mikel, 147–49, 151, 157, 158
Austrian count, 47, 54, 66
Axtell, L. V., 136
Axtell, Silas Blake, 132–34, 136, 165, 182, 203n7

Baldwin (treasury agent), 171, 172
Baltimore and Ohio RR Co. vs Henthorne, 152
Bank of Montreal (Victoria branch), 54, 55
Barkentine Puako Company, 132, 133, 135, 136, 193n4
Barkentine Rolph Company, 150, 151
Barnard, Ralph, 155
Barry (Rolph's attorney), 150, 155, 156
Bathing (*Puako* seamen's hygiene), 117
Belaying pin (symbol of "Red Record"), 175
Bell, John R., 174
Bellamy, Edward: *Looking Backward*, 14
Belsky, Frank, 36, 37, 66
Bendixsen, Hans, 143

215

Benjamin F. Packard, 177
Black Hands, 46
Blakeley, 137
Bligh, William, 201n2
Blume, Kenneth John, 195n4
Bordantown Colliery, 19
Bounty, HMS, 113, 201n2
Brasting, C. W., 143
British Admiralty, 61, 68
British Columbia Provincial Police, 199n7
British Military Intelligence, 66
British Naval Control (Cape Town), 68
Bruce, Ernest Allen, 12
Bryan, William Jennings, 96, 201n7
Bulman, J., 6, 10
Bureau of Navigation, 13, 36, 149, 161, 162, 171, 204n8. *See also* Steamboat Inspection Service
Burford (U.S. Immigration), 66

Caffey, Francis G., 89, 91, 94, 95, 132, 201n6
Calder (U.S. Senator from New York), 182
Cameron, John H., 93
Campbell, James (*Puako* able-bodied seaman), 55, 64, 97, 105, 110; assault against, 94, 127, 128; Cape Town, 22, 27; forced confession of, 52; joined *Puako*, 17, 19, 20, 110; libel against *Puako*'s owners, 135, 136, 138, 140; libel settlement, 141; medical condition of, 34; statements concerning, 28, 30, 38, 48 51, 97, 102, 103, 105; as witness against *Puako* officers, 64, 91, 95, 98, 99
Campbell, John Walter (*Puako* ordinary seaman), 55, 112, 125; Cape Town, 22, 56, 59, 63, 69, 105; describes water cure, 38, 69, 70; joined *Puako*, 17, 19; statements concerning, 31, 33, 45, 47, 58, 99, 100, 115, 117, 119; as witness against *Puako* officers, 64, 91, 92, 198
Canadian Pacific Railroad, 50
Cape Argus (Cape Town), 23
Cape Town boycott by ship owners, 131, 132
Carpenters. *See* Fredette, Frank (*Rolph* carpenter); Mattson, William (*Puako* carpenter)
Carr, Wilbur J., 130, 202n3 (chap. 11)
Challenger (A. C. Pedersen, master), 4, 5, 6, 10, 72, 73
Chamberlain, Eugene Tyler, 171
Chambers, V. G., 10, 11
Charles F. Crocker, 156
Christensen, Parley P., 132
Christian, Fletcher, 201n2
City of Bristol, 69
Clark, Cecil, 144, 199n7
Clayburn (tug), 18
Clear, Jack, 19
Coast Seamen's Journal, 6, 87, 142, 156, 175, 206n15
Coast Seamen's Union, 156, 172, 173, 175
Code of Visby, 167
Comax Logging Division of Crown Zellerbach, 161
Commentaries on the Law of Master and Servant (Bagott), 152
Committee on Merchant Marine and Fisheries, U.S. House of Representatives, 174
Conqueror, 144
Conscription affecting labor market, 16, 20
Consolato del Mare, 167, 168
Consular forms Nos. 79 and 82, 17, 195n5
Consular Regulations, Section 355, 65, 122, 149
Consul general, Cape Town. *See* Murphy, George H. (Cape Town consul general)
Consumption, 19, 175
Corporal punishment, 1, 2; Act of December 21, 1898, 177, 178; Act of March 4, 1915, 129; against *Puako* seamen, 34, 94, 110; Code of Visby, 167
Corron, George, 10, 11
Count Von Aulsdorf, 54. *See* Austrian count
Crimp system, 172
Crocker, R., 177
Crown Zellerback, Ltd., 161
CSU. *See* Coast Seamen's Union
Cullinghole, S., 112

Customs: Canada, 18, 66, 120; South Africa, 25; United States, 66, 69

Daily Colonist, 160, 199n7
Dana, Richard Henry, Jr.: *Two Years Before the Mast*, 165, 169–71, 202n4 (chap. 10), 206n16
Daniels, Josephus (secretary of the Navy), 70
Darrow, Clarence, 201n7
Del Rosa, 148, 149
Democracy, 182
Democratic Party, 179
Department of Commerce, 36, 61, 203n10; Hansen's license and, 204n8; and problems with ship owners, 131
Department of Justice, 36, 61, 133; A. C. Pedersen's claims, 66; evidence to New York grand jury, 90; F. Hansen charged, 143; praise for Murphy, 130; Smithson deserted, 201n1
Department of Labor, 88, 184
Department of State, 18, 36, 69, 133; A. C. Pedersen hearing and, 13; consul's authority and responsibility, 2, 65, 122; Hind, Rolph notified, 61; Lansing involved, 61; Malone's lie exposed, 202n3 (chap. 11); Murphy praised, 139; mutiny on *Puako*, 35, 66; *Puako* officers detained, arrested, 63, 70, 89; revoke F. Hansen's license, 149
Diary of *Puako* mates, 39, 41, 45, 67, 105, 130
Dolph. *See* Pedersen, Adolph Eric "Dolph" (*Puako* second mate)
Donkey engine, 194n8
Dooling, Maurice T., 150, 159
Dope, 52
Draft dodgers, 120
Drumwall (ex *Puako*), 161
Durham (treasury agent), 171
Dye, John W., 11, 12

Eastern Gulf Sailors Union, 139
Edward Lavidst. *See* Edward R. West
Edward R. West, 143, 156
Effects of seamen, handling of, 40, 42
Eiderkin, Per T. J., 174, 175
Enemy agents, collaborators. *See* German agents, spies, among *Puako* crew
Enemy surface raiders, submarines, 18, 120
Engelbach, Harold Augustus, 34, 200n5
Epilepsy, 70, 134
Eric, 162, 163
Erickson, Eric L., 156
Essex County Jail, 138
Examiner (San Francisco), 161

Fairhaven, California, 143, 203–4n4
Farmer-Labor Party, 132
Federal Penal Code, Section 291, 127
Federal Penitentiary, Atlanta, 138
Field, David Dudley, 201n7
Firearms: on *Puako*, 5, 30, 31, 33, 37, 47, 52, 53, 67, 99, 125; on *Rolph*, 144
Fletcher, J. A., 203n10
Flogging, 2, 89, 165, 170, 174, 177; abolishment of, 171
Fortner, Claude, 66
Fownes, William, 4
Francis, 177
Fredette, Frank (*Rolph* carpenter), 144–46, 165
Frueauff, Robinson and Sloan, 201n6
Furuseth, Andrew, 3, 14, 88, 156, 165, 177, 180, 182, 203n7, 207n22; alliance with J. Rolph, 178; Axtell's connection to, 133; death of, 184; liability of ship owners, 205n1 (Author's Reflections); as union activist, 172–74

Gabrielsen vs Waydell, 137
Galley, conditions of uncleanliness of, 46, 117
George U. Hind, 160
German agents, spies, among *Puako* crew, 3, 18, 24, 25, 27, 31, 34, 36, 48, 59, 60, 62, 63, 66, 97, 98, 100, 104, 119, 124, 125
Germany, and U.S. declaration of war, 9
Gilmour, (*Rolph* second mate), 145, 146
Goldfarb, Jacob J., 95
Gould (U.S. Congressman), 182

Index

217

Grielen, Frank (*Puako* able-bodied seaman): assaults against, 94, 128; Axtell contact, 133; confessions of, 31, 45, 46, 49; imprisonment of, 201n8; IWW involvement of, 201n9; joined *Puako*, 17, 18, 20, 21; libel against *Puako* owners, 135; libel settlement, 141; medical condition of, 34; rank of reduced, 39; statements concerning, 22, 26, 30, 35, 37, 38, 41, 44, 47, 51, 52, 53, 58, 62, 97, 110, 115–17, 119, 120, 124; as witness against *Puako* officers, 64, 66, 95, 99–102
Gronlund, Laurence: *Cooperative Commonwealth*, 14
Gusman (*Puako* seaman), 10

Hagen, Charles, 174
Hale, Henry Ewing, 95, 138
Hamilton vs US, 153
Hand, Learned, 90
Hannen, Charles, 143
Hanseatic League, 168
Hansen, Axel H. B. (*Puako* able-bodied seaman): death of, 4, 26, 31–33, 36, 38, 47, 90, 91, 104, 125; effects of, 42, 47; joined *Puako*, 17, 19; statements concerning, 45, 46, 52–54, 56, 92, 93, 101, 110, 115; union affiliation of, 196n9
Hansen, "Bully," 203n1 (chap. 14)
Hansen, Frederick (*Rolph* first mate): conviction of, 157, 158; and murder on *Edward R. West*, 143; and murder on *H. K. Hall*, 142, 143; description of, 142, 203n1 (chap. 14); hiring of, 152; joined *Rolph*, 144; license status, 149, 156, 157, 204n7 (chap. 15), 204n8; mistreatment of *Rolph* seamen, 145–47, 151, 153; paid off, 148; prison term of, 163; on *Puako*, 142, 143; reputation of, 154, 155
Harding, Warren G., 132
Harrison, Eric Morse (*Rolph* seaman), 145
Hauman, A. W., 60
Haywood, William D., 14
Heacock, Thomas E., 176, 177
Healy, Oswell Frank, 153, 154, 204n4
Hecate Straits Towing Co., 161

Hecla, 176
Heinrich, Lawrence (*Rolph* seaman), 147, 149
Heisler, Charles H., 9, 11–13
Helms, Charles Emil, 142, 143, 152, 160, 194n4
Hesperian, 160
Hill, Harry, 177
Hill, Joe, 51, 197n2 (chap. 5)
Hind, George U., 4, 139, 140, 193n4, 203n10
Hind, Rolph & Company, 2, 3, 15, 18, 72, 82, 114, 139, 143, 153, 178, 199n7, 203n10; attorney for Pedersen, 96; boycott of Cape Town, 131; built *Puako*, 6; Cape Town master hired for *Puako*, 63; charter market, 161; A. C. Pedersen hired by, 4, 5; and Pedersen's detention in Cape Town, 61–63; and Pedersen's reputation, 140; Smithson deserted, 118, 201n1
H. K. Hall, 142, 143
Hotel Occidental, Victoria, 55
Hough, Charles Merrill, 91, 93, 94, 199n4
Howe, Elliott, 56, 59, 76, 196n5 (chap. 3), 196n6, 197n8, 201n2; accused of lying, 109; examined crew confessions, 49; examined logbook, 39–48; questioned officers and seamen, 24–27; reported to consul general, 35, 70; searched *Puako*, 66, 67; Stewart's suicide, 57; as witness at trial, 91, 95, 104–7, 115, 116, 130
Hutton, H. W., 150–55, 205n1 (Epilogue)
Huycke, Harold, 162
Hypatia, 67, 68

Immigration: Canada, 28, 66; South Africa, 7, 9, 12, 25, 26, 60, 63, 104, 106, 198n12 (chap. 6); United States, 66
Industrial Worker (IWW), 14
Industrial Workers of the World (IWW), 14, 15, 50, 51, 57, 62, 105, 108, 115, 116, 123, 185, 197n2 (chap. 5), 201n9, 206n15
Influenza outbreak in Cape Town, 60, 67, 107, 198n5, 200n5, 201n10
Intaba, 70, 71
Iron Heel (London), 14

Irving (treasury agent), 171
Islander (Vancouver), 200n7
Island Tug and Barge Co., 161
IWW. *See* Industrial Workers of the World (IWW)
IWW Little Red Songbook, 57. *See also Songs of the Workers: To Fan the Flames of Discontent* (IWW songbook)
Iyo Maru, 9

Jack, George Whitfield, 95, 98, 101, 109, 110, 116, 119, 127–29, 199, 200n4
James Campbell, Libellant, vs The Barkentine Puako Company, 135, 136, 138, 140, 141. *See also* Campbell, James (*Puako* able-bodied seaman)
Jensen, Lester A. (*Puako* ordinary seaman, cook): assaults against, 38; cook duties of, 42; and galley condition, 117; hospitalized, 70; IWW connection, 57, 108; joined *Puako*, 17, 20, 21; libel against *Puako* owners, 132, 133, 135–38; libel settlement, 141; medical condition of, 34; statements by, 23, 43, 197n8; statements concerning, 22, 27–31, 35, 39, 45–48, 50–54, 58, 62, 97, 101, 115, 116, 121; Stewart's death, 63; as witness against *Puako* officers, 64
Jesus, 41, 195n5
Joe, Jack (*Puako* able-bodied seaman): assaults against, 94, 103, 104, 124; confessions of, 52; joined *Puako*, 17, 20; libel against *Puako* officers, 135, 136, 138; libel settlement, 141; medical condition of, 34; statements by, 36, 59; statements concerning, 22, 30, 39, 91, 96, 105, 116, 119, 125; as witness against *Puako* officers, 64, 95, 98
Jones, William (*Puako* able-bodied seaman): assaults against, 94, 128; confession of, 52; joined *Puako*, 17, 19; libel against *Puako* officers, 135, 136, 138; libel settlement, 141; medical condition of, 34; private agreement, 204n2; statements concerning, 22, 27, 28, 31, 33, 38, 48, 51, 58, 105, 115, 117, 124, 127; testimony of, 96, 97; as witness against *Puako* officers, 64, 95

Jorgensen, Peter (*Puako* able-bodied seaman): deserter of Canadian navy, 19; Hansen's effects, 47; joined *Puako*, 17, 19; medical condition of, 34; re-sailed on *Puako*, 63, 198n13; statements concerning, 22, 28, 30, 38, 48, 52, 70, 97, 112, 115–17; as witness, 64
Judgments of Oléron, 129, 168

Kaptein, John (*Rolph* seaman), 147, 149; assault against, 148; injuries to, 155; libel against *Rolph* owners, 151; libel settlement, 157
Kealy. *See* Keely, James
Kee, Cheng (*Puako* cabin boy), 6–9
Keely, James, 70, 198n10 (chap. 7)
Keet (Cape Town physician), 70
Killman, Daniel O., 143
King, William (*Puako* seaman): mysterious death of, 66
Knitzer, Alfred, 155
Knox, John Clark, 91
Knuckles. *See* Weapons
Kohilas, Demetrius (*Rolph* seaman): injuries to, 148, 149; joined *Rolph*, 147, 204n3; libels against *Rolph* owners, 150, 151, 153–55; libels settled, 157; Sorensen's refusal to discharge, 204n1
Kohilas vs Barkentine Rolph Company, 150
Kortum, Karl, 162, 165

Labatt, Charles Bagott: *Commentaries on the Law of Master and Servant*, 152
Labor market: manning shortage and, 2, 3, 16, 18, 194n7
LaFollette, Robert M.: as presidential candidate, 132, 203n5; Seamen's Act sponsor, 178, 179
LaFollette Act. *See* Act of March 4, 1915 (Seamen's Act)
Lansing, Robert, 13, 18, 63, 94, 130, 131; and order to detain *Puako* officers, 61
Larpent, A. J., 22
Larsen, George, 139, 155
Leder, Xavier H., 173

Lee, Sam, 6–8
Lee, Wai (*Puako* seaman), 6–10
Lemm's Outfitting Store, 13
Lester A. Jensen vs Barkentine Puako Company, 133
Levy, Maxwell, 20, 21, 196n8
Lillick, Geary and Olson, 203n9
Lillick, Ira S., 136, 137, 140, 203n9
Lipfert, Nathan, 206n17
Load Line Act, March 2, 1929, 16
Logbook protocol, 40
London, Jack, 35; *Iron Heel*, 14
London Sunday Times, 23
Looking Backward (Bellamy), 14
Low (Cape Town attorney), 9
Lubbock, A. Basil, 172
Ludlow Street Jail, 89
Ludwig Wiener, 25
Lumber, *Puako's* carrying capacity, 15

Macarthur, Walter, 175–77; as witness in *Rolph* libel, 156, 157
Magdalena, 22–25, 33, 59
Maguire, James G., 173, 174, 177, 178
Malone, Dudley Field: appeal of conviction, 130, 138; attorney in Scopes Monkey Trial, 201n7; cage for defendants, 199n7; challenge to venue for trial, 90; connection to Consular Service, 96, 122, 202n3 (chap. 11); defense phase, 92, 108–10, 112–15; dismissal request, 107; jibe by Miller, 123; joust with consul general, 106, 198n12 (chap. 6); on Smithson's desertion, 117; as presidential candidate, 132; prison file of A. C. Pedersen, 203n10; summation, 119–21; value of *Puako's* cargo, 202n1; witness list, 95
Manocal, Mario G., 202n3 (chap. 11)
Marie, 172
Martin, Daniel J., 163
Martin, William George, 22
Master: authority and responsibility of, 127; duties of, 152; use of term, 193n2
Masterson, William W., 131, 143
Mates. *See* Hansen, Frederick (*Rolph* first mate); Pedersen, Adolph Eric "Dolph" (*Puako* second mate); Pedersen, Leonard Roy (*Puako* first mate)
Matthews, Ben A., 92
Mattson, William (*Puako* carpenter): credibility questioned, 130; death of Stewart, 29; discharged, Cape Town, 63; plot against, 59; signed articles, 16, 17; statements by, 56; statements concerning, 22, 28, 33, 69, 98, 120, 125; testimony concerning, 105, 115, 117; testimony of, 103, 104; transport to United States, 68, 70; water cure, 70, 97; weapons identified, 103; as witness, 95, 198n12 (chap. 6)
May Flint, 176
McCarthy, Thomas D., 89, 91, 138, 198n10 (chap.7)
McDonald, E., 203n10
McGraph, J. J., 60
McNeil Island Federal Penitentiary, 85, 158
McQueen, James, 145
Military Intelligence Office, British, 66
Miller, S. Lawrence, 96, 106, 114, 120; and death of Hansen, 92, 196n5 (chap. 4); examined officers, 109–15; Mattson vacillates, 103, 104; resigned government service, 102n6; summation, 123–26; witness list, 95
Mines: coal, 19, 108, 204n2; floating, 18, 120
Mosher, R. B., 66
Murphy, George H. (Cape Town consul general), 6–12, *81*, 89, 92, 142, 143; boycott of Cape Town, 131, 132; claims A. C. Pedersen is insane, 38; consular authority and obligations, 65, 122, 149, 198n12 (chap. 6); death of, 163; death of Hansen, 38; death of Olsen, 60; death of Stewart, 38, *78*; detained officers, 61; discharged seamen, 80, 136; dispatches of 1917, 13; dispatches of 1918, 35, 36, 64; evidence shipped to United States, 69; hires new master, E. Pearson, 63; investigation of mutineers, 25, 26; investigation widens to officers, 27; logbook, 39; physical condition of seamen, 34; *Puako* searched, 66; transport of officers

and witnesses to United States, 67, 68, 70; as witness at criminal trial, 91, 95, 104, 106, 107, 121, 130; as witness at libel, 139

Navy Department: Office of Naval Intelligence (ONI), 36, 61, 65, 66; 13th Naval District, 65; transported *Puako* officers and witnesses to United States, 68, 70, 198n10; warned of enemy raiders, 120. *See also Rochester*, USS; *Woolsey*, USS
Nelson, Edward, 139
Newcomb, R. M., 16–18, 20, 66
New York Times, 89, 91, 92, 199n5
Nickels, E. D. P., 176, 177
Nixon Peabody, LLP, 203n9
Noling, Charles (*Rolph* seaman), 147, 149

Office of Naval Intelligence (ONI). *See* Navy Department
O'Hara, J. J., 204n8
O'Hare (S. Africa Immigration), 9
Ohlsen, Harry, 138
Olsen, Bjarne (*Puako* boatswain): assault of, 94, 98, 99, 102, 103, 123, 128; confessions of, 53–55; death of, 60, 79, 134, 197n6 (chap. 6); investigation of, 35, 62, 66; joined *Puako*, 17, 18, 20; medical condition of, 34; seamen qualifications of, 197n2 (chap. 6); statements by, 30, 31; statements concerning, 22, 33, 35, 38, 42, 45, 47, 52, 57, 58, 101, 110, 113, 114, 119, 124, 127; wages of reduced, 40; as witness, 64, 198n13
Olson, J. A., 136, 137
ONI. *See* Navy Department
Osborn (witnessed abuse), 13

Pacific Coyle Navigation Co., 161
Partridge, John S., 150, 157, 159
Paterson, T. W., 199n7, 200
Pearson, Eric, (*Puako* British master), 63, 142, 194n4, 201n1
Pedersen, Adolph Cornelius: background of, 4; Cape Town, 1917, 6–13; charges against in 1915, 6; command of *Challenger*, 4, 5, 6, 72; command of *Puako*, 5,

72, 193n4; connection to Hind, Rolph, 2; as "Hellfire," 5; marriage of, 73; Roeland Street Gaol, 81; Vancouver, 3, 15, 199n7
—April 1918–March 1919: alcohol use of, 99, 11, 34; charges against, 64; cost to U.S. government, 198n10 (chap. 7); crew makeup, 20, 21; crew signed, 16; crew as suicidal, 202n6; cut rations, 37; daybook of, 196n6, 198n8 (chap. 6); and death of Olsen, 60, 79; and death of Stewart, 4, 78; discharged, 63, 198n12 (chap. 6); enemy raiders, 18; German spies, 27; hearing of, 194n10; investigates crew, 35; letters and telegrams to Hind, Rolph, 61, 62, 153; IWW songbook and, 197n3 (chap. 6), 197n4; logbook entries, 39–48, 195n8, 197n8, 197n2 (chap. 5); and mutiny problems, 22–25; penalty assessment, 196n3; plot against officers, 49–55; private agreement with Jones, 19, 204n2; *Puako* searched, 66; Reilly's statement, 27–33; salary of, 18; statements by, 25, 56–59; statements concerning, 36–38; and tight labor market, 194n7; transport to United States, 68, 70, 71; value of cargo, 202n1; violent behavior, 68, 69; water cure, 69, 70; weapons found, 67
—March 1919–March 21, 1921: acquittal of murder charge, 93; appeal of conviction, 130, 137; arraigned, bail denied, 91; arrested, bail set, New York City, 89; assaults by, 134–36; demeanor at trial, 92; indictment, corporal punishment, 94; indictment, murder, 90; mates' testimony, 112–17; prison term of, 138; reputation of, 139; sentence of, 129; statements concerning, 119–26; testimony against, 96–107; testimony of, 108–11; trial preliminaries, 95; verdict, 128
—April 1, 1921–death: command of *Annie M. Rolph*, 161; connection to Hind, Rolph, 2; death of, 162; libel decision, 140; license renewed, 161; license revoked, 162; prison file of, 203n10; prison processing, 83, 84

Pedersen, Adolph Eric "Dolph" (*Puako* second mate): acquitted of murder, 93; arrested in New York, 89; assault verdict, 128; assaults by, 22, 34, 38, 134–36; bail denied, 91; bar pilot, San Francisco, 86, 163; consul general's dispatch, 35; and correspondence with A. C. Pedersen, 203n10; death of, 205n4; and death of Hansen, 4, 31, 32, 36, 91; and death of Olsen, 79; and death of Stewart, 29, 30, 41; detained Cape Town, 61; discharged Cape Town, 63, 66; indictment, assault, 90, 94; indictment, murder, 90; joined *Puako* 1918, 16, 17; lack of experience, 62; logbook entries, 39; plot against, 26, 44–48, 50–54; prison term of, 138; *Puako* Cape Town, 1917, 6, 8, 12; statements concerning, 25, 28, 33, 37, 56–59, 110, 119, 125, 127, 139; testimony concerning, 97–105; testimony of, 92, 110–15; transport to United States, 68; trial of, 95; and water cure, 70

Pedersen, Gertrude Thornlun, 4, 73

Pedersen, Leonard Roy (*Puako* first mate), 86; arrested in New York, 89; assaults by, 22, 31, 34, 38, 134–36; bail paid, 91; consul general's dispatch, 35; and correspondence with A. C. Pedersen, 203n10; death of, 163; and death of Olsen, 79; detained, Cape Town, 61; discharged, Cape Town, 63, 66; indictment, assault, 90, 94; interview in 1989, 162; joined *Puako*, 16, 17; lack of experience, 62; master of *Eric*, 162; plot against, 44–48, 50–54; prison term of, 138; *Puako* searched, 67; sentencing of, 129; statements concerning, 25, 28, 29, 33, 37, 39, 58, 59, 92, 110, 119, 125, 139; statements by, 56, 57; testimony against, 96–102; testimony concerning, 103–6; testimony of, 111–17; transport to United States, 68; trial of, 95; verdict, 128; and water cure, 70; as witness in libel, 137

Perjury (Mattson), 104

Perkins, Frances, 88, 184

Pilgrim, 169, 170

Pisar, Charles J.: influenza epidemic, 67; interviewed *Puako* seamen, 36, 38, 56, 59; praise for, 130, 131; statements concerning, 121; as witness for government, 95, 104, 106

Poison, 29; croton oil, 44, 197n6 (chap. 4); dishwater, 111; Lysol, 111; poisoned milk, 43, 50; ptomaine poisoning, 47; *Rough on Rats*, 111; soap, 111; strychnine, 111; tobacco, 111

Polk, Frank L. (acting secretary of state), 91, 95

Porter, Claude R., 89, 94

Portland Shipping Telegraph, 5

Preston, J. B., 143

Progressive Party, 203n5

Puako: cargo description, 114; cargo value, 18; carrying capacity, 15; command changes from Pearson to Helms, 142; command changes from Pedersen to Pearson, 63; command changes from Seeley to Pedersen, 5, 6; crew roster April 1918, 17; description of, 6, 193n4; documentation of, 6; 193n4; mechanical equipment of, 194n8; Pedersen's ownership share, 193n4; sold and renamed *Drumwall*, 161. See also *specific officers and seamen*

—timeline of: June 1917, 6; July 1917, 15; 1918 charted positions, 76; January 1918, 13; March 1918, 112; April 1918, 17, 18; May 23, 1918 (death of Stewart), 41; June 25, 1918, 43; July 12, 1918, 43; July 24, 1918, 45; August 6, 1918 (death of Hansen), 47; August 27, 1918, 22; December 27, 1918, 142; May 20, 1919, 142; June 6, 1919, 142; November 29, 1919, 142; June 1920, 142; August 9, 1920, 143; September 28, 1920, 160; December 20, 1920, 160; February 17, 1921, 161

Puritan (British bark), 19

Quincy Mining Company, 21

Rations, 1, 46, 169, 175. See also Scale of provisions

Red Record, *87*, 175–77
Reilly, Edward (*Puako* seaman): joined *Puako*, 18, 21, 39; libel against *Puako* owners, 135; libel settlement, 141; logbook entries involving, 43, 44, 46, 58; medical condition of, 34; statements by, 27–34; statements concerning, 22, 38, 51, 68, 120; testimony concerning, 92, 97, 104, 109, 115, 116; testimony of, 102, 103; as witness, 64, 91, 95
Republican Party, 179
Rhodian Law, 167
Rivera (*Puako* seaman), 10
Roberts, Chester E., 157
Roche, Theodore J., 150
Rochester, USS, *71*, 89, 90
Roeland Street Gaol, 7, 27, 63, 66, 69, *81*
Rolph: arrival in Mejillones, Chile, 148; crew carried, 144; crew discharged Melbourne, 146; crew signed Newcastle, 147; description of, 143; libel against owners, 150–54; libel settled, 157; surveyor's report, 159, 160. *See also specific officers and seamen*
Rolph, California, 143, 144, 203n4 (chap. 14)
Rolph, James, Jr., 150, 153, 157; and alliance with Andrew Furuseth, 178; career of, 163; Hind, Rolph & Co. established, 4; judgment against Rolph enterprise, 205n1 (Epilogue); Pearson's hiring approved by, 63; *Puako* ownership, 193n4; Rolph Shipyard established, 143, 144; supported Seamen's Act, 2, 3
Rolph Navigation and Coal Company, 12, 151, 154
Rolph Shipyard, 143, 204n4
Roosa, I. P., 69
Roosevelt, Theodore, 179, 199n6
Ross (*Susquehanna* first mate), 176
Rowe, John G., 5
Rudkin, Frank H., 140
Russell, Clark, 23, 195n3 (chap. 3)

Sabotage, 15, 62, 108
Sailor's Rule Book, 92

Sailors' Union of the Pacific (SUP), 138, 155, 156, 173
Sail vessel to steamship, transition of, 2, 77, 195n4
Salina (*Puako* seaman), 10
San Francisco Bay Bar Pilots Association, 86, 163
San Francisco Bulletin, 145, 161
San Francisco Chronicle, 145, 161
Scale of provisions, 37, 191
Scharrenberg, Paul, 184
Schoharie, 184
Scopes Monkey Trial, 201n7
Seaham Collieries, 154
Seamen's Bill. *See* Act of March 4, 1915 (Seamen's Act)
Seaworthiness: legislation regarding, 168, 173; *Puako* and, 135; *Rolph* and, 151, 153; test of, 153
Seeley, George, 6
Seppinen, Adolph (*Rolph* seaman), 149; assault against, 148; joined *Rolph*, 147; libel against *Rolph*, 151; libel settled, 157
Sewall, Edward Robinson (*Solitaire* master), 175, 176, 206n17
Sewall, Joseph Ellis (*Susquehanna* master), 176, 206n17
Shacknovis, J. B., 6
Siljan, 11
Sims, William, 70
Sjorberg, Avgot, 137
Smithson, L. A. (*Puako* cabin boy): confessions of, 49–52; and death of Stewart, 37; deserted in Australia, 117, 118, 201n1; joined *Puako*, 17, 18; logbook entry concerning, 43, 44, 46–48; medical condition of, 34; re-sailed on *Puako*, 3, 198n13; statements concerning, 22, 25, 28, 30, 53, 54, 57, 58, 70, 123–25; testimony concerning, 99, 100, 110, 111, 115; as witness, 64
Snyder (*Rolph* seaman), 147, 148
Sol Duc, 20, 21, 27, 195n9
Solidarity (IWW), 14
Solitaire, 175, 176

Somerset Hospital, 60, 79
Songs of the Workers: To Fan the Flames of Discontent (IWW songbook), 14, 57, 105, 108, 116, 123, 185, 197n3 (chap. 6), 197n4
Sophie Christenson, 10
Sorensen, Albert Henry (*Rolph* master): background of, 144; Hansen discharged, 148; statements concerning, 146, 147, 151, 204n1; testimony concerning, 156; testimony of, 152–54
Soultog. See *Sol Duc*
South African Police, 24, 33, 56, 78, 97. See also Howe, Elliott
Sowden, R., 56, 57
Spear, J. L., 155
Spies, accusations of *Puako* seamen as, 36, 68, 25–27, 31, 34, 48, 59, 62, 63, 66, 104, 125
Standard Oil, 46
Staring, Graydon S., 203n9
State Bank, Seattle, 35, 62
Steamboat Inspection Service, 13, 132, 149, 157, 161, 204n8
Steamshipmen's Protective Union, 173
Stephens, George (*Rolph* seaman), 147, 148
Stewart, John Henry (*Puako* cook): death report of, 78; effects of, 42; joined *Puako*, 17, 19; logbook entry concerning, 41; statements concerning, 45, 49–52, 54, 123, 125; statements concerning death of, 25, 28–30, 36–38, 44, 57, 63; testimony concerning, 100, 104, 110, 111
Stewart, R. P., 130
Sullivan and Sullivan, 150
SUP. See Sailor's Union of the Pacific
Susquehanna, American, 176
Susquehanna, British, 95
Sweeney, Charles P., 138, 203n10
Sweet, E. F., 131

Tacoma Maru, 9
Tacoma Sunday Ledger, 5
Taft, William Howard, 179
Talking as offense on sailing vessels, 206n16
Tam O'Shanter, 177
Thompson (*Pilgrim* master), 170

Thompson, John Vance, 206n15
Tietjen, B. H., 159
Titanic, 178
Tombs, the (prison) 89
Tourice, Raoul, 142, 143
Treasury Department, 171
Tully, Wilfred, 150
Tuohy, Edmund Joseph, 70, 198n10 (chap. 7)
Two Years Before the Mast (Dana), 165, 169–71, 202n4 (chap. 10), 206

U.S. Consular Service, 7, 65, 149; Malone's false claim, 122, 202n3 (chap. 11); Murphy's connection to, 106, 163
U.S. Employment Bureau, 20, 27
U.S. Navy. See Navy Department
U.S. Public Health Service, 155
U.S. vs Frederick Hansen, 142

Vancouver Harbor Commissioner, 112
Vancouver Police, 145, 151
Van Trojen, Victor J., 11, 12
Victoria Daily Times, 18
Voetter, Thomas W., 148, 149, 154, 156, 204n1
Von Aulsdorf (Austrian count), 54

W. A. Boole and Son, 6
Wallace and Ames, 133, 136
Wann, Fred, 6, 11
Ward, Joseph, 139
Water cure, 38, 69, 70, 82, 92, 99
Weapons: belaying pin, 1, 38, 66, 98, 147, 148, 151, 172, 174–77; blackball, 38; boots, 1, 7, 148, 172; brass knuckles, 38, 96, 98, 105; clubs, 1, 31, 37, 38, 100, 101, 103, 105, 124, 125, 130, 134, 135; feet, 29, 38, 41, 98, 151; fists, 7, 38, 99, 148, 151, 177; hammers, 176; hand cuffs, 37, 38; handspike, 175; iron bar, 31; marline spike, 1, 98, 176; rope ends, 1, 105; sheath knives, 105; slingshot, 38; table board, 38; tiller stick, 31, 38, 92, 96, 98; truncheon, 30
Weaver, J. B., 204n8
Webb, Thomas F., 184
Welles, Roger, 66

Welte, William H., 202n3 (chap. 11)
Westport, 131
White Act. *See* Act of December 21, 1898 (White Act)
William H. Smith, 204n7 (chap. 15)
Wilson, Woodrow, 1, 9, 96, 179, 180, 199n6, 202n3 (chap. 11), 207n22
Wilvers, Albert C., 131

Windward-Anchor Societies, 171
Winterling, John, 163
Wobblies. *See* Industrial Workers of the World (IWW)
Woolsey, USS, *71*, 198n12 (chap. 7)
World Sailing Ship Routes, 61

Zerbst, Fred G., 138

E. Kay Gibson lives in Midcoast Maine. She and her husband, Charles Dana Gibson, alternate their time ashore with long-distance cruising on *Hannah II*, their 38-foot Downeast cruiser. *Brutality on Trial* is Kay's first full-length history. She has previously assisted her husband on eight books dealing with maritime history. The most recent, *Over Seas: U.S. Army Maritime Operations, 1898 through the Fall of the Philippines*, was named an Outstanding Academic Title by the American Library Association. Two earlier books of which she was coauthor with her husband received the John Lyman Book Award as 1995's best books in maritime history. In 2004 the Gibsons were corecipients of the K. Jack Bauer Award, presented annually by the North American Society for Oceanic History in recognition of a body of work in the field of maritime history.